First Words
On Dostoevsky's Introductions

The Unknown Nineteenth Century

Series Editor

Joe Peschio (University of Wisconsin, Milwaukee)

Editorial Board

Angela Brintlinger (Ohio State University, Columbus)
Alyssa Gillespie (University of Notre Dame, South Bend, Indiana)
David Powelstock (Brandeis University, Waltham, Massachusetts)
Ilya Vinitsky (University of Pennsylvania, Philadelphia)

First Words
On Dostoevsky's Introductions

LEWIS BAGBY

Boston
2016

Library of Congress Cataloging-in-Publication Data:
A catalog record for this book as available from the Library of Congress.

Copyright © 2016 Academic Studies Press
All rights reserved

ISBN 978-1-61811-813-4
ISBN 978-1-61811-483-9 (electronic)

Cover design by Ivan Grave

Published by Academic Studies Press in 2016
28 Montfern Avenue
Brighton, MA 02135, USA
press@academicstudiespress.com
www.academicstudiespress.com

This study is dedicated to

Donna Peters Bagby

In Memory of

Grover C. Bagby

(1916–2010)

and

Dorothy Waters Bagby

(1917–2010)

They could not wait for this book

One feels an urge to smoke
Dostoevsky out with the question,
"Who's talking?"

—John Jones, Dostoevsky

On this occasion I shall include
"The Notes of a Certain Person."
That person is not I,
but someone else entirely.
I think no further foreword is needed.

—Dostoevsky, "Bobok"

Table of Contents

	Note on Transliteration	viii
	Acknowledgments	ix
	Introduction	xi
CHAPTER 1	Model Prefaces from Russian Literature	1
CHAPTER 2	Dostoevsky's Initial Post-Siberian Work	28
CHAPTER 3	Playing with Authorial Identities	61
CHAPTER 4	Monsters Roam the Text	91
CHAPTER 5	Re-Contextualizing Introductions	119
CHAPTER 6	Anxious to the End	144
	Conclusion	164
	Bibliography	171
	Index	193

Note on Transliteration

Russian names in the text are spelled either in the form most familiar to readers who know no Russian or in such a way as to facilitate pronunciation. For all other Russian words I have followed the Library of Congress transliteration system.

Acknowledgments

A work of this many years in the making inevitably involves a large collection of people and institutions. I would like to express my gratitude for support and assistance to my colleagues, Elizabeth Cheresh Allen, who challenged me in this and other work on Dostoevsky to not only use my mind but to trust my intuition in attempting to get to the heart of the matter; and Gene Fitzgerald, a friend and colleague of over forty years, for his astute commentary on the figure of the narrator and the constitution of the subject in Dostoevsky. Their insights have proven most helpful to me. To my friend and colleague of over thirty years at the University of Wyoming, Pavel Sigalov, I also extend my gratitude for assistance. His advice about the Russian language has proven both broadly educational and useful specifically in my work on this project. Irina Paperno, William Mills Todd, III, and Boris Gasparov were very supportive in my initial efforts to get this study off the ground, and their recommendations for research holdings, publishing outlets, and critical literature have kept me on the straight and narrow at every step of the way. Victor Brombert holds a special place in my grateful heart for his seeing the potential of my initial discoveries on Dostoevsky's introductions. He assisted me in locating the first outlet for my work, *The Modern Language Review*, to whose editors I express my gratitude for the opportunity to present my ideas about *Notes from the House of the Dead*'s first paragraph, but also for allowing portions of that first publication to appear in this study. And to Gerald Janecek, former editor of *The Slavic and East European Journal*, I also express my appreciation for permission to print portions of an article on the preface to *The Brothers Karamazov*.

The library at Stanford University, the Hoover Institute of War and Peace, the University of California at Berkeley, as well as the

New York Public Library have opened their doors to me and provided original manuscripts and journals. Without those materials, I would have been lost. The University of Wyoming Interlibrary Loan division and its friendly and persistent staff have always been ready to secure a ton of tomes for my research. I am forever in their debt. I express my appreciation, too, to Maggie Farrell, former dean of the University of Wyoming Libraries, for creating and sustaining such a wonderful, open institution on campus.

The acquisitions editors at Academic Studies Press, Sharona Vedol and Meghan Vicks, have been most helpful and encouraging in all our dealings, and the copyeditor, Elizabeth F. Geballe, has made this study better with her keen eye and sensitive ear. It has been a distinct pleasure to work long distance with her on this study. Joe Peschio, editor for the Academic Studies Press series on "The Unknown Nineteenth Century," has been kind enough to inaugurate the series with my study of Dostoevsky's introductions. I am grateful to him, and not only for his generosity, but for his friendship and enthusiastic support of this project. It goes without saying (as I say it nonetheless), that I am responsible for the final product. Please read it; pray not weep.

Behind every researcher there are the deepest of friends who over the years have supported my tilting at windmills no matter how big or small. I thank them all for sticking with me. And then there are the generations of a greatly supportive and rather large extended family down to fourth cousins. My thankfulness flies to them along with an invitation, à la Nikolai Gogol's Rudy Panko, to feast at the cabin and listen to yarns on the high plains. At its pine-scented center lives a great heart. To her I have dedicated this book. Each day's first words are to her and for her. The final ones, too.

Introduction

I found myself in the fallow field of Dostoevsky's introductions many years ago at a National Endowment for the Humanities summer seminar on world literature directed by Victor Brombert at Princeton University. Professor Brombert asked me to make comments to our group of mostly non-Slavists on the adequacy of the translation we were using for Dostoevsky's *Notes from the House of the Dead*. I began by comparing the original's first words against the translation's. Those words appear in a fictional editor's introduction to Dostoevsky's novel-memoir of his protagonist's life in a Siberian prison. In performing my assignment, I discovered that the translation did not serve the original adequately. The first paragraph alone seemed insurmountable for any translator to capture in another language, for it is coded with a secondary narrative, folkloric in structure and imagery that for linguistic reasons cannot be rendered into English while doing justice to both the overt and covert levels of the discourse. The subsurface story of the hero's quest is encoded in the very roots of Dostoevsky's language and in the motion suggested by his use of prefixes. I was on my way.

Introductions have a long, distinguished, but sometimes zany history in world literature. We dip into a moment of time in that history by taking a close look at Dostoevsky's use of introductions in his fiction. No systematic study has been undertaken of Dostoevsky from this perspective. True, the focus is narrow, but in terms of a narrative's discourse, introductions are important in that they represent the author's first words, the opening into a text. As Edward Said argues, "Every writer knows that the choice of a beginning for what he will write is crucial not only because it determines much of what follows but also because a work's beginning is, practically speaking, the main entrance to what it offers."[1] Consider Genesis: "In the beginning God created the heaven and the earth. And the earth was without form, and void."[2] Introductions often take us to origins, to tales of beginnings, even to ideas about the very beginning of beginnings, or at least to the illusion of beginnings. What would we make of the narrative in the Book of John without its philosophical opening, a prolegomenon to his account of the life of Jesus: "In the beginning was the Word, and the Word was with God, and the Word was God"?[3] Compare these impactful beginnings with the mundane, even blunt, prologue: "The words of Nehemiah the son of Hachaliah."[4] A mere glance tells us that introductions do many different things.

Fast forward millennia and recall Tolstoy's first sentence of *Anna Karenina*, a stunningly brief prologue with immense import: "All happy families resemble one another; each unhappy family is unhappy in its own way."[5] Compare Tolstoy's authoritative voice with the first words of the introduction to Dostoevsky's *The Brothers Karamazov*: "Starting out on the biography of my hero, Alexei Fyodorovich Karamazov, I find myself in some perplexity. Namely, that while I do call Alexei Fyodorovich my hero, still, I myself know that he is by no means a great man, so that I can foresee . . . inevitable questions . . ."[6] While we may be confident that Tolstoy's words represent the direct address of his surrogate omniscient narrator, in Dostoevsky's case we cannot be so sure even though his introduction is entitled "From the Author." Perhaps Dostoevsky has another author in mind, someone other than himself. Might this always or frequently be true of his introductions?

First words are nearly always important, marked in a special way for their being the initial utterances we encounter as we enter into the world of the text. Furthermore, initial remarks that occur in introductions

---

[1] Edward Said, *Beginnings: Intention and Method* (New York: Basic Books, Inc., 1975), 3.
[2] Genesis I: 1–2 in *Holy Bible: King James Text, Modern Phrased Version* (New York: Oxford University Press, 1979).
[3] John I: 1–2.
[4] Nehemiah I: 1.
[5] Leo Tolstoy, *Anna Karenina*, trans. Marian Schwartz (New Haven: Yale University Press, 2014), 3.
[6] Fyodor Dostoevsky, *The Brothers Karamazov*, trans. Richard Pevear and Larissa Volokhonsky (San Francisco: North Point Press, 1990), 3.

are yet another set of originating utterances of special value (as distinct from those that appear in the body of the work, usually beginning with something often labeled Chapter One). The discourse that appears in introductions represents something of a puzzle if for no other reason than it occupies an indeterminate space between the narrator's and the writer's respective positions. At one extreme, the preface may be wholly in accord with what follows, as we see in Tolstoy, and (questions of authorship aside) in Genesis, John, and Nehemiah. But at the other, it can detach from the text that follows and drift toward an identification with another ontological order, one that appears less continuous with the text, something more problematic than straightforward. The introduction to *The Brothers Karamazov* represents this second variety. Between these two we find many gradations. John Steinbeck's *Tortilla Flat*, for instance, begins with the author's direct address in which he disparages both conventional thinking about verbal art and the opinion of literary critics, then transitions almost seamlessly to the voice of the story's narrator (who occupies a different discursive plain).

Prefaces as an object of literary study have drawn attention over the course of time, but in more recent history Gérard Genette's *Paratexts* presents something more comprehensive than any study preceding it.[7] Genette provides a helpful typology of introductions to works of verbal art. We shall soon have recourse to it. Edward Said has contributed to the topic, as has a wide range of articles on introductory words, signs, and symbols as coded phenomena of literary texts. Turning to specific examples, Pushkin's and Gogol's famous introductions to their first published pieces of prose fiction, *The Tales of the Late Ivan Belkin* (1831) and *Evenings on a Farm Near Dikanka* (1831–1832), have been treated extensively in the critical literature.

In contrast to Pushkin's and Gogol's introductions, however, Dostoevsky's have received short shrift.[8] There is no study of his use of

---

[7] Gerard Genette, *Paratexts: Thresholds of Interpretation*, trans. Jane E. Lewin (Cambridge: Cambridge University Press, 1997).

[8] Not to mention Sir Walter Scott, whose famous *Waverley* prefaces, separated from their narratives entirely, have been published in a single volume, *The Prefaces to the Waverley Novels by Sir Walter Scott*, ed. Mark A. Weinstein (Lincoln: University of Nebraska Press, 1978). See also Charles W. Eliot, ed., *Prefaces and Prologues to Famous Books*, in *The Five Foot Shelf of Books*, vol. 39 (New York: Collier and Son, 1910); Herbert S. Greshman and Kernan B. Whitworth, Jr., eds., *Anthology of Critical Prefaces to the 19th Century French*

introductions as a device—as strategy, frame, authorial stance—in his prose fiction. From reading the literature, it would appear that his forewords more than any other response have caused consternation. This is certainly understandable. Dostoevsky's novels hold so many riches that their prefaces pale in comparison. His introductions are quickly forgotten in the forward press of his powerful narratives. Do Dostoevsky's beginnings have anything to contribute to our understanding of the works in which they appear? Or do they hang by an almost invisible thread to the work's great bulk?[9] Dostoevsky's creative power is so great, his ideas so challenging, his narratives so deeply engaging, that the functions of the introduction, minor subgenre that it is, have found no significant place in the critical literature on Dostoevsky's art, at best appearing as afterthoughts, and at worst judged useless verbiage.

This study finds that introductions are complex, multifunctional, variegated rhetorical phenomena. They are a literary artifact we should not take for granted, least of all in Dostoevsky's neglected case.

Dostoevsky provides clues that introductions hold greater importance to him than readers have acknowledged previously. He never used them in his pre-exile work of the 1840s, when it was a fairly common practice, but in his fiction of the post-exile years he delivered up many an introduction when it was less normative to do so. From the first work out of Siberian imprisonment and exile, *The Village of Stepanchikovo and its Inhabitants* (1859), to his last, *The Brothers Karamazov* (1880–1881), Dostoevsky published forewords on many occasions. The list of works with prefaces is quite impressive. In addition to these two novels, we find forewords in *Notes from the House of the Dead* (1860–1862), *Notes from the Underground* (1864), and *Demons* (1871–1872). To this list we can add the nonfiction *Winter Notes on Summer Impressions* (1863) and four short stories that emerge within his *The Diary of a Writer*, "Bobok" in 1873, and for the year 1876, "The Boy at Christ's Christmas Party," "The Peasant Marei," and "A Gentle Creature," the last being one of Dostoevsky's greatest short stories. None of his other works from this period (*Crime and*

Novel (Columbia: University of Missouri Press, 1962); Richard P. Blackmur, ed., *The Art of the Novel: Critical Prefaces by Henry James* (New York: C. Scribner's Sons, 1934); and A. S. Demin, ed., *Tematika i stilistika predislovii i posleslovii* (Moscow: Nauka, 1981).

[9] As Genette mentions, readers often bypass prefaces (*Paratexts*, 4).

Punishment and *The Idiot*, for example) includes a foreword labeled as such.[10] Rather than this fact rendering introductions irrelevant, it instead marks their occurrence as unique. We are immediately forced to ask: Why does he use an introduction in one text but not another? Is the absence of a preface as significant as its presence? What characteristics of a given work militate toward the use of a preface or its avoidance? These and related questions are addressed when sufficient information has been amassed to turn to them productively.

Other than using prefaces in some very significant works, Dostoevsky engages in a signaling strategy to underscore their non-trivial nature. First, he uses different labels for them in all but two instances. Second, in his fiction he never utilizes the most common form of preface of his day—direct authorial address. Except for his non-fiction, where he does use his own voice, in his fiction Dostoevsky casts the voice emanating from his prefaces as someone else's. He is completely consistent in this practice.

Regarding these two signaling strategies, Dostoevsky utilizes a wide variety of synonyms to identify his introductions:

- An Introductory (*Vstuplenie*) for *The Village Stepanchikovo and its Inhabitants*
- Introduction (*Vvedenie*) for *Notes from the House of the Dead*
- Instead of a Foreword (*Vmesto predisloviia*) for *Winter Notes on Summer Impressions*
- [A zero label] for *Notes from the Underground*
- Instead of an Introduction (*Vmesto vvedeniia*) for *Demons*
- [A zero label] for "Bobok"
- "A Boy with his Hand Outstretched for Alms" ("Mal'chik s ruchkoi") for "A Boy at Christ's Christmas Party" in *The Diary of a Writer*
- "On Love of the People" ("O liubvi k narodu") for "The Peasant Marei" in *The Diary of a Writer*
- From the Author (*Ot avtora*) for "A Gentle Creature" in *The Diary of a Writer*
- From the Author (*Ot avtora*) for *The Brothers Karamazov*

---

[10] Dostoevsky never includes an introduction when he uses an omniscient narrator. This point is discussed in the Conclusion.

Only in the final two cases are the labels the same. I shall address this anomaly later. For the moment, let us simply note that a constant feature of the titles is their variety. His consistency in using different forms suggests that his practice was most probably intentional. Just what his intent was in shifting labels from one work to the other will be discussed in due time. For now, we need only acknowledge that Dostoevsky wished to highlight his introductions and that he did so by calling them by different names almost every time he used them.

To alert us to the notion that his introductions are to be accorded more than passing attention, Dostoevsky also avoids their most commonly attested form—direct authorial address. This point requires some amplification. To this end we turn to Gérard Genette's typology of prefaces to see where Dostoevsky's fit.

Genette identifies three general types of preface—authorial, allographic, and actorial. The first represents any foreword that comes directly from the implied author, "the second self," who "chooses, consciously or unconsciously, what we read."[11] Except in his *Diary of a Writer*, Dostoevsky avoids them in his prefaces. As we shall see, this is true even when he affixes his name to the preface. The second of Genette's types denotes a preface that comes from a third party, someone either real, living (once living), or fictional, but certainly not the author. Dostoevsky only once uses an allographic preface in his fiction. The third general type identifies introductions that come from a character, fictional or authentic, who figures in the subsequent narrative. Autobiography supplies the most examples here, but not exclusively. Dostoevsky's practice moves toward this type over time.

Genette divides each of these preface types into three subcategories—authentic, fictive, and apocryphal. Thus, an authentic authorial preface would be one that comes to us in the voice of the implied author. A fictive authorial preface is one that issues from the voice of a character who also serves as narrator. And an apocryphal authorial foreword is one cast in the speech of someone ("an author") other than the person to which the foreword is explicitly ascribed. In other words, let us say that Dostoevsky signs the preface of his work of fiction, thus

---

[11] Booth explains that readers "infer [the implied author] as an ideal, literary, created version of the real man; he is the sum of his own choices" (*The Rhetoric of Fiction* [Chicago: University of Chicago Press, 1961], 74–75).

leading us to believe that the preface represents his direct authorial address. Then, by clues he provides, we learn that it isn't his person at all, but someone else. That makes it apocryphal. Dostoevsky employed this ruse, in fact, in *Notes from the Underground*, but not only there.

Rather than describing each of the permutations and combinations of Genette's main types and subtypes, we shall look into the forms relevant to Dostoevsky's fiction that we are treating in this study, specifically, works with clearly demarcated forewords duly indicated, with rare exception, as such. They provide a shorthand for us as we work through the prefaces. His forewords represent a solid portion of Genette's typology:

	Authorial	**Allographic**	**Actorial**
Authentic	*Winter Notes on Summer Impressions*; *Notes from the Underground*; "Bobok"; "A Boy at Christ's Christmas Party"; "A Gentle Creature"; *The Brothers Karamazov*		*Winter Notes on Summer Impressions*
Fictive	*The Village of Stepanchikovo*; *Demons*	*Notes from the House of the Dead*	*The Village of Stepanchikovo*; *Demons*
Aprocryphal	*Notes from the Underground*; *The Brothers Karamazov*		*The Brothers Karamazov*

Given the overlap of Dostoevsky titles across Genette's categories, as we see here in the case of *The Village of Stepanchikovo*, *Winter Notes on Summer Impressions*, *Notes from the Underground*, *Demons*, and *The Brothers Karamazov*, I suggest in this study that Dostoevsky engages hybrid forms of Genette's typology. They cannot be pigeonholed into one part of the grid at the expense of another. We shall examine these instances in due time.

Dostoevsky did not operate in a preface vacuum. There are myriad examples of preface, introduction, prologue, and foreword in the literature with which he was familiar, indeed, in the literature he most loved to read and that influenced his practices. Consequently, in Chapter One we first take a look at the models Dostoevsky had before him when he began using forewords with some regularity. This is not meant to be a mere academic exercise, but one that allows us to accomplish three things simultaneously: to identify many of the purposes to which introductions are put as part and parcel of Dostoevsky's literary heritage; to enjoy the play that inheres in those models; and to put flesh on the bare bones of Genette's typology as it applies to Dostoevsky's work.

After examining Dostoevsky's models from Russian literature of the early nineteenth century, we turn our attention in Chapter Two to Dostoevsky's work in the last years of his exile and the first years of his return to St. Petersburg. This is the period when Dostoevsky first began to put introductions to work. He quickly transitioned from some awkward first steps in *The Village of Stepanchikovo and its Inhabitants* to the kind of astounding aesthetic achievement, in *Notes from the House of the Dead*, that we associate with his name. Through the remainder of the 1860s and 1870s, Dostoevsky alternately did and did not use forewords to his work. We examine the texts containing prefaces in Chapters Three and Four, then turn in Chapter Five to *The Diary of a Writer* with its unusual application of forewords. In the final chapter we take up an analysis of the curious introduction to *The Brothers Karamazov*. Its preface may not represent the summit of Dostoevsky's achievement as a writer of prefaces (*Notes from the House of the Dead* and "A Gentle Creature" hold that place), but it discloses the man behind his masks as few others did before it. A Conclusion hazards informed guesses about the function of Dostoevsky's use of forewords, when he used them, why he used them, and what they tell us about verbal art as authors choose how to set their readers loose to inhabit the worlds they create for us.

Before turning to introductions as a literary phenomenon, it might be helpful first to establish the technical vocabulary to be used throughout this study. Genette opts for "preface" because it is predominant in French. Since it is a finely tuned and well-oiled lexical item, derived from seventeenth-century French, Medieval Latin, and Ancient Greek, it has pedigree. But I intersperse it with synonyms: foreword, introduction, and introductory—lexical items Dostoevsky himself was most inclined to use.

There are also a variety of permutations on these terms, all denoting initial remarks made to the reader by another party. In Dostoevsky's first words alone we find attested "From the Author" ("Ot avtora") and "In Place of an Introduction" ("Vmesto vvedeniia"). More striking than the mutability of the signs, or the fixity of the notion of what is denoted by the signs, are the spatial and temporal suggestions each contains—that is, their chronotope.[12]

Imagine a medieval illuminated manuscript for a moment, for example, the eleventh-century *Marvels of the East*.[13] The text demonstrates two phenomena that pertain to prefaces: their framing capacity in both a literal and figurative sense and their images' inspired, if fitful, transgressions of the frames. Prefaces, and the range of synonyms that represent them as verbal signs, possess this duality. In the *Marvels*, there are figures (monsters) that illuminate the pages, often representing the verbal text's first letter or word. They do not move outside the clearly and ornately adorned frames in which they are located. But there are other figures whose appendages—a foot, head, or an arm, for instance—cross into the frame's space. They are still wholly contained within the outer edge of the frame, but they now form a part of it. Then there are monsters that have broken through the frame border, torn it open in such a way that they might step or gesture out into the text they accompany. There are also partially as well as completely splintered frames. Here the monster transgresses the space of the discourse, sometimes even producing in cartoon boxes the folio's first words as quoted speech from the mouth of the beast. And finally, there are frames that have wholly disappeared. The monster roams the page freely.

Introductions, prefaces, forewords, prologues, and their other synonymous forms do something quite similar. Like the monsters' feet, prefaces are contained in time and space in distinct ways. Their labels' roots indicate those differences in a way conventional usage appears to

---

[12] This is Mikhail Bakhtin's term for the space-time continuum in discourse, "Forms of Time and of the Chronotope in the Novel," in *The Dialogic Imagination: Four Essays by M. M. Bakhtin*, ed. Michael Holquist, trans. Caryl Emerson and Michael Holquist (Austin: University of Texas Press, 1981), 84–258; M. M. Bakhtin, "Formy vremeni i khronotopa v romane. Ocherki po istoricheskoi poetike," in *Voprosy literatury i estetiki* (Moscow: Khudlit, 1975), 234–407.

[13] *Marvels of the East* (British Library, Cotton MS Vitellius A XV), https://imagesonline.bl.uk/?service=search&action=do_quick_search&language=en&q=Marvels+of+the+East.

me to have lost. For example, "introductions" conduct across a threshold (*intro+duct*). In this sense, they move discourse from one qualitative level to another (the fictional narrative's). Like its usage in common parlance, when we are introduced to someone or something, we move from a state of not knowing to knowing. Introductions in literature perform a similar service. They take our familiarity with the object (which we might best imagine as zero) and conduct us into a level of initial knowing. Introductions thus prepare us to become even more familiar with the object. The chronotope of introductions involves movement in time across discursive space. It suggests a dynamism. It gestures outside the frame toward utterance.

"Preface" comes from Medieval Latin *prefatia*; *pre+fari*, speech beforehand or in advance of some other speech act. It suggests something more static, something oriented to a prior condition in and of itself and before something new (once introduced) is encountered. It is preparatory. Its prefix and root suggest a chronotope that focuses on the moment and on the current discursive space of utterance. Its root emphasis is on itself as a speech act. It stands within the frame structure and does not break out of it.

A "prologue" is related, as forebear, to "preface." It derives from Greek *pro+logos*. It is speech before other speech, discourse in advance of another level of discourse. When thinking of presentations in drama wherein a *dramatis persona* steps forward (perhaps in front of the curtain) and pronounces on the play that follows, think prologue. It is already outside the frame and stalking the narrative on its own stage. But its discourse is qualitatively distinct from that of the characters whose speech floats next above the boards. Fictional though it may be, the prologue plays at the level of narrative discourse, but only by having stepped out of a traditional prefatorial frame. It frames, but is not chronotopically bound within a traditional frame discourse or introduction. Nor does it occupy a space within the text (play) that unfolds in its aftermath. It is a pointer directed at the drama about to unfold. Having broken through the frame, it stands on the same stage that the actors will, but it does not wander.

"Foreword" (German *Vorwort*, which is modeled on Latin *praefatio*, whence "preface") indicates a moment of discourse that precedes the one when readers enter into the text of fiction. It is marked by a decided differentiation of the discourses in the foreword and in the ensuing story. Like a preface, it marks out a speech act that precedes other speech acts, which are, of necessity, of a qualitatively different order. Its temporal and spatial orientation is the same as in a preface—it is more static and implies a speech act rather than motion across a threshold.

When not marshaled as synonyms with differing suggestive potentials, I use the four terms—introduction, foreword, preface, and prologue—to reflect Dostoevsky's own language usage. For example, when he says "Introduction" ("Vvedenie"), I use it when referencing his term; and when Dostoevsky uses an apparent variant of it, "Introductory" ("Vstuplenie"), I employ his term, too.[14] When speaking more generally about a given work without reference to Dostoevsky's specific term or phrase, I utilize the synonyms rather freely.

Use is also made of the notion of frames. There are three ways in which the term is used to indicate distinct phenomena. It would be wise to keep them separate for they impact discussions of Dostoevsky's introductions in meaningful ways. In the first instance, frames are conceived in spatial terms, as verbal structures very much like those in the plastic arts that separate the object from a larger, containing context. Think here of the images from *Marvels of the East*. In verbal art, the spatial nature of framing occurs when the preface is marked off in terms of voice, style, and spatio-temporal setting from the narrative discourse that follows (the fictional tale). In a second sense of framing, the term is used to indicate the means by which an argument or a theme is prepackaged in order to sway reader or target audience response in a particular direction. The third sense refers to the phenomenon of narrative framing, a phenomenon of verbal art through which the discourse, setting, and spatio-temporal (chronotopic) elements interact with the fictional narrative to generate a covert message or a third tale which synthesizes the elements of story and frame.

I offer apologies for introducing what might seem to be unnecessary distinctions so early in the game. I only do so because I feel they shall prove useful as we examine the first words Dostoevsky and some

---

[14] "Introductory" (*Vstuplenie*) possesses its own etymology. It is made up of the prefix meaning "in/inward" (*v-*) and "step" (*stup-*) and thus suggests motion, not across a threshold, but into a new space. Note: Dostoevsky usually puts the label "foreword" (*predislovie*) in the mouth of his narrator and tends not to use it himself.

of his immediate Russian predecessors committed to the page in their verbal art. I should note, too, that in large measure, I conduct close readings of Dostoevsky's prefaces guided by formalist, structuralist, and semiotic practices.

One final clarification before proceeding: I have named the study "First Words" in a narrow sense to indicate the first complete utterances of any text penned by the author. The titles and epigraphs attached to a literary text also represent first words, but not necessarily as complete or sustained utterance. Needless to say, titles and epigraphs deserve treatment every bit as much as do introductions.[15] By my definition, they lay beyond the scope of this study.

---

[15] See, for example, A. N. Andreeva, et al., *Poetika zaglaviia* [*The Poetics of Titles*] (Moscow-Tver': Liliia print, 2005).

Model Prefaces from Russian Literature

CHAPTER 1

I

AUTHENTIC AUTHORIAL INTRODUCTIONS

We begin our examination of model prefaces with the type of introduction—authentic authorial discourse—Dostoevsky eschewed until the end of his career when writing fiction for *The Diary of a Writer* and when composing the opening to *The Brothers Karamazov*. In all other instances, Dostoevsky shied away from appearing to speak in his own voice in his prefaces. There are reasons for this that we shall address when we turn to his late work. It serves our purposes now, however, to examine models of direct authorial address in representative examples of early nineteenth-century Russian prose.

To give us a jumpstart on that century, we turn first to Vasily Narezhny (1780–1825) and his foreword to his once-popular *A Russian Gil Blas* (1814). The introduction is presented in his own words and from his own authorial position: "The most excellent work of Lesage, known under the title *The Adventures of Gil Blas de Santillana*, has brought and continues to bring as much pleasure and utility to the reading public as it has honor and surprise to its publisher."[1] Finished with the bombast, Narezhny continues by articulating his rationale for writing: "France and Germany have their own heroes [of this type] whose

---

[1] I have translated the passage faithfully to reflect Narezhny's syllepsis. I believe what he wished to say was ". . . to the honor of the author and to the surprise of his publisher." V. V. Narezhnyi, *Izbrannye sochineniia* I (Moscow: Khudlit, 1956), 43.

adventures fall under the titles *A French Gil Blas* and *A German Gil Blas*. And for this reason I have taken it upon myself, following these examples, to publish this new work of mine under this well-known title and thus to unburden those [had I entitled the work differently] who would otherwise have labored to discover with whom I, in this composition, might be compared."² Narezhny has fun with his readers, but also with Alain René Lesage, a Frenchman who inexplicably, for Narezhny, chose to situate his hero in Spain: "For Russian folk I have fashioned a Russian personage, considering it so much more proper to take up the business of a fellow countryman rather than that of a foreigner. Why Lesage could not have done this one can only guess."³

Genette notes that the most common function of the preface is to identify the work's genre.⁴ Here we see Narezhny engaged in that task. His work is a picaresque. But, he also goes to some length to poke fun at his reader, whose tastes, he anticipates, may not be satisfied by a Russian Gil Blas. It turns out, too, that he had more than the public's taste to contend with. Generations of censorship kept his *Russian Gil Blas* from unexpurgated publication for a very long time indeed—until 1938.⁵

Readers and censors aside, there is the matter of the literary model, Lesage. Narezhny's query of Lesage's intent in situating his hero in Spain hints at the superiority of his (Narezhny's) own work vis-à-vis the model narrative. In the inchoate Romantic Age in Russia, this was no small matter, for nativeness (*narodnost'*) was becoming all the rage. Common as it might be for authors of imitative works, Narezhny's need to vault himself above Lesage underscores a level of tension, of insecurity, relative to his own achievement. Never mind surpassing it; does Narezhny's hold up to the original? Furthermore, there is a degree of anxiety to be ascertained, too, in Narezhny's own identity relative to his work—a Ukrainian writing a Russian *Gil Blas* into Russian literary history, while simultaneously chastising Lesage for placing his hero in a country other than Lesage's France. Clearly, more goes on in prefaces than the mere introduction of genre. It is also a locus of emotion, where

---

2   Narezhnyi, *Izbrannye sochineniia*, 43.
3   Narezhnyi, *Izbrannye sochineniia*, 44.
4   Genette, *Paratexts*, 222.
5   Narezhnyi, *Izbrannye sochiineniia* II, 615–617.

the author's sometimes hidden, sometimes overt, desires as well as his anxieties are encoded.

It is the locus, too, of many a scrape and bow. Even sycophancy has a place. Faddei Bulgarin's preface to his re-make of Narezhny's re-make of Lesage's *Gil Blas* was published in 1829. (It first appeared in serial form in the mid-1820s.) The foreword to *Ivan Ivanovich Vyzhigin*, Bulgarin's vain attempt at imitation, is cast in the form of a dedicatory letter addressed to "His Highness [Count] Arsenii Andreevich Zakrevskii." This is not someone whose name will pop up soon in a history of Russia, but someone who, for Bulgarin, had pull in the right places—at Court: "Twenty years have passed . . ." Bulgarin writes bombastically, "since I first saw you on the field of battle in Finland when the unforgettable Count Nikolai Mikhailovich Kamensky led us to victory after victory and together with us overcame incredible challenges . . ."[6] Bulgarin then turns to genre; his work is a satire. He cites Peter the Great's instruction for writing in this genre and rolls out the shortest of short lists of Russian authors who have inspired him in his endeavor, Prince Antiokh Kantemir and Catherine the Great.[7]

Despite having this most distinguished and excellent cover, Bulgarin nonetheless foresees that his readers will be offended by his work. He reinvents the jock wisdom "A strong defense is a strong offense": "[My] *Vyzhigin* will not be appreciated by people who take every truth loudly proclaimed as an act of self will [*svoevol'stvo*], every exposure of abuse an act of ill intent . . ."[8] He casts himself here as radical and heroic—he will man up against the barbs and jibes sent to afflict him.

Bulgarin is not an author whose name is associated with willfulness, with challenges to authority, or with attempts at overturning the status quo. He serves grand figures of authority—we surely noticed his reference to Catherine II—not to challenge them, but to bask in the glory of their mere mention. And also to underscore his obeisance to them: "Well-intentioned people of all classes feel to the full extent the

---

[6] Faddei Bulgarin, *Sochineniia* (Moscow: Sovremennik, 1990), 24.
[7] Bulgarin, *Sochineniia*, 25. Antiokh Dmitrievich Kantemir (1709–1744), ambassador to England and France, wrote nine satires in which Russian backwardness vis-à-vis Europe was taken to task. He had trouble with the censors and his satires were first published posthumously in 1749, but only in French translation. They appeared in Russian in the second half of the eighteenth century.
[8] Bulgarin, *Sochineniia*, 25.

magnanimous intentions of our wise rulers and are prepared to the extreme to serve the greatest good. The Bureau of the Censor, having been ratified on the twenty-second of April 1828, is a durable memorial to the love of Enlightenment and to the Eternal Truth, beloved by us all, and propagated by Our Very Orthodox Monarch—a memorial worthy of our century and of the greatness of Russia!"[9] Bulgarin does not mask his desire to have Zakrevskii represent him in the higher echelons of society. We note, too, that Bulgarin (pity him) does not belong to those higher echelons. But he longs to belong. His rhetoric encodes insecurity, hope, and strategy.

Modesty is absent in Bulgarin's remarks: "Thanks be to God, we still have authentic Russian Nobles of Old [*vel'mozhi*] among us who through their service to the Crown have acquired the right to approach the Sacred Steps of the Throne."[10] Bulgarin is not shy in his efforts to align himself with these Nobles of Old. (He flatters Zakrevskii that he is one.) In fact, in an act of performative rhetoric, he claims himself to be one of them, too, if only literarily, for he distinguishes himself heroically on the page as much as the *vel'mozhi* have by the sword: "Will my readers enjoy the simplicity of the plot movement and of the narration? I hardly know. Let them forgive me any imperfection [in my tale] for the sake of my honorable goal [in writing it], but [let them also recognize] that mine is the first original Russian novel in this genre."[11] Narezhny raises an eyebrow.

Bulgarin attacks the current state of literary arts in Russia (the done thing in the early nineteenth century), roundly assaulting the incapacities of authors, readers, and critics alike. That is to say, he indicts the entire complex of individuals who make up these key components of the institutions of literature. His most stinging barbs are aimed at critics:

> I haven't focused on contemporary [criticism in] my satire, for in our day [literature] needs more assistance than opposition—it is not yet of sufficient age and it is burdened by many ills that are inimical to good morals [to warrant my barbs]. Few are the number of the literarily engaged among us. They do not comprise a distinct class such as

---

[9] Bulgarin, *Sochineniia*, 26.
[10] Bulgarin, *Sochineniia*, 27.
[11] Bulgarin, *Sochineniia*, 28.

they do in other countries.[12] [Critics] do not address what is harmful [in their essays], but instead make the odd remark about literary art and then denigrate worthy writers. Their opinions carry no weight with the public, but bring shame to the most biased and immature of their ilk. I [leave] them in peace—one doesn't beat a sleeping dog.[13]

Bulgarin's insecurities are glaring in these remarks. Anticipating criticism of his re-issued novel, and not without cause given the blows he had received during its serial publication, Bulgarin attempts to shore up his case. In his preface, therefore, he kisses up and kicks down. He flatters Zakrevsky and chastises his opponents. This was his signature in literary society.

Introductions bring literary debate to the fore. In Bulgarin's instance, his preface highlights unwittingly a raw ambition undergirded by personal, professional, and cultural insecurity. As much as Narezhny was anxious about writing as a Ukrainian in the dominant Russian culture, so, too, was the Pole, Faddei Bulgarin. A renowned stooge of Nicholas I's infamous creation, the Third Section (the secret police), Bulgarin suffered for his national origins and social status in Russia. He sought good cover.[14]

If Bulgarin in his introduction was hard on his critics and literary opponents, he was kinder to his readers. The same can't be said of Mikhail Lermontov who began publishing pieces of *A Hero of Our Time* within a few years of *Ivan Vyzhigin*'s publication. When the novel, considered the first novel of psychological realism in Russian literature, first appeared in print in 1841, it contained no preface. It sold

---

[12] Bulgarin mistakes class for profession, a normative thing to do in the Age of Pushkin, but less so as the third decade commenced. See William Mills Todd III, *Literature and Society in the Age of Pushkin* (Cambridge, MA: Harvard University Press, 1986), 10–105.

[13] Bulgarin, *Sochineniia*, 28.

[14] See Sidney Monas, *The Third Section: Police and Society under Nicholas I* (Cambridge, MA: Harvard University Press, 1961). "[Bulgarin's] own profitable literary activities depended upon the support of the Third Section of His Majesty's Imperial Chancery, which helped finance Bulgarin's newspaper, protected him from other censorship organs, restrained his literary competitors, and even sought promotions for him from the Ministry of Education" (Todd, *Literature and Society*, 75). For more on Bulgarin's origins and his role as informer, see Joe Peschio, *The Poetics of Impudence and Intimacy in the Age of Pushkin* (Madison: The Wisconsin University Press, 2012), 110–113.

out quickly, and in 1842 a second edition was published. This time it contained a word from the author, one written in response to what the critics had said about the first edition.

Lermontov's authentic authorial preface was akin to Bulgarin's in that it was published only in subsequent editions. Readers and critics get scathing treatment in equal measure. But, unlike Bulgarin's preface, Lermontov's lacks a sycophantic note. In fact, the preface is not out to make friends and influence people. It comes dripping jet black from Lermontov's bilious pen. Readers receive the first jab:

> In every book the preface is the first and also the last thing. It serves either to explain the purpose of the work or to justify it and answer criticism. But readers are generally not concerned with moral purposes or with attacks in reviews, and in result, they do not read prefaces. It is a pity that this should be so, particularly in our country. Our public is still so young and naïve that it fails to understand a fable unless it finds a lesson at its end.[15]

Lermontov's pugilistic stance is not unusual for him. He attacks the premises of prefaces—genre identification, self-justification, self-defense—as the paltry concerns of lesser critics and faint-hearted writers. These are not the concerns of readers whom he imagines sweeping

---

[15] M. Iu. Lermontov, *Polnoe sobranie sochinenii v piati tomakh* V (Moscow: Akademiia, 1936–1952), 30; Mikhail Lermontov, *A Hero of Our Time*, trans. Vladimir and Dmitry Nabokov (Ann Arbor: Ardis, 1988), 1. (Subsequent citations provide page numbers, first for the English translation, then for the Russian. This convention holds for the remainder of my study, save in those instances where it is only essential to cite the English translation.) In saying that prefaces are first and last things, he means that they are most often written last, but placed first. He is at least correct in regard to *A Hero of Our Time* and to the contemporaneous *Russian Nights* (1844) by Prince Vladimir Odoevsky, who wrote an introduction to his tales later (for his collected works) even though he had already attached one to the original publication (*Sochineniia v dvukh tomakh* 1 [Moscow: Khudlit, 1981], 31–33); Vladimir F. Odoevsky, *Russian Nights*, trans. Olga Olienikov and Ralph E. Matlaw (New York: E. P. Dutton & Co., 1965), 221–234. Cf. Narezhny's introduction, which comes first, but was hardly written last. The same is generally true of Dostoevsky's forewords; they are rarely, if ever, written last. They are attached to the first installment of his serialized fiction, i.e., long before he had written much, if any, of the narrative's later parts. Exceptions come in his *The Diary of a Writer*. See Todd, "'To Be Continued': Dostoevsky's Evolving Poetics of Serialized Publication," *Dostoevsky Studies* 18 (2014): 27, 30–31.

past introductions as so much uninteresting flotsam on the messy shore of clean story. Lermontov's audience, however, does not escape his scorn. They come in for harsh treatment as gaping rubes: "[Our readers miss] a humorous point and [do] not feel irony; they are, quite simply put, brought up badly. . . . Our public resembles a provincial who, upon overhearing the conversation of two diplomats belonging to two warring Courts, is convinced that each envoy is betraying his government in the interest of a most tender mutual friendship."[16] Despite his condescension toward the general reading public, which was small but burgeoning at the time, Lermontov nevertheless provides ample opportunity for a projected *ideal* reader to participate with him in his jests.[17] Through the metaphor of diplomatic niceties between warring parties he suggests his preferred relationship with a public made up of naïve readers and inept critics. But with intimates and kindred spirits he imagines quite different relations.[18]

Alas, Lermontov is hoisted on his own petard. His aggressiveness merely obscures the similarity between his preface and those of his opponents. *A Hero of Our Time* has been subjected to mindless interpretation, he claims. It has been misread, and his intentions in writing the novel have been mistaken. So, Lermontov defends himself from the mindlessness and the naïveté of his detractors by engaging in the three rhetorical forms he denigrates at the outset—purpose, self-justification, and defense.[19]

> The present book has only recently suffered from the unfortunate faith that certain readers and even certain reviewers have in the literal meaning of words. Some were dreadfully offended, quite in earnest, that such an immoral person as the hero of our time should be set as a model to them; others very subtly remarked that the author had drawn

---

[16] Lermontov, *Hero*, 1; 185.
[17] Donald Fanger, *The Creation of Gogol* (Cambridge: Harvard University Press, 1979), 24–44.
[18] For an expanded treatment of authors targeting distinct audiences, see Peschio, *Poetics of Impudence*, 34–59.
[19] Lermontov exaggerates the degree to which his work was unappreciated. At the time there were many a positive review, some quite astute. His arrows were aimed only at his detractors, but Lermontov overstates their representativeness. To examine some of the earliest reviews of the novel, see my *Lermontov's "A Hero of Our Time": A Critical Companion* (Evanston: Northwestern University Press, 2002), 145–195.

> his own portrait and the portraits of his acquaintances . . . What an old and paltry jest! But apparently Russia is created in such a way that everything in it changes for the better, except this sort of nonsense. With us the most fantastic of all fairy tales would hardly escape the reproach of being meant as some personal insult.[20]

Lermontov's sword is double-edged. On the one hand he argues that forewords engage in the task, useless to the general public, of self-defense. Then, on the other hand, he roundly defends his work from what he has misconstrued as injudicious readings of his novel. Furthermore, Lermontov chastises reviewers and readers "of a certain type" for taking as a slight the depiction of his protagonist and of the dramatis personae surrounding him. Lermontov, in equal measure, takes personally the barbs aimed at him and his novel in the reviews.

Lermontov gives with one hand and takes with the other. Having poked fun at those who take personal offense at the portrait of Pechorin, claiming that they read out of false vanity, he next asserts that they should indeed take offense, that he has aimed his protagonist at society, like a fist into its face. Can he then claim that there is no moral purpose to his novel? Hardly, for in presenting an amoral hero to the public for their censure, he simply flips the coin on how moral lessons are constituted in fiction:

> You will say that morality gains nothing from this. I beg your pardon. People have been fed enough sweetmeats; it has given them indigestion: they need some bitter medicine, some caustic truths. However, do not think after this that the author of this book ever had the proud dream of becoming a reformer of mankind's vices. The Lord preserve him from such benightedness! He merely found it amusing to draw modern man such as he understood him, such as he met him—too often, unfortunately, for him and you. Suffice it that the disease has been pointed out; goodness knows how to cure it.[21]

Lermontov overtly disavows (but covertly asserts) the moral intent of his depiction of "the vices of our generation." He will not accept the mantle of prophet that might be placed on the likes of those who wish to enlighten the public and edify them through art—he will leave that role to the likes of Bulgarin. However, identifying one of the purposes

---
[20] Lermontov, *Hero*, 1–2; 185–186.
[21] Lermontov, *Hero*, 2; 186.

of *A Hero of Our Time*, Lermontov aligns himself with those who would indeed edify and instruct through art. Deny the role as he might, he assumes it nonetheless. Lermontov had a choice to publish his late authorial introduction or to refrain from doing so. He didn't restrain himself. It's a fool's game, as he knows, for it is not up to him alone to decide whether he is a moralist or not. *A Hero of Our Time* puts the decision into others' hands, and he resents it. As a result, his preface becomes a house divided against itself.

Lermontov's example suggests yet again that prefaces, whether in the hands of epigones or masters, not only perform diverse services—genre identification, self-justification, defense against anticipated criticism—but also form a shaky ground on which to stand, even for the wary. To summarize from our handful of examples, the functions of authentic authorial introductions are many, the voices cast in them diverse, their purposes broad, their projected readerships disparate, and their authorial intentions sometimes quite divergent. In all of the cases we have so far examined, the configuration of author, text, reader, critic, and publisher gets modified on the basis of each author's conscious or unconscious anxieties and concerns. In more or less direct ways, the author who pens the preface places a self-generated definition on how each party is to play his or her role. Lermontov would have his reader be as keen and wary as he. Bulgarin would have his reader be grateful to him for his labors and helpful to him in opening doors to power, security, and financial reward. Narezhny would only have the reader accept him as a genuine Russifier of European literary models.

Each author's preface demonstrates that much is left in the hands of the audience. Once the work is set loose into the public, some idea of the author emerges beyond the writer's capacity to control. Readers collectively gain a rather high degree of autonomy in fixing the meanings of the text, or, alternatively, in realizing the potential meanings the writer has made available in his or her text. The circumstances under which works are evaluated become problematic. Narezhny prompts his readers' responses, but can hardly be assured they will be forthcoming. Bulgarin focuses on the mediators of the public's literary tastes and attempts to bypass them through appeals to higher authorities who might fix the value of his work in accord with his desires. Lermontov rails at the whole circumstance of miscommunication via literary activity and rejects any endeavor to pigeonhole him and his novel. But he unintentionally cuts himself as he thrusts at his detractors. What these authors, perhaps all authors, long for are ideal readers who conform completely to the projected reader the author wishes them to be: "My audience grasps completely what I intended."

Better yet to have readers aid the author in the constitution of the text itself. How then could they possibly complain? This notion is our starting point in examining the last of our examples of authentic authorial prefaces. In this instance we turn to Nikolai Gogol, whose foreword, published with the second edition of his *Dead Souls* in 1846, is a glaring, perhaps even tragic example of an author's attempt in a foreword to have readers conform to his ideal.

Gogol's novel was first published in 1841 to wide acclaim. It was hailed as a phenomenon unlike anything encountered previously in Russian literature. But it was not enough for Gogol. He was not satisfied with his accomplishment and wished for the moral, spiritual and social transformation of his reader. Gogol sought, through the mediation of the text, to establish a complete unity with his audience.

Gogol's concern over relations with his readers was acute. It is significant that his fiction is loaded with prefaces. He rarely did without them. They are a locus for the demonstration of his anxieties as a writer.[22] For example, even after the success of his *Dead Souls* had been thoroughly secured for posterity, he felt compelled to add an introduction to the second edition of the novel. It is a late authentic authorial preface, unique in how deeply troubled the author was in his attempt to generate, if not force, an ideal response to his already well-received novel. For Gogol that ideal consisted in the formation of a complete unity between author and reader, a unity that would inevitably lead to personal renewal and moral regeneration: "Reader, whosoever or wheresoever you be, and whatsoever be your station—whether that of a member of the higher ranks of society or that of a member of the plainer walks of life—I beg of you, if God shall have given you any skill

---

[22] Bojanowska treats the tensions that lurk in Gogol's prefaces, particularly those he shared with Narezhny, both being Ukrainians writing for a Russian reading public. See Edyta M. Bojanowska, *Nikolai Gogol: Between Ukrainian and Russian Nationalism* (Cambridge: Harvard University Press, 2007), 37–88.

Model Prefaces from Russian Literature

in letters, and my book shall fall into your hands, to extend to me your assistance."[23]

Gogol here engages a literary convention, by his time entirely trite—he seeks his readers' forbearance, etc., etc. But the preface turns out to be more than a cliché. In fact, it is something we should worry about on Gogol's behalf, for he wishes the reader to be more than receptive to his tale, kindly disposed toward it, enthusiastic about it. He asks readers to participate in it, help constitute missing parts, more specifically, to provide him with examples from their lives to underscore the novel's verisimilitude. He would then add their comments when revising the work for republication in the future:

> I beg of you not to deprive me of your comments, seeing that it cannot be that, should you read my book with attention, you will have *nothing* to say at some point therein. For example, how excellent it would be if some reader who is sufficiently rich in experience and the knowledge of life to be acquainted with the sort of characters which I have described herein would annotate in detail the book, without missing a single page, and undertake to read it precisely as though, laying pen and paper before him, he were first to peruse a few pages of the work, and then to recall his own life and the lives of folk with whom he has come in contact, and everything which he has seen with his own eyes or has heard of from others, and to proceed to annotate, in so far as may tally with his own experience or otherwise, what is set forth in the book, and to jot down the whole exactly as it stands pictured to his memory, and lastly, to send me the jottings as they may issue from his pen, and to continue so doing until he has covered the entire work![24]

The length of Gogol's second sentence surely suggests the extent of his anxieties about the reception of his work. But more than its reception, he is still concerned with its status as a moral instruction (*pouchenie*) to the world. He wishes now that his reader, one apparently superior in knowledge and experience than he, constitute the next iteration of the text with him, perhaps even *for* him. Gogol wishes that each successive edition of *Dead Souls* be better than the last: "Honestly can I say that to consider these points [gathered by my readers for me] against

---

[23] N. V. Gogol, *Dead Souls*, trans. D. J. Hogarth (London: J. M. Dent and Sons, 1931), 1.
[24] Gogol, *Dead Souls*, 2.

the time when a new edition of my book may be published in a different *and a better form* would give me the greatest possible pleasure."[25] Consequently, he begs his readers to compose notes for his edification so that he might improve what has become, even without them, a classic. Desire and insecurity meet tragically in Gogol's introduction.

To secure his real-world wishes (rather than those of some authorial persona winking at us from the wings), Gogol tells his willing readers how to post their suggestions to him: "Inscribing the package with my name, let [my readers] then enclose that package in a second one addressed either to the Rector of the University of St. Petersburg or to Professor Shevyrev of the University of Moscow, according as the one or the other of those two cities may be the nearer to the sender."[26] Petersburg is where Gogol was teaching at the time he wrote his preface. It was his real address. These were his authentic wishes.

Gogol's preface is not a game, it is not relieved by Lermontovian irony, and it is not addressed, like Bulgarin's, to a select well-established reader, but to everyone ("whosoever," "wheresoever" the reader might be). Within the Genette category of authentic authorial prefaces, Gogol's may be one of the most direct of direct forms of discourse we are ever to encounter. Its guilelessness tests severely the commonplace notion that implied authors and implied readers are as close as two actual parties (real author and real reader) ever get. But here we sense persona-less Nikolai Gogol thrusting himself face to face before living readers in an act of direct communion. In his belated preface to *Dead Souls*, Gogol's raw and troubled being obliterates rhetorical distances assumed to normally inhere in verbal art.

We find in Gogol's foreword another order of significance, another function of discourse to be enclosed within authentic authorial prefaces. In Gogol's dramatic display of mental fragility—which is well beyond any run-of-the-mill authorial anxiety or insecurity—we catch a glimpse of his imminent breakdown. We observe, too, the risk inherent in any aesthetic communication that attempts to breach the divide that separates readers and authors, particularly during the first decades of the nineteenth century when Russian literature struggled for an identity. Gogol's anxieties make those of Narezhny, Bulgarin, and Lermontov

---

[25] Gogol, *Dead Souls*, 3 (my emphasis).
[26] Gogol, *Dead Souls*, 4.

seem paltry.[27] But they flowed from his character, not from the condition created by engagement in verbal art.

By the 1850s many changes had been wrought in literature. Literary style had shifted toward omniscience, authoritativeness, and god-like perspectives on the issues of the day. Consequently, prefaces almost completely disappeared from major texts. Turgenev and Tolstoy did not invoke them in any of their varieties—authorial, allographic, or actorial; authentic, fictional, or apocryphal. But the form persisted to a degree. Alexander Herzen and Nikolai Chernyshevsky used authentic authorial prefaces to their fiction, *Who is To Blame?* (1845) and *What is to be Done?* (1863), respectively. Herzen's preface was penned more than a decade after his novel appeared in an expurgated edition. Its direct authorial address takes a matter-of-fact approach in recounting the history of his novel's publication. It is brief, informative, neutral in tone, and enlivened somewhat by the use of occasional literary anecdotes.[28]

Chernyshevsky's preface, by way of contrast, is more aggressive in its direct authorial discourse. Its author's insecurities are overtly presented, but assertively and as a matter of pride. As if it were merely a matter of will to accomplish the feat, Chernyshevsky turns defect into virtue: "But now that I've warned you that I have no talent whatever, you know that any merit to be found in my tale is due entirely to its truthfulness."[29] This kind of claim that abounds in the novel incensed Dostoevsky. It is surprising that Chernyshevsky's novel was as successful as it was given that it insults readers outright:

> Yes, the first pages of my story reveal that I have a very poor opinion of my public. I employed the conventional ruse of a novelist: I began my tale with some striking scenes taken from the middle or the end, and I shrouded them with mystery. You, the public, are kind, very kind indeed and therefore undiscriminating and slow-witted. You can't be

---

[27] For a more thorough treatment of Gogol's art and insecurities, see Anne Lounsbery, *Thin Culture, High Art: Gogol, Hawthorne, and Authorship in Nineteenth-Century Russia and America* (Cambridge, MA: Harvard University Press, 2007).
[28] Alexander Herzen, *Who is To Blame? A Novel in Two Parts*, trans. Michael R. Katz (Ithaca: Cornell University Press, 1984), 45–48.
[29] Nikolai Chernyshevsky, *What is to Be Done?*, trans. Michael Katz (Ithaca: Cornell University Press, 1989), 48.

relied upon to know from the first few pages whether or not a book is worth reading. You have poor instincts that are in need of assistance. . . . My name could not have attracted you [to my novel]. So I was obliged to bait my hook with striking scenes. Don't condemn me for it: you deserve all the blame. It's your own simpleminded naiveté that compelled me to stoop to such vulgarity. But now that you've fallen into my hands, I can continue the story as I see fit without further tricks.[30]

But tricks are exactly what Chernyshevsky was into. He waylays the naïve and unsuspecting, turning away the unwashed mass reader while simultaneously holding out an olive branch to those who prove willing to follow him. It was and is the appeal made by cult leaders.[31] Engage in disparagement, then supply a route to enlightenment:

> As far as the worth of its execution is concerned, you can confidently place my tale side by side with the most famous works of your well-known authors. Perhaps you'd not do wrong to place it even higher than theirs! It certainly contains more artistry—rest assured on that point.
>
> You may thank me. You so love to cringe before those who abuse you; so now you can cringe before me, too.
>
> Yet there is among you, dear readers, a particular group of people—by now a fairly sizable group—which I respect. I speak arrogantly to the vast majority of readers, but to them alone, and up to this point I've been speaking only to them. But with the particular group I just mentioned, I would have spoken humbly, even timidly. There is no need to offer them any explanation. I value their opinion, but I know in advance that they're on my side. Good strong, honest, capable people—you have only just begun to appear among us; already there's a fair number of you and it's growing all the time. If you were my entire audience, there'd be no need for me to write. If you did not exist, it would be impossible for me to write. But you're not yet my entire audience, although some of you are numbered among my readers. Therefore, it's still necessary and already possible for me to write.[32]

---

[30] Chernyshevsky, *What is to Be Done?*, 47.

[31] For the many ways Chernyshevsky exploited behavioral codes to manipulate his readers, see Irina Paperno, *Chernyshevsky and the Age of Realism: A Study in the Semiotics of Behavior* (Stanford: Stanford University Press, 1988), 159–218.

[32] Chernyshevsky, *What is to Be Done?*, 48–49.

Like Gogol in his preface to the second part of *Dead Souls*, Chernyshevsky expresses a deep desire for an ideal readership, that is, one that coincides in its thinking with his vision of a new reality that he conjures in a performative act of utterance. Where Gogol failed, Chernyshevsky succeeded. Young readers flocked to him and his call for a new social order. As Irina Paperno puts it, "Chernyshevsky succeeded in promoting cultural mechanisms for ordering human reality and organizing individual behavior in an era of ultimate disarray, when 'everything came up for rearrangement.'"[33]

Chernyshevsky's manipulations, both aesthetic and social, worked within radical circles, which Chernyshevsky ineptly portrayed, ironically, to great success in *What is to Be Done*? The response from Dostoevsky in both philosophical and literary terms came within two years with the publication of *Notes from the Underground*. We might surmise that Dostoevsky's suspicion of authentic authorial prefaces derives from his reception of Chernyshevsky, a barely qualified writer of fiction who takes the risks of speaking in one's own voice to new lows. Bulgarin looks like an old piker in comparison.

Dostoevsky, it turns out, was to use authentic authorial introductions only on rare occasions in his fiction. When he did turn to them, it was in a threshold form where both the print context in which the tale occurs and the reliability of the voice contained in the preface challenge the diverse range of possibilities we observe in Narezhny, Bulgarin, Lermontov, Gogol, and Chernyshevsky. More often, however, Dostoevsky found greater scope for his first words in what Genette labels fictional authorial and allographic introductions.

II

FICTIVE AUTHORIAL INTRODUCTIONS

An introduction that projects an imaginary figure as its author is a form attested widely in the Romantic period by the likes of Sir Walter Scott, Washington Irving, Nikolai Gogol and, it has been argued, if speciously, Alexander Pushkin. Walter Scott's Laurence Templeton of

---

[33] Paperno, *Chernyshevsky*, 38.

Ivanhoe (1820) is a famous case in point.[34] Templeton, in fact, served as a model for many a Russian Romantic prose writer. Scott's *Ivanhoe*, for example, begins with Templeton's preface cum dedication in which the real author depicts both addresser and addressee, each as fictional as the dust that forms the latter's surname:

> Dedicatory Epistle to The Rev. Dr. Dryasdust, F. A. S., Residing in the Castle Gate, York.
>
> Much esteemed and Dear Sir, It is scarcely necessary to mention the various concurring reasons which induce me to place your name at the head of the following work. Yet the chief of these reasons may perhaps be refuted by the imperfections of the performance. . . . I fear I shall incur the censure of presumption in placing the venerable name of Dr. Jonas Dryasdust at the head of a publication which the more grave antiquary will perhaps class with the idle novels and romances of the day. I am anxious to vindicate myself from such a charge; for, although I might trust to your friendship for an apology in your eyes, yet I would willingly stand convicted in those of the public of so grave a crime as my fears lead me to anticipate my being charged with.[35]

If some level of anxiety runs through prefaces, we detect it in Scott's stepping out of his established role as poet into that of prose writer. This shift in literary mode may account for the fictive prefaces of his Waverley Novels. The literary crimes with which Templeton fears he might be charged merely mask Scott's concerns with his "crime" of altering his authorial persona from poet to prosaist.

Whatever the case may be, Scott's fictional authorial introductions to the Waverley Novels (in *Ivanhoe* as elsewhere) give way after a decade of deception to an authentic authorial preface. In it Scott outs his fictional counterpart and lays claim to his own work. In a preface of 1830, Scott writes: "The author of the Waverley Novels had hitherto proceeded in an unabated course of popularity, and might, in his peculiar district of literature, have been termed *l'enfant gâté* of success.

---

[34] Scott's introductions have become artifacts in their own right; they have been liberated from the narratives they introduce. See Walter Scott, *The Prefaces to the Waverley Novels*, ed. Mark A. Weinstein (Lincoln: University of Nebraska Press, 1978). For a study of Scott based in significant measure on his prefaces, see Caroline McCracken-Flesher, *Possible Scotlands: Walter Scott and the Story of Tomorrow* (Oxford: Oxford University Press, 2005).

[35] Sir Walter Scott, *Ivanhoe* (Norwalk, CT: The Heritage Press, 1950), xvii.

It was plain, however, that frequent publication must finally wear out the public favor, unless some mode could be devised to give an appearance of novelty to subsequent productions."[36] No longer does Scott fear his readers' censure for turning from poetry to prose, for by 1830 he can rest assured that he, like his Templeton, is covered in Waverley glory. He signs his name to the introduction.

Scott's concerns shift from persona to pen, from authenticity to irony. He fears now that the Waverley Novels are becoming tedious. What better remedy, he claims, than to provide the "appearance of novelty" by providing a new type of introduction, as though prefaces held magical powers sufficient to rescue the narrative they introduce. Scott's jest comes at the expense of a naïve readership that has been mistaking Templeton for a real person for a solid ten years. Time has come for him to be rewarded for his accomplishment. Time, too, for readers to wise up. Time it was, too, for Scott to put his insecurities to rest, which he could now do with every assurance of success.

Scott spawned imitators of which there were many in Russia, some of whom were in fact tedious from the first words. Others were more clever. Nikolai Gogol belongs, of course, to the second camp. His *Evenings on a Farm Near Dikanka*, in which fictional authorial introductions appear, is a case in point. Part One (1831) and Part Two (1832) of the *Dikanka Tales* are introduced to readers by the beekeeper, Rudy Panko. Gogol's "author," Rudy, takes solid shape before our eyes.[37] We learn about him from what he has to say about the narrators whose oral tales he transcribes. We also discover something essential about him from the editorial remarks he makes that dot the landscape of the tales he passes on to us. The social context in and through which the storytelling in the village of Dikanka takes place also gives us a sense of Rudy's character:

> "What oddity is this: *Evenings on a Farm near Dikanka*? What sort of *Evenings* have we here? And thrust into the world by a beekeeper! God protect us! As though geese enough had not been plucked for pens and

---

[36] Scott, *Ivanhoe*, ix.
[37] Nikolai Gogol, *Sobranie sochinenii v piati tomakh* I (Moscow: Akademiia nauk, 1960), 11–303; *The Complete Tales of Nikolai Gogol*, vol. I, ed. Leonard J. Kent (Chicago: The University of Chicago Press, 1985), 3–206.

rags turned into paper! As though folks enough of all classes had not covered their fingers with inkstains! . . . ."

I had a premonition of all this talk a month ago. In fact, for a villager like me to poke his nose out of his hole into the great world is—merciful heavens!—just like what happens if you go into the apartments of some fine gentleman: they all come around you and make you feel like a fool . . .[38]

Rudy knows he is stepping beyond the social and literary boundaries that would normally apply to the likes of him. But he has a mission. And he has pretensions. The first is to bring a world hitherto unrepresented in Russian fiction to the fore, and the second to be the one to do it, literate, if lowly, beekeeper that he is. He knows (like his creator) that he has something new to present to the public. Furthermore, given that he is cognizant of his station in life and knows that his assumption of the author's mantle challenges social and cultural norms, he is aware that the reading pubic may not appreciate what he is up to:

At home, my dear readers—no offense meant (you may be annoyed at a beekeeper like me addressing you so plainly, as though I were speaking to some old friend or crony)—at home in the village it has always been the peasants' habit, as soon as the work in the fields is over, to climb up on the stove and rest there all winter, and we beekeepers put our bees away in a dark cellar. At the season when you see no cranes in the sky or pears on the trees, there is sure to be a light burning somewhere at the end of the village as soon as evening comes on, laughter and singing are heard in the distance, there is the twang of the balalaika and at times of the fiddle, talk and noise . . . Those are our *evening parties*! . . .[39]

It is in Rudy Panko's "hut" that the storytelling takes place. He describes the scene in his domicile—who listens, who narrates, how the audience responds to the stories, and how their spell is cast.[40] Then Rudy concludes (in the preface to Part One of the collection)[41] with an invitation to us, his readers, to come visit him so that we might enjoy more of the

---
[38] Gogol, *Complete Tales*, 3; 11.
[39] Gogol, *Complete Tales*, 4; 12.
[40] Gogol, *Complete Tales*, 4–6; 11.
[41] Each of the two parts of the *Dikanka Tales* is introduced by Rudy Panko. Gogol understood that a good deal of the charm of his tale had to do with Rudy's role, so he gave him full vocal range in the second part.

same. He provides directions on how to find his hut and delivers up a long list of the foodstuffs with which we will be regaled upon arrival.[42]

There is no mystification in Gogol's prefaces. They are clearly fictional. The pleasures to be derived from them are direct. This is not to say, however, that the prefaces, particularly the first, are not rife with worries. Rudy Panko's anticipation of his readers' response to him as a writer is significant for being overt. Covertly, those anxieties may well stand in for Gogol's own, something of the type made in the extreme, as we have seen, in his introduction to the second edition of *Dead Souls* fourteen years later. His previous efforts at publication had proven disastrous, so much so that he either scorched the earth of his labor or consigned his manuscript to his desk to await a more propitious moment. All it took was the loud acclaim accorded his *Dikanka Tales* for Gogol to move on with alacrity. He issued Part Two within a year.

The second introduction reveals a voice more confident in its aesthetic purposes, more sanguine about the reader's response, and consequently less self-defensive and cautious. It plays on the strengths hard won in Part One:

> Here is a second part for you, and I had better say the last one! I did not want, I did not at all want to bring it out. One should not outstay one's welcome. I must tell you they are already beginning to laugh at me in the village. "The old fellow has become stupid," they say, "he is amusing himself with children's toys in his old age!" And, indeed, it is high time to rest. I expect you imagine, dear readers, that I am only pretending to be old. Pretend, indeed, when I have no teeth left in my mouth! Now, if anything soft comes my way I manage to chew it, but I can't tackle anything hard. So here is another book for you![43]

The mature Gogol is already apparent in the presentation of the narrator, whose speech engages in misdirection, allogism, slang, Ukrainianisms, and an orientation toward oral performance, all eventual stylistic trademarks.[44]

---

[42] Gogol, *Complete Tales*, 7; 16–17.
[43] Gogol, *Complete Tales*, 89; 137.
[44] In Parts One and Two, Gogol's introductions include a glossary of Ukrainian vocabulary.

But anxiety yet again sticks out its mug. In bidding farewell to his reader, Rudy Panko expresses a persistent fear of Gogol's—that he might be forgotten, never amount to anything, disappear without a trace: "Goodbye. It will be a long time before we meet again, if we ever do. But then, it would not matter to you if I had never existed at all. One year will pass and then another—and none of you will remember or miss the old beekeeper, Rudy Panko."[45] Here questions concerning his ultimate value bedevil Gogol, barely masked as Rudy Panko. They presage the implosion we witness in the preface to Part Two of *Dead Souls*, an authentic authorial introduction that hardly obscures the ache of anxiety.

III

FICTIVE ALLOGRAPHIC INTRODUCTIONS

Allographic prefaces represent third-party introductions, that is to say, they are not written by the work's author, but by another party altogether. Allographic introductions include those written by real historical personages or by fictional personages.[46] Of the two, Dostoevsky only uses the second subtype—fictional allographic prefaces. We examine two instances in which they occur in Russian literature of the Romantic period, Pushkin's *Belkin Tales* and Lermontov's *A Hero of Our Time*.

In taking up pen, ink, and paper to "poke one's nose out into the great world [of letters]," to cite Gogol's Rudy Panko again, there would seem to be little recourse for burying one's trepidation other than to hide behind a set of masks. In the direct authorial prefaces we have seen, Narezhny, Bulgarin, and Lermontov all wear their misgivings in more or less full view. Fictional authorial forewords, likewise, are hard-pressed to hide authorial anxiety. Both Scott's and Gogol's trepidations can be adduced through the discourse of their fictionalized authorial characters.

---

[45] Gogol, *Complete Tales*, 91; 140.
[46] For example, see Prince Peter Viazemsky's preface to Alexander Pushkin's "The Fountain of Bakhchisarai" (1824): http://feb-web.ru/feb/pushkin/critics/vpk/vpk-152-.htm.

Alexander Pushkin, cognizant of his own anxieties about turning from poetry, where his persona was well established, to prose, where it was not, attempted something different in his preface to *The Belkin Tales* (1831). He used a set of masks to filter out his authorial persona altogether. Like Scott, awaiting positive reader response before revealing himself to the public, Pushkin delivered up his story cycle anonymously. But, unlike Scott and Gogol, he did not present a fictional character who parades as the work's author. Instead, he provides a set of figures enrolled in the institutions of literature—a publisher, whose introduction we read; a collector of tales (who has literary pretensions), the eponymous Ivan Ivanovich Belkin; and four narrators, the "authors" of the tales that Belkin transcribes for publication. It is a complex structure that fictional allographic forewords more readily accommodate.

Pushkin's introduction follows the pattern of Scottian prefatorial mystification. Pushkin's fictional author, however, is not an author, like Templeton, but the publisher, "A. P." Pushkin's initials suggested to critics and readers in 1831 that Alexander Pushkin was that very publisher. In other words, they viewed A. P. as Pushkin in the barest of disguises. A cursory reading of the introduction, however, convinces one rather quickly that the mentality represented in and through A. P.'s discourse does not, indeed cannot, point directly to Alexander Pushkin's identity.[47]

Pushkin hardly buries allusion to this fact. For example, A. P. promises to give us a thoroughly satisfactory account of Belkin's identity, the person who has transcribed the tales for posterity. To that end A. P. states that he will provide the entirety of Belkin's neighbor's epistolary account of him, the only reliable source of information he has on Belkin's character: "We print [the neighbor's letter describing Belkin] without any change or annotations, as a precious document testifying to a noble frame of mind and to a touching bond of friendship, and, at the same time, as a perfectly adequate biographical sketch."[48] A. P.

---

[47] This is not meant to suggest that Pushkin is not the author of *The Belkin Tales*. Here, I address the voice presented in the preface. It belongs to A. P., not to Pushkin, who has invented it for A. P. to use. Dostoevsky imitates Pushkin in *Notes from the Underground*.

[48] A. S. Pushkin, *Sobranie sochinenii v desiati tomakh 5* (Moscow: Khudlit, 1960), 45; Alexander Pushkin, *Complete Prose Fiction*, trans. Paul Debrezeny (Stanford: Stanford University Press, 1983), 62.

nevertheless annotates the neighbor's letter, expunges parts of it on the grounds that it can be of little interest to the reader, and derives nothing from the letter that would allow either him or us to indeed perceive in Belkin "a noble frame of mind" or to find evidence of "a touching bond of friendship" between the letter writer and Belkin.[49] Pushkin's clues are hardly subtle. But readers missed them nevertheless.

It cannot be said that either A. P. or Belkin is the author of the tales. A. P. merely discovers the manuscript of the tales (he doesn't explain how) and publishes it. Belkin, for his part, has merely recorded the tales. He did not invent them or write them down from direct experience. They are stories he has been told by four individuals whose identities we are excluded from knowing.[50]

In the introduction to *The Belkin Tales* Pushkin plays with reader curiosity about the relationship between authorial identity and authorial personae. Pushkin's preface parodies the assumption that authors are their characters in mufti. He also satirizes the reader's willingness to believe that fiction and life coincide, not only in the figure of the author, who mediates the two, but also in the figures of the dramatis personae. Critics' reviews in which A. P. was taken as Pushkin only fueled the satiric fire that warmed the only readers Pushkin seems to have cared deeply about—his friends, almost all elite literati. Pushkin could count on them to know who A. P. wasn't.[51]

Fictional allographic prefaces provide perfect cover for the author's identity. Any risks associated with "sticking your mug out" before the reading public can be effectively nullified by burying one's identity behind a set of narrative filters of the type Pushkin developed for *The Belkin Tales*. As we have seen in our treatment of authentic authorial prefaces, Mikhail Lermontov's pugnacious relations with readers led him to expose himself more than he might have wished. He might better have chosen to follow Pushkin's example of narrative layers in *The Belkin Tales*'s first words. And, if not A. P., then Lermontov perhaps might have followed the model he embedded in his own novel— the "Introduction to Pechorin's Journal."[52] In *Hero of Our Time*,

---

[49] Pushkin, *Prose Fiction*, 63–64; 46.
[50] We are given their initials along with their station in life only.
[51] Peschio, *Poetics of Impudence*, 94–124.
[52] Lermontov, *Hero*, 63–64; 228–229.

Model Prefaces from Russian Literature | 23

Lermontov parodies the conceit of having a traveling narrator discover a story that then finds its way into print. This traveler delivers up the first two tales of the five that comprise the novel. Like Panko and Belkin, Lermontov's traveler has acquired the first story, "Bela," from his temporary companion, a *kavkazets*, Maksim Maksimich.[53] Then the traveler relates the second story, "Maksim Maksimich," which he narrates as a direct experience. At the conclusion of that second tale, the traveler describes how he acquired Pechorin's personal notes from Maxim Maksimich, who gives it up in a fit of pique. Pechorin's journal makes up the novel's last three chapters or stories. The traveling narrator provides an introduction to Pechorin's journal roughly mid-way through the novel. It represents a fictive allographic preface, structurally much like A. P.'s in *The Belkin Tales* but without creating the illusion of its coming from his (Lermontov's) hand.

Lermontov's novel is rather unique in that it contains two introductions. The first is in the normal place at the outset of the narrative (the late authentic authorial one I have already sketched). The second is the traveling narrator's inserted fictive allographic preface, allographic in the sense that Pechorin's journal is introduced to us by a third party who did not compose the text we are about to read, and fictive in that the speaker/writer is not a real, living third party.

The traveler's preface performs four functions. First, it introduces the text's genre—diary/journal. Second, in an attempt to verify the authenticity and reliability of the first-person narratives that comprise the journal, the traveler attests to the uncensored nature of Pechorin's confession: "While reading over these notes, I became convinced of the sincerity of this man who so mercilessly exhibited his own failings and vices. The history of a human soul, be it even the meanest soul, can hardly be less curious or less instructive than the history of an entire nation—especially when it is the result of self-observation on the part of a mature mind, and when it is written without the ambitious desire to provoke sympathy or amazement. Rousseau's *Confessions* have already the defect of his having read them to his friends."[54] In other words, the traveler would have us believe that Pechorin did not write his notes for

---

[53] A *kavkazets* was a Russian common soldier who had served so long in the Caucasus that he had become bi-cultural.
[54] Lermontov, *Hero*, 63–64; 229.

public consumption. At the moment of his recording a diary of his life in the Caucasus, Pechorin is both author and sole audience, enclosing communication in a solipsistic circle very much in keeping with his personality and in his self-absorbed disregard of others.

Third, the traveler's introduction replicates the ironic stance of the preface Lermontov subsequently added. The traveler begins his preface saying, "I learned not long ago that Pechorin had died on his way back from Persia. This news gladdened me very much, for it gave me the right to publish these notes, and I took advantage of the opportunity to sign another man's work with my own name. God grant that readers do not castigate me for such an innocent forgery."[55] These tightly packed first words underscore the irony that is the novel in its entirety—its play with genre expectations chapter by chapter, its scathing attitude toward human behavior that is cut from one thin cloth, its reorganization of the plot's chronology, its claim that it has nothing to teach through its depiction of casual immorality while simultaneously educating through negative example nonetheless.

Fourth, the traveler's introduction to Pechorin's journal clarifies that the novel, *A Hero of Our Time*, is his and his alone: "Perhaps some readers will want to know my opinion of Pechorin's character. My answer is the title of this book. 'But this is wicked irony!' they will say. I wonder."[56] At this point the traveling narrator's stance and Lermontov's coincide, but not their status one vis-à-vis the other. The traveler is the fictional author of the novel, Lermontov the authentic one. But, if their respective ontological statuses differ, their purposes are one—the exposure of "all the vices of a generation."

There are other vices of "our time" exposed in the preface as well. They have to do with the legal status of the text within society. The traveler has patched together disparate elements of his own writings (his travel notes) along with Pechorin's travel journal. He overtly discloses the problem for writers of the time—they are not protected from theft. The traveler considers it a minor crime that he has affixed his name to Pechorin's own work. In this way another risk-filled feature of the institutions of literature come to the fore in the embedded fictional allographic preface we find here: theft.

---

[55] Lermontov, *Hero*, 63; 228.
[56] Lermontov, *Hero*, 64; 229.

We have already seen the depiction of the sundry figures who constitute the literary moment—publishers, writers working to become authors, authors themselves, collectors of tales, oral storytellers and transcribers of oral tales, compilers, and editors. In various combinations they figure in the introductions we have examined. But in *A Hero of Our Time* Lermontov's traveling narrator announces forthrightly the problem of copyright, the legal ownership of one's own creation. It was a serious problem, as Prince Vladimir Odoevsky (1804–1869) attests in the introduction to his *Russian Nights* (1844) only one year before Dostoevsky entered the field.

In closing this chapter in order to turn to Dostoevsky's prefaces, it is worth noting Odoevsky's experience in regard to the theft of his work, something he did not consider, unlike Lermontov's traveling narrator, a minor crime. Writing a foreword to *Russian Nights* for an 1860s edition of his collected works, a foreword, incidentally, which did not appear in print until the twentieth century, he noted:

> [Some] good people took advantage of the fact that my book had become a bibliographic rarity and on the sly began pilfering out of it whatever anyone needed in his art. Some followed the literary practice, that is, they borrowed in a very refined manner under various guises; some were less ceremonious and simply replaced the names of personages in my works by those of their own choice, changed the time and place of action, and claimed it as their own; there were also some who without further ado took, say, a whole story of mine in its entirety, called it a biography, and signed their name to it. There are plenty of such curious works wandering around in the world. For a long time I did not protest against such *borrowings*, partly because this particular kind of edition of my works seemed rather amusing to me. Only in 1859 did I consider it necessary to warn certain gentlemen about the possible consequences of their unceremonious fraud. . . . Thus, the fate of my book was as follows: people pilfered it, distorted what they took, and abused it; and the majority of readers did not have any means of checking these frauds. All these reasons taken together, which are of such importance to a person for whom the rights and obligations of a literary man are sacred, have prompted me to proceed with a new edition of my works.[57]

---

[57] V. F. Odoevskii, *Sochineniia v dvukh tomakh* 1 (Moscow: Khudlit, 1981), 305–306; V. F. Odoevsky, *Russian Nights*, trans. Olga Olienikov and Ralph E. Matlaw (New York: E. P. Dutton & Co., 1965), 22–23.

FIRST WORDS On Dostoevsky's Introductions

When Dostoevsky published his first work of fiction, *Poor Folk*, in 1845, he entered a print world fraught with dangers, not only of the type described by Lermontov in fiction and Odoevsky in truth of fact, but of the several types we have examined in the works from the first decades of the nineteenth century. Prefaces constituted an entry point not only into a given work of art but into the fictional enterprise itself. It is a hallway that leads to several doors at once: toward the complexities of the communication process (from writer's motivation to reader response, from misreadings to ideal forms of communion); toward the individual writers' psyches and the anxieties that accompany their forays into creativity; toward bombast and egocentrism as well as toward raw ambition and unsettling insecurity; toward the playground of verbal art and toward sometimes striking earnestness.

Little wonder then that Dostoevsky avoided prefaces completely in the 1840s. Not a single one of his publications prior to his arrest for seditious activity in 1849 is preceded by a foreword, preface, introduction, or prologue.[58] This fact may be ascribed to the emergence of realist narrative tendencies in the 1840s, but this rings hollow as an explanation. Clearly, including an introduction was a matter of choice for any author at this historical moment. Dostoevsky opted out, one can conjecture, because he was most interested in the narrative and its function independent of a prejudicial word from his (or another's) point of view. He clearly did not feel the urge to direct readers toward an understanding of genre. He let the text do that, feeling no need to interject his own voice between the reader and the text. The work would stand on its own without interference.

Nor did Dostoevsky wish to have another voice prepare readers for their entry into the text, neither the voice of a living third party, say for example his apartment mate, Dmitry Grigorovich (1822–1899), nor the voice of his text's narrator. Dostoevsky was not interested in prodding his reader to form an ideal relationship with him via the text, that is, to decode his text in complete accord with his intentions. He did not seek

---

[58] There is one possible exception. In "A Faint Heart" ("Slaboe serdtse"), the fictional author belatedly refers to the first paragraph of his account as a foreword (*predislovie*). Dostoevskii, *PSS*, II, 16; Fyodor Dostoevsky, *White Nights and Other Stories*, trans. Constance Garnett (New York: Grove Press, Inc., 1960), 57.

the protection of a high-placed addressee à la Bulgarin. Neither did he wish to communicate with a narrow readership as Pushkin did or with an intellectually challenged one as Lermontov felt he must. He simply chose to have his narratives stand on their own, naked.

In many ways, his decision was a courageous one that ran against the norms of the period (prerogative of the young artist). After his incarceration and exile from 1849 to 1859, however, he altered his approach and made judicious decisions about the use of prefaces, introductions, and forewords. Again he went against the prevailing norms of a new generation of authors, including the realists Turgenev, Tolstoy, Goncharov, and Saltykov-Shchedrin, who eschewed prefaces for the most part. When Dostoevsky did turn to introductions, he invented hybrid forms out of the types we have encountered in the models available to him. We turn to his unique practice now.

Dostoevsky's Initial Post-Siberian Work

Dostoevsky was granted permission to return to European Russia in 1859, ten years after his arrest. By this time he had served four years in a convict prison in Western Siberia (Omsk), another four years of military service in Semipalatinsk, and somewhat more than one year in active pursuit of return to St. Petersburg while in retirement from military service. Upon his return, Dostoevsky entered a literary fray much transformed from what he had known and experienced in the 1840s. But Dostoevsky longed to hold the center stage he had held briefly upon the publication of his first two works of prose fiction, *Poor Folk* (1846) and *The Double* (1846). Other than these two works, he had departed the scene with a record of subsequent publications that mystified and disaffected an originally enthusiastic readership. Belinsky, who hailed Dostoevsky's first work in the press even before it appeared in print, had subsequently grown cool toward him. Then, not long before his arrest for sedition, Dostoevsky had parted ways with Belinsky over the function of art, first and foremost, but secondarily over Belinsky's assessment of the aesthetic quality of Dostoevsky's work published hard on the heels of *Poor Folk* and *The Double*: "Mr. Prokharchin" (1846), "A Novel in Nine Letters" (1847), *The Landlady* (1847), "Polzunkov" (1848), "A Faint Heart" (1848), "Another's Wife and a Husband under the Bed" (1848), "The Honest Thief" (1848), "The Christmas Tree and the Wedding" (1848), and *White Nights* (1848). None of these tales produced a positive critical response. Truth be told, even *The Double* had raised many an eyebrow. A return to the literary scene in 1859 represented a double challenge for Dostoevsky. First, he was not familiar with that scene in a personal way, except as mediated by journalists and correspondents. He was playing catch-up. And second, he was facing an informed critical opinion that thought he may have exhausted his literary capacities as early as 1846.

Against his practice of avoiding introductions in the 1840s, Dostoevsky put them to use immediately. This is not to suggest that he saw them as a magic bullet that would propel him into the center of his target audience's heart. Such an opinion would exaggerate mightily both the limited function and aesthetic reach of the device. Rather, Dostoevsky may have turned to prefaces because of what he had learned about himself as an artist from years of contemplating both his failings and his promise. He conducted his introspections both in the privacy of his mind while lying on the hard board bed of his prison barracks and also in communication with his brother, Mikhail. His strength as a young writer was in the point of view he captured in his stories and novellas, in perspectives that belonged to his dramatis personae, not to any (apparent) omniscient authorial personage. Through the voices of his protagonists—directly rendered in Makar Devushkin's and Varvara Dobroselova's speech in *Poor Folk*; sometimes directly, at other times indirectly in Iakov Golyadkin's in *The Double*—Dostoevsky sweeps us up into the turmoil of his protagonists' rising hopes and dashed dreams. One of his great artistic virtues lay in creating narrative forms that depict inner consciousness, not through omniscience, but by means of his characters' sometimes scant intellectual powers, their gross subjectivity, emotional instability, inner struggle, and their deep longing to get right with self and world.

Dostoevsky highlights this strength by featuring it in his prefaces. Within the first utterances he formalizes the process of narration-from-within by indicating to his readers from the beginning that they are encountering an Other who narrates the tale. Two of his first three post-Siberian novels put prefaces to quick use—*The Village of Stepanchikovo and its Inhabitants* (1859) and *Notes from the House of the Dead* (1860–1862).[1] These two introductions announce immediately that someone other than Dostoevsky's alter ego speaks to us directly. Furthermore, the voice issues from out of the fictional discourse and not from a source occupying an abstract intermediate

---

[1] The exception is *The Humiliated and Injured* (1861).

ground somewhere between authorial persona and protagonist. Because Dostoevsky in large measure eschews conventional omniscience, his prefatorial narrator is not someone privy to all the information necessary to deliver up a more or less complete and comprehensive view of the action. Unreliability inheres in his narrator types. In *The Village of Stepanchikovo* and *Notes from the House of the Dead* Dostoevsky experiments with two of them.

I

THE VILLAGE OF STEPANCHIKOVO AND ITS INHABITANTS

In *Stepanchikovo*, the tale's narrator is an actor, if a peripheral one, in the drama. His "Introductory" (*Vstuplenie*) forms the whole of the novel's Chapter One. Temporally, it marks the same time stamp as the novel's "Conclusion" (*Zakliuchenie*), which, like the introductory, forms its own chapter (Chapter Six, Part II). Character and plot development occur between these two framing points. All the plot action (the other sixteen chapters) takes place over a two-day period. Within the frame, the plot unfolds, reaches a climax followed by a comedic anticlimax in which the (laughable) status quo is restored. Both the preface and the conclusion, in other words, are entirely conventional. The capacity of frame narratives to deliver up a hidden message is not realized in the least.[2] Then again, because most of the characters are the butt of Dostoevsky's joke, there really is little more to discover about them, or the narrator, other than what has already been exposed to ridicule in the course of the story.

These features of the Introductory indicate the degree to which Dostoevsky relied on tried-and-true narrative techniques for his re-entry into literary activity. Neither a first person narrator nor a frame structure represented any kind of literary innovation. Well attested though they may have been in Dostoevsky's time (and long before it),

---

[2] The "third message" is the focus of Charles Isenberg's *Telling Silence: Russian Frame Narratives of Renunciation* (Evanston: Northwestern University Press, 1993). The covert tale represents a synthetic form of the themes presented in the frame and insert tale. We shall first have recourse to Isenberg's thesis in treating *Demons*.

these elements could in no way guarantee what Dostoevsky wished most for his novel: critical acclaim. Most likely, the work's conventionality doomed it to a fate worse than failure—it went unnoticed. Before the novel's publication, Dostoevsky wrote to his brother, Mikhail, with a mixture of trepidation and excitement: ". . . the novel has very great defects, perhaps its worst being that it's too drawn out; but I am sure of one thing, as of an axiom, that at the same time it also has the greatest qualities and that it is *my very best work*. I have been writing it for two years, with a break in the middle to complete 'Uncle's Dream.' The beginning and the middle portions are already completed, the end [will be] soon. But here I place my whole soul, my flesh and blood. . . . [If] the public receives it coldly, then, I confess, I may very well fall into despair. I base all my fondest hopes on it, and—this is the main thing—the restoration of my literary reputation."[3]

Even after the work had been turned down outright by a string of publishers, Dostoevsky remained hopeful. In August of that same year, he wrote: "I am convinced that there are many weak and bad things in my novel, but I am also convinced—cut my throat if I'm wrong—that there are very fine things in it, too. They poured forth from my soul. There are scenes of high comedy, scenes Gogol himself would have put his name to in a trice."[4]

Stepanchikovo is a farce. It is also a satire aimed at the Nikolai Gogol of *Selected Passages from Correspondence with Friends* (1846), disaster that it was.[5] Despite Dostoevsky's insistence to the contrary, there is very little "high" comedy to be found in *Stepanchikovo*. Something rather more slapstick, sometimes even crude, stands in its stead. One doubts that Gogol would have claimed any part of it and not simply because he is pilloried in the novel. It's because an important element of Gogol's humor is missing—that part that lifts us upward

---

[3] Dostoevskii, *PSS*, XXVIII/1: 326.
[4] Dostoevskii, *PSS*, XXVIII/1: 334.
[5] See Ruth Sobel, *Gogol's Forgotten Book: Selected Passages and its Contemporary Readers* (Washington, DC: University Press of America, 1981); Alexander Zholkovsky, "Rereading Gogol's Miswritten Book: Notes on *Selected Passages from Correspondence with Friends*," in *Essays on Gogol: Logos and the Russian Word*, ed. Susanne Fusso and Priscilla Meyer (Evanston: Northern Illinois University Press, 1992), 172–184. Cf. Donald Fanger for a highly nuanced, even moving, reading of the text in his *The Creation of Nikolai Gogol* (Cambridge: Harvard University Press, 1979), 209–222.

and leavens, quite often, the more base elements of his humor.[6] Yet the Introductory does allow Dostoevsky to highlight the aforementioned strength of his narrative technique: unreliable narration from within that encompasses two time dimensions—the time of the events of the tale and the time later on when the narrator pens his tale, thus providing perspective on the narrated events.[7]

Although Dostoevsky's preface introduces the complication adequately and provides us immediately with a notion of the narrator's capacities, it in no way prepares us for the repetitive, drawn-out, wearying soap opera *Stepanchikovo* in fact proves to be. Despite heroic attempts by critics to salvage some aesthetic value from the work's wreckage, *Stepanchikovo* is not a narrative ship we wish to sail on for long.[8] It is not a narrative proper, but a series of scenes in which the same dynamic (reversal of roles, for instance) is repeated *ad nauseam*. To borrow a term from Gary Saul Morson, *Stepanchikovo* lacks something we associate with Dostoevsky's work, to wit, "narrativeness."[9]

As we have seen, Dostoevsky calls the preface "Introductory," not the most conventional of labels in the panoply of rough synonyms we see him use over the course of the ensuing twenty years, but an attested one in Russia nevertheless. What is important to note is that the label belongs to the implied author, not to his narrator, who refers to the "Introductory" as "my foreword" (*moe predislovie*).[10] Dostoevsky's use

---

[6] See Alexander Slonimskii, "The Technique of the Comic in Gogol," in *Gogol from the Twentieth Century: Eleven Essays*, ed. and trans. Robert A. Maguire (Princeton: Princeton University Press, 1974), 323–374.

[7] *Demons* is also structured in this way, that is, with a "narrating-I" and an "experiencing I."

[8] See, for example, Joseph Frank, *The Years of Ordeal: 1850–1859*, 297–304; Ignat Avsey, "*The Village of Stepanchikovo* or 'There's a man with no clothes on,'" in *Dostoevsky's Polyphonic Talent*, ed. Joe E. Barnhard (New York: University Press of America, Inc., 2005), 153–172. The value of the text, these authors argue in large measure, is to be found in the way it presages major themes of Dostoevsky's subsequent art. Cf. Kristin Vitalich, "*The Village of Stapanchikovo*: Toward a (Lacanian) Theory of Parody," *Slavic and East European Journal* 53, no. 2 (2009): 203–218.

[9] Gary Saul Morson, *Prosaics and Other Provocations: Empathy, Open Time, and the Novel* (Boston: Academic Studies Press, 2013), 33–53. To represent "narrativeness," Morson argues, a text must deliver up a sense of contingency, process, presentness, and open time. These features are entirely lacking in *Stepanchikovo*.

[10] Fyodor Dostoyevsky, *The Village of Stepanchikovo and its Inhabitants*, trans. Ignat Avsey (Ithaca: Cornell University Press, 1987), 42; Dostoevskii, *PSS*, II: 18.

of two distinct labels for the introduction is meant to delineate implied author and narrator and to differentiate the author's novella from the narrator's text. Another indication of Dostoevsky's desire to separate the two levels, he has his narrator identify the genre of the work:

> Allow me to say something, as a conclusion to this chapter [the Introductory], about my own relationship with my uncle [the protagonist, Colonel Rostanev], and how it came about that I was so unexpectedly brought face to face with Foma Fomich [Opiskin, a comic villain cum tyrant in Rostanev's household] and thrown headlong into the midst of the most momentous events that had ever disturbed the peaceful routine of the blessed village of Stepanchikovo. In this manner I intend to conclude my introduction and pass on to the story [*rasskaz*] proper.[11]

Note the variety of labels Dostoevsky affixes to his text. Dostoevsky's "tale" (*povest'*)—which he calls a "comic novel" (*komicheskii roman*) in his letters—is his narrator's "story" (*rasskaz*).[12] The genre differences are significant. They indicate that Dostoevsky needed to differentiate himself from his narrator because his plan was to both ridicule his characters and to belittle his narrator. But, as Tynianov demonstrated long ago, the real butt of Dostoevsky's satire is Nikolai Gogol and his unfortunate *Selected Passages*.

In his Introductory, Dostoevsky's narrator, Sergei, tells the tale self-consciously, as both witness to the myriad vaudeville-inspired twists and turns in the plot, and also as a marginal participant in those events. He often records his emotional responses to events. And he reports those occasions when he enters the fray to defend his uncle, Colonel Rostanev, set upon as he is by his mother and the now wheedling, now abusive, power-monger Opiskin. For example, the narrator remarks in his foreword: "I must confess, it is with more than a little awe that I introduce this new personage. He is undoubtedly one of the principal characters of my tale. But what sort of claim he has on the reader's attention I shall not presume to judge: the reader will be better able to make up his own mind."[13] He provides perspective on what transpires

---

[11] Dostoyevsky, *The Village*, 42 (with minor changes); 17–18.
[12] Cited in Iurii Tynianov, "Dostoevskii i Gogol': k teorii parodii," in *Literaturnaia evolutsiia: izbrannye trudy*, ed. V. Novikov (Moscow: Agraf, 2002), 320.
[13] Dostoyevsky, *The Village*, 28; 7.

(as if it is necessary to do so in this over-the-top romp) and summarizes what even half-awake readers can surmise for themselves. We are forced to align ourselves with the narrator's perspective, of course, but it says little for our capacities as readers that we do.

There are occasions when we must distance ourselves from the narrator, for example, when he tells us what we have already realized on our own. Readers may agree with the narrator along ethical lines, but intellectually it is less easy to do. To make up for this deficiency—this is a distinct weakness in the work's conceptual design—Dostoevsky has his narrator explain away his inadequacies on the basis of his youth. Thus, when he accepts his uncle's offer to marry the family's nanny, Sergei Alexandrovich jumps at the chance even though he has never even met the girl: "I hoped to bring happiness to the unfortunate . . . young girl by my offer of marriage, and so on and so forth. Little by little I became so carried away that, by dint of my youth and having no other prospects [*po molodosti let i ot nechego delat'*], I went to the opposite extreme: instead of doubting [my uncle's offer] and hesitating, I was now consumed by a desire to perform great and prodigious deeds."[14]

Clearly, the narrator records his tale when he is older, although just how much older is impossible to tell from evidence in the text. But that is hardly the point. What galls is Dostoevsky's flimsy pretense built on the narrator's suspect gullibility. Verisimilitude be damned, especially in a farce. But this was a bit much to ask of his readers in 1859. Dostoevsky perpetrates this kind of conceptual error, and others like it, on more than one occasion in the course of the narrative. It becomes part of the work's wreckage.

We are meant to join Dostoevsky in seeing the deficiencies or limitations of our narrator, Sergei Alexandrovich.[15] We are also asked to record, through Sergei's foreword, Dostoevsky's perception of literary

---

[14] Dostoyevsky, *The Village*, 44; 19.
[15] The narrator's surname is withheld. In this singular fact a network of mysterious family and kin relations are secreted. Colonel Rostanev is the narrator's uncle. That is all we know for certain. It is difficult to ascertain how the narrator is or is not related to Rostanev's family at Stepanchikovo. Sergei, however, is not the grandson of Rostanev's mother, so it is logical that it is through the colonel's wife (deceased) that he was uncle to the lad. This renders the cousin relations in the text ambiguous as well. It's all a tease that, upon consideration, amounts to very little, which, I suppose, is meant to be funny in itself.

matters as they pertained in the 1850s. Sadly, his argument is built upon a defunct literary apparatus, that of the 1840s when Dostoevsky was in fact *au courant*. Hiding this defect by situating the story back a decade hardly works in Dostoevsky's favor. But, as we have seen in our examination of prefaces prior to Dostoevsky's entry into literary practice, there is a degree to which Dostoevsky, through his narrator, expresses his own anxieties about returning to the scene:

> I stated that Foma Fomich was an exception to the general rule. And so he was. He had once tried his hand at literature, and had suffered disappointment and rejection; but, of course, literature has ruined mightier men than Foma Fomich—especially rejected literature. It is also likely . . . that attempts to establish himself prior to his literary period had been none too successful either, and that wherever he turned, a smart kick in the pants had been his due rather than a decent wage. I have no definite facts in hand, but according to some enquiries I made, it seemed that Foma Fomich had actually produced a "novel" rather resembling such works as *The Liberation of Moscow*, *Ataman Storm*, *Filial Love—or Russians in 1104*, etc., etc., which in the thirties used to appear every year by the score and afforded such delectable food for the wit of Baron Brambeus.[16] All this, of course, is past history, but the serpent of literary self-love bites deep and the wound never heals, especially when its chosen victims are the insignificant and the feeble-minded. Humiliated at his first literary attempts, Foma Fomich there and then joined the countless ranks of the embittered whence all hapless spiritual vagrants and God-forsaken simpletons emerge. I presume that his monstrous vainglory, his need to be universally acclaimed, admired and applauded, also dated from that particular moment.[17]

This final remark might be devastating to Dostoevsky from an extraliterary perspective. We recall that Dostoevsky, upon the publication of his acclaimed *Poor Folk*, suffered a similar vainglory in his youth.[18] The narrator's remark about Foma Fomich can be seen as a covert criticism

---

[16] Brambeus was the penname of Osip Ivanovich Senkovsky (Józef Julian Sękowski, 1800–1858), editor, publisher, critic, and author. For a literary biography, see Louis Pedrotti, *J. J. Sękowski: The Genesis of a Literary Alien* (Berkeley: University of California Press, 1965), and for a consideration of his contribution to Russian journals, see Melissa Frazier, *Romantic Encounters*: Writers, Readers, and the *Library for Reading* (Stanford: Stanford University Press, 2007).
[17] Dostoyevsky, *The Village*, 34–35; 12.
[18] See Frank, *Seeds of Revolt*, 159–171.

that Dostoevsky levels at himself.[19] Dostoevsky's insecurities might even be disclosed when Gogol is referenced directly:

> I know he seriously tried to convince my uncle that he, Foma, was destined one day to perform a great feat, a feat for which he had been expressly summoned into this world, and that in hours of solitude and darkness a winged creature or something of that kind was providing him with the necessary strength and inspiration. Namely, he was to compose a profoundly searching *magnum opus* of a spiritually edifying nature that would shake the world and stun all Russia. And then, after all Russia had been stunned, he, Foma, scorning glory, would withdraw to a monastery, spend the rest of his days and nights praying in the caverns of Kiev for the salvation of his motherland. My uncle, of course, was deeply impressed by all of this.[20]

There are several occasions in the text when Sergei cites Gogol's *Selected Passages* verbatim. Here, in the foreword, we find the first instance. It is a ventriloquist act by Dostoevsky, who identifies the target of his farcical narrative in order to set himself apart from one of the more significant models he relied on in his early work.[21]

In terms of the text's aesthetics, however, Dostoevsky's callow narrator ends up in a no-man's land of rhetorical ambiguity. We readers depend on him to relay reliable information, which he does in the main. But his youth gets in the way on occasion. For instance, it is simply dumbfounding that he would rush off at the drop of a hat to marry the nanny to his uncle's children—this error of judgment, sadly enough, supplies the motivation for the entire story. Had he seen his uncle's request in the first instance as silly beyond belief, he would not have made the trip and uncovered such a madhouse of topsy-turvy relations. There would have been no story to relate. As it is, the tale hangs entirely on the improbable. Dostoevsky makes certain the narrator's response to his uncle's unreasonable request is seen by readers as more than youthful

---

[19] Metaliterary debate was something Dostoevsky often engaged in his work, starting with *Poor Folk*.
[20] Dostoyevsky, *The Village*, 35–36; 13.
[21] For an indication of how widely this phenomenon occurs in the novel, see Part II of the aforementioned essay by Tynianov (320–339) and Ignat Avsey's translation of *The Village of Stepanchikovo* (249–255). Cf., N. V. Pervushin, "Dostoevsky's Foma Opiskin and Gogol'," *Canadian Slavonic Papers/Revue Canadienne des Slavistes* 14, no. 1 (Spring, 1972): 87–91.

enthusiasm—it is madcap impulsiveness. That Sergei comes around to understanding his foolishness hardly salvages the story's motivational force. Nor does it salvage reader relations with the narrator.

There are many design errors in Dostoevsky's novella, but we hardly need review them all. What is important to note is that they are readily apparent in the narrator's foreword. Rhetorical relations are mishandled. Implausibility of motivation weakens the farce's pretext. And the satire is damaged by a crude slapstick that reaches down to the underbelly. In this last instance, it is worth noting as an example that Foma Fomich Opiskin's surname references the lower body principle of the carnivalesque that Bakhtin has described so imaginatively in Dostoevsky's work.[22]

We come upon the (mis-)workings of private parts first in relation to the surname of Colonel Rostanev's servant, Vidopliasov ("See-Me-Dance," an absurd name of Dostoevsky's invention). Vidopliasov wishes to change his name so as to avoid any more ridicule than he has already suffered. But he selects equally strange names to replace it. People make fun of whatever he chooses by rhyming his new name with something jocular, silly, or belittling. When Vidopliasov, in his final attempt, selects Tantsev as his new name (from German, "to dance"), the humor compounds, since he is not changing his name in any substantive sense at all. But when a rhyme comes back to him based on Tantsev he "daren't even repeat it" to Rostanev and the narrator.[23] Neither the narrator nor Dostoevsky outs the rhyme. But it can be imagined—*zasrantsev* is the genitive plural of *zasranets*, a verbal noun of *zasrat'sia*, meaning "to shit oneself" or "to shit one's pants." From here it is but one small step to Opiskin and the front end of Dostoevsky's rude joke. In fact, it is but one small accent shift to make the linkage. To "miswrite" (*opisát'sia*) satirizes Foma Fomich's literary pretensions. But *opísat'sia*, with the accent shifted back one syllable, means to "piss oneself." This is the lowest rung on the ladder of humor in *Stepanchikovo*. How did Dostoevsky descend to this point?

---

[22] Mikhail Bakhtin, *Problems of Dostoevsky's Poetics*, ed. and trans. Caryl Emerson (Minneapolis: University of Minnesota Press, 1984), 101–180. See Zholkovsky (173) for the usually accepted meaning of Opiskin as surname (*opiska*, miswriting).

[23] Dostoyevsky, *The Village*, 159; 105.

Part of the problem of the text, other than its egregious farcicality, is that it seems to have misconceived its audience. Joseph Frank, among others, notes that a vaudeville piece, written about provincial life at a time when conditions in Russia were about to change with immense consequences for the nation, was hardly timely.[24] I am suggesting, however, that Dostoevsky's exclusion of contemporary issues was more than a failure in historical timing. Where Dostoevsky failed was in imagining his audience.

Dostoevsky conceived of his story while in Siberian imprisonment and continued to mull it over through his military service all the way to his return to St. Petersburg. He worked on it between 1856 and 1858. Only late in his exile could he begin to acquaint himself with the new faces on the literary scene, their new work, the issues of the day, and the turn toward post-Romantic western philosophies—positivism, materialism, utilitarianism—and the scientific revolution, particularly Darwin's theory of evolution which was then, as it is now, frequently misapplied to social, economic, and political phenomena. All this affected the arts in ways Dostoevsky was only beginning to understand.

The audiences he knew most thoroughly belonged either to the 1840s or, most recently for him, to the prison camp. In Dostoevsky's *Notes from the House of the Dead* an entire chapter is dedicated to an evening of performances staged, acted, and directed by convicts. In this chapter, titled "Theatricals" (*Predstavlenie*), the narrator, Goryanchikov, reveals how closely text and audience were aligned. First he records what, for the audience, amounts to elevated anticipation: ". . . the actors had taken everything on themselves, so that the rest of us did not even know what was the state of affairs or what was actually being done; we did not even know properly what was to be performed."[25] What will come at them on stage is to be entirely fresh. This seems to turn them into an ideal audience ready to meet the production on its own terms. When it comes to the performance, they respond to each and

---

[24] The emancipation of the serfs was just two years away. The intelligentsia could hardly tolerate a work that was so detached from the buildup to this event. Furthermore, Dostoevsky's novel seemed to insist on an old norm of master-serf relations, hardly a popular position at the time.

[25] Fedor Dostoevsky, *Memoirs from the House of the Dead*, trans. Jessie Coulson, ed. Ronald Hingley (New York: Oxford University Press, 1983), 175; Dostoevskii, *PSS*, IV: 116.

every scene, gesture, plot twist, dance, pantomime, skit, and slapstick maneuver in complete accord with what is intended by the actors. The audience laps it up in delighted howls of laughter. Goryanchikov notes: "In a word, the play was concluded to the complete general satisfaction. There was no criticism; how could there be?"[26]

Next the second sketch, a fragment from a bedroom comedy, is performed. Again, the response is at one with the intent: "The spectators' delight knew no bounds . . . everybody was laughing with pleasure."[27] The final act consists of a set of pantomimes set to rousing folk music: "This was the *gopak* in its fully glory and really Glinka would have learned a great deal if he had chanced to hear it in our prison."[28] Even the narrator, an educated man, succumbs to the pleasures to be derived from the farces. The audience so thoroughly suspends disbelief that it happily overlooks glaring deficiencies: "I must remark that our scenery was very poverty-stricken. In this scene, as in the preceding play and all the other scenes, one supplied the deficiencies from one's own imagination rather than saw with one's eyes." This is because ". . . the spectators were not looking for defects and were content to supplement the actuality with their fancy, especially since prisoners are well versed in doing this." [29]

Dostoevsky's *Stepanchikovo* involves a long series of farces similar to those viewed by the prisoners. In fact, it may be that he conceived the novel first as a play. How he would have enjoyed to have had a response to his novel in the St. Petersburg press to match that of the prison theatricals by the convicts. Instead, there was only silence from both the public and, most gallingly, from critics. Dostoevsky misunderstood his audience entirely. By assuming that his readers would respond to *Stepanchikovo*'s antics with the refreshingly direct, "childlike" qualities of his barrack mates, Dostoevsky revealed just how thoroughly detached from literary life he had become.[30]

---

[26] Dostoevsky, *House of the Dead*, 191; 125.
[27] Dostoevsky, *House of the Dead*, 194; 127.
[28] Dostoevsky, *House of the Dead*, 194; 128.
[29] Dostoevsky, *House of the Dead*, 195; 128.
[30] Goryanchikov's most common descriptions of the prisoners in response to the theatricals are "childlike," "childish," and similes and metonyms based on the same root (Dostoevsky, *House of the Dead*, 118, 178, 183, 186, 188, 190, 198; 81, 118, 120, 122, 123, 125, 130). For more on Dostoevsky's use of vaudeville techniques as they apply to his pre-exile work, see Susanne Fusso, "Husbands and

Dostoevsky did not despair when *Stepanchikovo* fell on its face. He pushed ahead. And when he did move on, he dispensed with the formulaic first-person preface cast in the voice of a fictional author-narrator. He would not return to this type of preface (or to the label "Introductory" again). Stung by his story's failure, he attempted to capitalize on public interest in his return from exile by working all the more diligently on his *Notes from the House of the Dead*, the third novel published out of exile, one he had conceived as far back as 1854.[31] In it he turned to a tradition-bound form of preface, the kind we have encountered in Pushkin's *The Belkin Tales* and Lermontov's *A Hero of Our Time*, the fictional allographic form made famous even earlier in the Romantic Age by, among many others, Sir Walter Scott. To remind ourselves, the fictional allographic preface is one presented to readers by a personage invented by the author.

II

NOTES FROM THE HOUSE OF THE DEAD

With the first installment of the serially published semi-autobiographical novel *Notes from the House of the Dead*, Dostoevsky discovered an entirely new form of introduction. He rights the wrongs of his *Stepanchikovo*, particularly in its lack of gravitas and its misreading of his audience. If he achieved nothing unique in the introductory to *Stepanchikovo*, in *House of the Dead* he set a high bar for any future introduction to surpass. It is a remarkable achievement rooted, as always in Dostoevsky, in the voice of an Other. Like the narrator of *Stepanchikovo*, here we encounter a voice in the first-person. But unlike *Stepanchikovo*'s Sergei Alexandrovich, the narrator of the introduction does not continue to control the narrative thread for the remainder of the novel; nor does he create its discourse, which belongs to the protagonist, Goryanchikov, whose memoirs of his time in prison form the

---

Lovers: Vaudeville Conventions in 'Another Man's Wife,' 'The Jealous Husband,' and *The Eternal Husband*," in *Before They Were Titans: Essays on the Early Works of Dostoevsky and Tolstoy*, ed. Elizabeth Cheresh Allen (Brighton, MA: Academic Studies Press, 2015), 61–92.

[31] Dostoevskii, *PSS*, IV, "Zapiski iz mertvogo doma: Istochniki teksta," 275.

body of the novel. The narrator of the introduction claims the role of editor of a previously undiscovered text.

Much like the editor A. P. who supposedly penned the introduction to *The Belkin Tales* and Lermontov's traveling narrator in *A Hero of Our Time*, in this introduction Dostoevsky's narrator announces his acquisition of a manuscript he discovered while engaged in what was most likely government service in Siberia. If the introduction sounds time-worn in its adherence to convention-bound rules, it is. But only at the surface level:

> Circumstances took me away from our town for about three months. Returning home after the beginning of winter, I heard that Alexander Petrovich [Goryanchikov] had died in the autumn, died alone and never once called in a doctor. He was already almost forgotten in the town. His room was empty. I lost no time in making myself known to his landlady, with the intention of finding out from her what her lodger had done with his time and whether he had not been writing something. For twenty kopecks in silver she brought me a basketful of papers left behind by the dead man.[32]

The greatest portion of the introduction is taken up by the unnamed editor's description of Goryanchikov, the conditions under which he lived, his reclusive life, his adamant refusal to join Siberian society, his anxieties, psychological quirks, and his generous heart. As mentioned previously, introductions often announce the genre that readers are about to encounter. They represent a way of instilling in the reader expectations appropriate for the text. If in *Stepanchikovo* the positing of the work's genre can only be affirmed with qualifications, it was Dostoevsky's manifest intention to make genre transparent in *House of the Dead*. It is a form he frequently used, specifically, notes (*zapiski*).[33]

---

[32] Dostoevsky, *House of the Dead*, 5; 8.
[33] In *Stepanchikovo*, the narrator calls his work "a short story" (*rasskaz*). Dostoevsky claims, in a letter to Mikhail Dostoevsky, that it's a longer work similar in length to *Poor Folk*, which would make it a short novel. As regards Dostoevsky's use of the "notes" or fragment form, many of his works were labeled thus, for example, "The Honest Thief (From the Notes of an Unknown Person)" (1848); "The Christmas Tree and A Wedding (From the Notes of an Unknown Person)" (1848); *Notes from the House of the Dead* (1860–1862); and *Notes from the Underground* (1864).

Dostoevsky's genre claim is undercut by the editor at almost every turn. His suggestions for the work's genre are manifold:

> I took his *papers* away with me and spent a whole day going through them. Three-quarters of them were blank sheets, meaningless fragments, or pupils' copy-books. But there was one fairly bulky *notebook* filled with small handwriting, but unfinished, abandoned and perhaps forgotten by the author himself. It was a *description*, although a rather disconnected one, of the ten years' penal servitude undergone by Alexander Petrovich. In places it was broken by another *narrative*, some kind of strange and terrible *reminiscences*, written in cramped irregular characters, as though under some compulsion. I read through these *fragments* a few times and almost convinced myself that they had been written in madness. But the prison *memoirs*—"Scenes from the House of the Dead," as he himself called them somewhere in the *manuscript*—appeared to me to be not without interest. The completely strange world, unknown until that time, the strangeness of some of the facts, some particular notes on those lost souls, attracted me, and I read with curiosity. I may, of course, be mistaken. As a test, I have picked out two or three *chapters* to begin with; let the public judge . . .[34]

The editor, manuscript discoverer that he is, gives a variety of genre identifications to the work he presents to his reader. He calls them by many names, of which only one seems to capture the notion he seeks amidst the variety—fragments. His fragments represent "scenes" (*stseny*), or what Dostoevsky calls "notes" (*zapiski*). Perhaps it is the sum of these parts that get at the heart of the novel as practiced by Dostoevsky. Gary Saul Morson views Dostoevsky's texts of this type as experiments in the delineation of chaos in which "[the narrator] writes in order to make sense of his life by arriving, in the process of composition, at a coherent account [of his life. This narrator is] unable to comprehend either himself or his world [and therefore] creates not a finished work but 'notes' and fragments that end as uncertainly and abruptly as they begin. Whatever order there is is often attributed to an 'editor' who has shaped the text just enough to make it readable at all."[35]

---

[34] Dostoevsky, *House of the Dead*, 6; 8 (Dostoevsky's ellipsis; my emphases).
[35] Gary Saul Morson, *The Boundaries of Genre: Dostoevsky's Diary of a Writer and the Traditions of Literary Utopia* (Austin: University of Texas Press, 1981), 9–10.

The editor's voice brings the fictionality of *House of the Dead* to the reader's attention, rendering interpretations of the text as autobiography or socio-political commentary suspect.[36] The artistic reworking of the narrative implied in the fictional introduction to the text suggests that it might be considered novelistic, at least in a Bakhtinian sense. For Bakhtin, the extended and fragmentary literary form often represents the novel, not in a traditional nineteenth-century guise, but as an historically validated force which periodically challenges the codified definition of what is literary to encompass those texts which might otherwise be excluded from the canon.[37] Since "in the second quarter of the nineteenth century the mere idea of a truly Russian novel was problematic," and considered by some "a debased form of literature," there may be some logic to the assertion that it is precisely a work such as *House of the Dead* that may be considered novelistic, if not a novel proper.[38] Let us refer to *House of the Dead* conditionally as a novel in the capacious sense Bakhtin gives the genre, that is, as a boundary genre intermediate between "the structure of the novel and the structure of life"[39] which is forever open to change and transformation, a genre we would today call fictional non-fiction or literary non-fiction.[40]

Dostoevsky was aware of the literary innovations he was making in *House of the Dead*, and not only in relation to the subject matter (which had not been treated in Russian literature previously). He was quite conscious of the literary tradition out of which he worked in forming the discourse, particularly in his use of an ironic introduction where the fictional editor's voice dominates surface utterance only to be challenged by another hidden point of view secreted in that voice. In the dialogue between covert and overt speech which suffuses

---

[36] V. Ia. Kirpotin, "Zapiski iz mertvogo doma," in *Tvorchestvo Dostoevskogo*, ed. N. L. Stepanov (Moscow: Nauka, 1959), 101–127.

[37] M. M. Bakhtin, "Epic and the Novel," in *The Dialogic Imagination: Four Essays*, ed. Michael Holquist, trans. Caryl Emerson and Michael Holquist (Austin: University of Texas Press, 1981), 33.

[38] Simon Franklin, "Novels without Ends: Notes on *Eugene Onegin* and *Dead Souls*," *Modern Language Review* 79 (1984): 372–383.

[39] Christopher Pike, "Formalist and Structuralist Approaches to Dostoyevsky," in *New Essays on Dostoyevsky*, ed. Malcolm V. Jones and Garth M. Terry (Cambridge: Cambridge University Press, 1983), 187–214.

[40] John Warnock, *Representing Reality: Readings in Literary Nonfiction* (New York: St. Martins, 1998).

the introduction to *House of the Dead*, readers are propelled along a channel of reception uniting genre considerations and linguistic technique through which Dostoevsky grasps humankind in all its depth. With *House of the Dead* we meet the emergent great writer Fyodor Dostoevsky.

Turning to the theme of our humanity, Robert Louis Jackson states that "a continual cycle of death and resurrection (the structure of the story provides an impression of a continuous cycle or circular movement) expresses the tragic optimism of *House of the Dead*, its triumph over the finite."[41] This view represents a vast improvement over Viktor Shklovsky's pessimistic or D. S. Mirsky's optimistic reading of the novel.[42] Taking Jackson's position as the starting point of our analysis, the question before us relates specifically to the "continual cycle of death and resurrection" in the life of individual men, or, more specifically, in the life of Goryanchikov. How early can it be detected in *House of the Dead*?

Dostoevsky's cyclical patterning of existence occurs as a covert theme in the fictional introduction to the novel. In fact, its first paragraph alone is laced with it. Yet in the novel's persistent focus on murderers, deserters, child abusers, wife beaters, burglars, master pickpockets, and petty thieves, all thrown together in the most degrading of circumstances, *House of the Dead* itself seems so unrepentantly gloomy as to preclude the complex picture of humanity (particularly men) associated with Dostoevsky's later fiction. Indeed, the novel's brutally evil Gazins, Orlovs, and Zherebyatnikovs overwhelm the meek, often simple-mindedly good Sushilovs, Luchkas, and Aleys. This is the tragedy, not only of the novel, but of existence. Yet the work in fact does not lack a profound vision of man, which combines extreme, opposite types. Dostoevsky makes this point in the introduction. Once deciphered, the first paragraph of the introduction in itself teaches us how to read the dark and pessimistic pages of *House of the Dead* in pursuit of a complex hope that absorbs, but does not preclude, the horrific impression of humanity emanating from the novel's dark surfaces.

---

[41] Robert Louis Jackson, *The Art of Dostoevsky: Deliriums and Nocturnes* (Princeton: Princeton University Press, 1981), 41.
[42] See Shklovsky, *Za i protiv: Zametki o Dostoevskom* (Moscow: Sovetskii pisatel'*,* 1957), 108; D. S. Mirsky, *A History of Russian Literature*, ed. Francis J. Whitfield (New York: Knopf, 1958), 282.

The introduction exploits the plasticity and expressive potential of its medium in order to transcend habitualized perception and narrow convention.[43] And if the introductory paragraph instructs us how to read the novel, then in the symmetry of fictional beginnings and ends we are informed how to go about our reading at the text's conclusion. In the final chapter, Dostoevsky's narrator, the ex-convict and former nobleman, Goryanchikov, writes that prior to his release from a penal servitude of ten years he was allowed to receive books. They were a revelation to him, just as they had been for Dostoevsky as he emerged from his four years of imprisonment. But, there is a difference between Goryanchikov and Dostoevsky. Goryanchikov states, "I worried [over] every word, read between the lines, tried to find secret meanings, any hint at the past."[44] Dostoevsky's irony here consists of Goryanchikov's negative evaluation of his reading method, for this is precisely the way Dostoevsky would have us approach his novel, reading between the lines, attempting to find its secret meanings, and seeing more than appears to be there at first glance.

Goryanchikov's remark serves another purpose. It represents an aperture through which to enter Dostoevsky's text and penetrate its gruesome mask in quest of its most profound insights. Goryanchikov's example models an approach essential to a more complete understanding of Dostoevsky's poetics. Bypassing literal readings, the text can be viewed as something more than mere medium of social and political import (as in "we must reform our prison system"). Rather, Dostoevsky would have us experience this book as Goryanchikov experiences his books, sensing the words not as mere signifiers of some reality but as the signified element itself, as the tangible matter of the fictive discourse. Goryanchikov's self-criticism notwithstanding, Dostoevsky would have us see more in his text than an artificially restricted or automatized approach to language and its uses allows. In fact, through a rich and

---

[43] On the importance of treating Dostoevsky's language as a point of departure into his fictional universe, see M. M. Bakhtin, *Problemy poetiki Dostoevskogo* (Moscow: Khudit, 1972), 210, 311; P. M. Bitsilli, "K voprosu o vnutrennei forme romana Dostoevskogo," in *O Dostoevskom: Stat'i*, ed. Donald Fanger (Providence: Brown University Press, 1966), 3–71. See, too, Iu. N. Karaulov and E. L. Ginzburg, eds., *Slovo Dostoevskogo 2000: Sbornik statei* (Moscow: Azbukovnik, 2001).

[44] Dostoevsky, *House of the Dead*, 357; 229.

suggestive utilization of language as medium, Dostoevsky attempts to take us across a threshold that the gross details of his novel make uninviting. In this way, the introduction to *House of the Dead* serves a dual purpose. At the surface level, it transports us from the discourse of the detached editor figure to the discourse of Goryanchikov's "Scenes of a Dead House." At the subsurface level, it plunges us deeper into the language through which the discourse is fashioned, that is, into a second level of meaning formation that connects, even unifies, the introduction and the memoir.

For Dostoevsky and his Goryanchikov, a larger and more accurate image of man lies within their grasp only through having experienced the prisoner both in his inhuman depravity and in his humane potential. A more accurate image of humankind can be considered authentic only if it is shorn of illusion; is not blinded by idealism or pessimism (which Dostoevsky considered enticing, if illusory, antitheses of his time); does not reduce the infinite complexities of life into pattern, category, and mundane coherence; and is constituted of a language which reflects its deepest insights. It unifies humanity's basest and loftiest essences and fuses our fundamental contradictions and paradoxes in a complex intuition of our uniqueness. In short, a fusion of the sensory or phenomenal world with another symbolic order must be experienced if we are to penetrate Dostoevsky's novel in a manner that duplicates his and Goryanchikov's prison revelation.

If near the novel's conclusion Goryanchikov instructs us how to read the editor's introduction, the introduction itself with its tradition-bound literary cues informs us that it is precisely here that we must attend if we are to comprehend the novel more fully. In recalling that Pushkin, Gogol, and Lermontov all embed ironic intentions within the utterances of their editors, we follow this traditional cue and examine Dostoevsky's editor's remarks for their hidden significance. As we read behind the *House of the Dead* editor's matter-of-fact descriptions of life in Siberia, we are thrust into the vital core of Dostoevsky's understanding of the multi-voiced aesthetic word as it signals simultaneously two rather contradictory phenomena: first, the bourgeois mediocrity of the editor's enthusiasm at finding Goryanchikov's manuscript; second, continuous cycles of fall and redemption central to Dostoevsky's vision of humankind, a vision he thereafter sought to express more thoroughly over the ensuing twenty years. For in the editor's introductory description of Siberia, masked by the casual utterances of bourgeois materialism, are located the novel's key concerns: life is a riddle and to solve the riddle we must make a journey, and as we travel toward illumination, we are impeded on the way by our own reticence and perceptual blindness. The figure of the pilgrim and the image of a metaphysical journey enacted within a figurative space came to Dostoevsky from Dante, a fact readers have long noted and which Dostoevsky did not attempt to hide.[45] Both texts, in their first lines, refer to a dark or impenetrable forest, and the protagonist of each narrative makes his primal descent at the age of thirty-five.[46] Dostoevsky's pilgrim journey, however, is markedly contemporary. Purgatorio is not subterranean. The underground is where we live.

The editor begins his description in a matter-of-fact style typical of the period's travelogues:

> In the remotest parts of Siberia, amid the steppes, the mountains, and impenetrable forests, here and there lie scattered small towns of one, or at most two, thousand inhabitants, drab little towns built of wood, with two churches—one in the town itself, the other in the churchyard—towns which are more like a prosperous village [*selo*] of the Moscow region than a [real] town [*gorod*].[47]

Dostoevsky immediately exploits both the semantic ambiguities of the language and its root structure to deepen the significance of his editor's initial utterance. They suggest the problem of seeing (of adequate perception), the idea of necessary limits to people's freedom, and humanity's fall as both social and existential fact. We shall consider each point in turn.

The act of seeing in the special sense Dostoevsky wants to evoke requires penetration of surface phenomena. Apropos, Goryanchikov

---

[45] Jackson, *Art of Dostoevsky*, 6, 40; Kirpotin, "Zapiski iz mertvogo doma," in *Tvorchestvo Dostoevskogo*, ed. N. L. Stepanov (Moscow: Akademiia nauk, 1959), 119.

[46] Additional reminders of *The Divine Comedy* come in Goryanchikov's narrative, for example, the famous bath house scene (Dostoevsky, *House of the Dead*, 144–155; 98–104), and references to "la perduta gente" (e.g., Dostoevsky, *House of the Dead*, 6; 13). See also A. V. Toichkina, "Obraz ada v 'Zapiskakh mertvogo doma': K teme Dostoevskii i Dante," *Dostoevskii i mirovaia kul'tura: Al'manakh* 29 (2012): 52–66.

[47] Dostoevsky, *House of the Dead*, 1; 5.

himself makes reference to the binary opposition of exterior and interior: "[A] general tone consisted outwardly [*snaruzhi*] of a certain personal dignity"; "There was some sort of surface [*naruzhnoe*] peace"; "It is doubtful that even one prisoner admitted to himself [*vnutrenno*] to being guilty."[48] The notion of movement from one level of perception to another occurs twice in the editor's first utterance. It is used explicitly to describe Siberian forests. Impenetrability here refers to one's ability to "pass through" (*pro* + *khod*) a physical object (the dense forest of Russian folklore through which the hero must pass at risk of life and limb). But if we are to pierce life's meaning in these surroundings, penetration must come from some medium other than physical locomotion. The adjective denoting "ugly" or "drab" (*ne* + *v* + *zrach*[*ok*]: "not to admit through the pupil of the eye") also connotes the visual impenetrability of an object, in this instance, Siberian towns and the prisons located in their environs. We are to enact with Goryanchikov our pilgrimage with the interior eye, breaking through the deformed or repugnant surface of the apparent to apprehend the concealed but immanent.[49]

Overcoming visual or physical obstruction involves the notion of limit, barrier, and border, things that do not permit intrusion or transgression. *Krai*, the noun here indicating a geographical area as in "remotest *parts* of Siberia," refers also to the idea of a boundary or limit in general. The impenetrability of the Siberian forests implies the restriction of movement into it. Yet we must enter if we are to initiate our pilgrimage. The key to crossing this physical threshold, it is suggested as though in a folk riddle, is through the eye. We shall see our way through it. But even here we meet again with impenetrability, although of yet another order. The "ugly" or "visually impenetrable" towns of Siberia represent the boundary our eyes cannot pierce, just as the forest blocks accessibility. To perceive the town and its inhabitants in their essence we must penetrate their surface appearances and encounter what, upon first glance, does not impinge upon the pupil of

---

[48] Dostoevsky, *House of the Dead*, 13; 13. Binary oppositions of this type occur regularly in the first paragraph's initial sentence. For example, the town holds 1–2,000 inhabitants; it houses two churches.

[49] For confirmation of the semantic value of prefixes in Russian, see Laura A. Janda, et al., *Why Russian Aspectual Prefixes Aren't Empty: Prefixes as Verb Classifiers* (Bloomington: IN: Slavica, 2013).

the eye. As we shall see, the key to passing over the visual threshold lies in an illumination of the possibilities of language to express the human condition in this "wealthy and happy land."

The third notion rooted in the language Dostoevsky's editor uses (albeit unconsciously) refers to people's failure to lift the veil of appearances. Indeed, from Dostoevsky's point of view, one's inability or unwillingness to remove the veil of the phenomenal world represents a most basic human error (modeled for us by the editor himself) that conditions one type of submission to illusion, a failure in reaching perceptual or cognitive adequacy in life. In religious terms this amounts to a fall from grace. Signaling the notion of a Biblical-like Fall, the colloquial verb for locating objects in space (*popadat'sia*) is used instead of a more standard, neutral verb (for example, *nakhodit'sia*, "to be found or located," or *raspolozhen*, "to be situated or spread out"). Significantly, the root of the verb the editor uses here suggests motion downward, that is, falling. Thus, within the very notion of Siberian wealth and wellbeing presented by the editor, there is an allusion to a fall, one conditioned, as already suggested, by an unwillingness to perceive the essence within the phenomenal order. But it also suggests that being located in the physical universe in itself constitutes a fall from some primal or imagined condition of grace. It should be noted that passage here into the phenomenal world ("here and there lie scattered [fall] small towns") is marked by motion across a threshold (*krai*), but in this instance it is a vertical threshold rather than a horizontal one of the type we encounter in the text's "impenetrable forests." In the small Siberian town we arrive at a point of intersection between the vertical and horizontal dimensions, the spirit and material worlds. It seems that these towns do not spring into existence; they *fall* into existence.

It is worth mentioning that the spatial location of these towns "here and there" (*izredka*) is rendered by a temporal construction in Russian. Its primary meaning is "from time to time" or "now and then." This shift, too, can serve as a small indication that alteration and change lie at the heart not of the editor's description but of Dostoevsky's. The transformation of the temporal into the spatial, the alteration of the phenomenal world into its noumenal potentialities, and an interpenetration of social and moral dimensions, suggest a reading of the editor's first remark quite beyond his comprehension: "From time to time villages fall," and with them, of course, their inhabitants.⁵⁰

Since Goryanchikov's prison is located in just one such town, it might be said that where the prison signifies overtly the socially-defined locus for those who have fallen in man's eyes, this town in Dostoevsky's imminent view is the prison's moral equivalent. It is the geographical location of those who have unwittingly fallen spiritually (but who believe the contrary to be true). Such a reading is not entirely out of the question as indicated by the editor's second utterance in which he describes social links between the prisoner's world and the mundane social order of the town: "As a rule [these towns] are abundantly furnished with district police inspectors, assessors, and other minor officials."⁵¹ Here we meet the functionaries of a governmental apparatus who are vested with the power to determine who may and who may not reside within the normal social order. It is the job of the officials to make these determinations, more often than not referring to the proper authorities higher up the chain of command. They are therefore required *not* to pierce the repugnant surface of the criminal visage. Unlike Goryanchikov, officials must not "see" the criminal in a redemptive light. It is their task to keep order, to represent wholly the commonly accepted view (which the editor also represents by his morbid curiosity about Goryanchikov "the misanthrope"). But in the very next remark, Dostoevsky's language undermines the editor's description of hierarchy, and the social domain is suddenly transformed into a spiritual equivalent: "Generally speaking, Siberia, though its climate may be cold, allows one to get on quite warmly [*sluzhit' chrezvychaino teplo*]."⁵² Playing with the contrast between the notions of cold weather and personal gain in government employ (getting on warmly), the editor, without appreciating the implications of his remark, uses a term which denotes both government service and a religious service (*sluzhba*). This is a minor point, since there are no other possibilities within the language for him. But Dostoevsky realizes the potential link between the two. In this manner the editor's profane linguistic play on

---

⁵⁰ T. S. Karlova, "O strukturnom znachenii obraza 'Mertvogo doma,'" in *Dostoevsky: Materialy i issledovaniia*, ed. G. M. Fridlender (Moscow: Nauka, 1974), 135–146.
⁵¹ Dostoevsky, *House of the Dead*, 1; 5 (translation altered).
⁵² Dostoevsky, *House of the Dead*, 1; 5 (translation altered).

words (warm/cold) is mirrored by Dostoevsky's fusion of the horizontal and vertical axes (government and religious service). We again encounter a point of intersection between the material and spiritual worlds, where each reflects the other in a transcendent unity of service itself. At a more subversive level, however, we note that the distinction between the criminal element behind the stockade walls and the criminal impulse lurking within the breast of the corruptible government official (who "gets on warmly" [takes bribes] in his dealings with small town society) has been effaced.

For Dostoevsky, the question of humanity's recurrent fall and redemption lies at the root of existence. Similarly, the key to the description of this fundamental verity is to be found in the roots of language. The editor continues his description of the Siberians and those who have moved there in a manner that at first sight might appear to be positive. But economic desire and licentious urges are joined in this description and serve to undermine his evaluation of this land of milk and honey: "The officials, who play the part of a virtual Siberian aristocracy, are either natives, dyed-in-the-wool Siberians, or migrants from Russia chiefly from the capital, attracted by the supplementary salaries, the double allowances for expenses, and alluring hopes for the future."[53] An existence founded on the pursuit of base human desires (which, as Aristotle reminds us, are infinite) rather than on basic human needs (which are finite) lies at the very heart of man's sinfulness. Officials from Great Russia come to this *a priori* fallen little town with petty bourgeois desires of monetary gain. The words "enticement" and "seductive" signal the moral category into which they can be placed. They are doubly fallen, it seems, first by the very nature of their desires, and second by their arrival in this town. They have fallen into a fallen town.

Yet Dostoevsky does not separate these two types of error, the spiritual/existential from the economic/social. Rather, he sees them as a single reality undifferentiated at some presumed point of contact. Towns "falling" into existence represent "sin" plotted spiritually along a vertical axis; the seductive enticements of life in such a place constitute the horizontal organization of the same fall from grace. At their intersection they become one, and another locus at which

---

[53] Dostoevsky, *House of the Dead*, 1; 5.

the phenomenal and noumenal orders meet is identified. But in this instance the fusion is not primarily spatial. It is, instead, a union of temporal and spatial orders originally suggested in Dostoevsky's use of the adverb *izredka* ("from time to time"). This, too, is an interior or moral point of intersection and indicates the psychological terrain that is to be traversed as the editor's description continues. It is, in other words, our impenetrable forest.

Elevating the discourse to this abstract level, Dostoevsky has his editor raise the value of his officials' pursuits, albeit unconsciously, to ethical and metaphysical heights by breaking into two categories the official who comes from Russia to secure wealth in Siberia. What separates the two groups, in the editor's depiction, is their respective abilities to solve the riddle of life: "Those among them who are capable of solving the riddle of life almost all remain in Siberia and gladly take root there. The fruits they subsequently bear are sweet and abundant."[54] Clearly, in our bourgeois editor's view, selfish desire and sensual urges lie at the foundation of one's ability to solve the riddle, for the phrase (like "getting on warmly") is a euphemism for taking bribes. The riddle's solution is synonymous with learning how to succeed economically through illegal acts. The editor's exploitation of Goryanchikov's "Scenes from a Dead House" for personal gain may represent a variant of this type of success.[55]

It is significant that Dostoevsky likens the "deep-rooted" successful Siberians and the successful newcomers from Russia in terms of roots. They partake of the same being. These deep-rooted Siberians and the Russians who "take root" in Siberia are linked linguistically through the word denoting roots: *koren'*.[56] People so given over to the world of pleasure, material gain, and illegal activity are surely fallen creatures. Out of their comfort they have no need to penetrate the surface of existence in search of a redemptive core. They are sufficiently

---

[54] Dostoevsky, *House of the Dead*, 1; 5.
[55] We recall that Lermontov's traveling narrator happily accepts the charge of exploitation for personal gain: "[Pechorin's death] gave me the right to publish these notes [of his], and I took advantage of the opportunity to sign another man's work with my own name" (Lermontov, *Hero*, 63). Perhaps his travels took him twenty years later to Semipalatinsk.
[56] "Deep-rooted" and "to take root" in Russian are *zakorenelyi* and *ukoreniat'sia*, respectively.

blessed, at least by all overt material evidence. As the Gospel says, they already have their reward.[57] In Dostoevsky's view, the contrary is true, for these officials see their fall in redemptive terms, confusing the horizontal and vertical planes in what amounts to a corrupted notion of transcendence. Dostoevsky has already instructed us earlier (and later in Goryanchikov's example) that transcendence comes when we "see" through the darkness of physical existence to the luminous and hallowed interior of ethical aspiration enacted in the world. Unlike the editor and the petty officials who live at the ambiguous intersection of these two orders and who mistake the source of their so-called well-being, Dostoevsky asserts that humans are as deeply rooted in redemptive potential as they are in misguidedness or evildoing. Where Dostoevsky's editor and his town officials see their material bounty, Dostoevsky sees their fall.

In contrast to these "fortunates," those who do not choose to reside in Siberia any longer are outside the parameters of the editor's description. They don't interest him too terribly much: "The others, the frivolous ones, who cannot guess the answer to life's riddle, soon grow weary of Siberia, and, disheartened, ask themselves why they ever came there. Impatiently they serve out their statutory term of three years and as soon as it has expired begin to petition for transfer, and go back home reviling and ridiculing Siberia."[58] This remark is as rich as the introduction's first sentences and consequently requires comment. In it Dostoevsky provides the first clues to the solution of the riddle he embeds in the editor's foreword.

The editor's initial comparison of the native folk and successful European Russian officials is developed, as we have seen, into a contrast between two types of bureaucrat, the one who has solved the riddle of life and the one who has not. Remembering the bourgeois nature of the editor's understanding of this riddle, he considers those who leave Siberia frivolous and light-minded people who have succumbed to melancholy. The Russian noun for melancholy, *toska*, refers to a special emotional state familiar to the reader as an

---

[57] The Gospels were given to Dostoevsky upon his entry into prison. It was all he had to read for four years. See Joseph Frank, *The Years of Ordeal: 1850–1859* (Princeton: Princeton University Press, 1983), 72–75.

[58] Dostoevsky, *House of the Dead*, 1; 5.

existential form of isolation and despair, a longing for a better place or another, superior world. Read in reverse, however, the editor's judgment of this "unsuccessful" group of officials is itself frivolous in that it cannot acknowledge the contaminating force of its earthly values, not to mention its illegal impulses. Dostoevsky's irony, again consisting of a play with roots, revalues the editor's position. This is particularly apparent in the structure of the lexicon indicating ridicule. For in the editor's negative description of the malcontents (who, to put it explicitly, either do not wish to take bribes or do not succeed in the endeavor) there is a sarcastic note directed against the posture of superiority assumed by the editor. In Russian, the preposition that is the necessary complement of the verb for ridicule, derision, and laughter, is *nad*, meaning "over/above" ("to laugh over/above"), whereas in English we either use a direct object or use the object of a preposition, as in "laugh *at*." *Nad* indicates the subject's superior position in a figurative spatial orientation relative to the object of ridicule. Thus, the horizontal sphere (financial gain), which the editor glowingly describes, undergoes a vertical reorientation. Those who live in material abundance in remote Siberian towns are located *below* those who leave. As they depart "ridiculing Siberia," the departing officials assume a morally superior position in relation to the successful bureaucrats who remain behind. They laugh "over" them.

It is also suggested that those who depart from Siberia are saved, if only momentarily. For implicit in the root of the expression "to return home" is an upward movement across a threshold that carries one back to one's own self. And its opposite. The Russian verb "return" is constructed of the Old Church Slavonic prefix *voz-* denoting upward motion and a root which indicates a turning or revolution, *vrashch-*. This root is joined thematically, too, to the idea of limits or boundaries encountered in the editor's first utterance. Dostoevsky is most assuredly concerned with each of these notions, both literally and figuratively; cycles of life, transgressions of limits, and a reorientation or turn related to culturally-acquired ideas about transcendence suffuse much of Dostoevsky's fiction. Embedded in the language of return, therefore, is concealed a cyclical patterning of life along the vertical and horizontal axes. But, those who rise can also fall. Those returning "home" (*vosvoiasi*) are being renewed, they are making an upward movement (*voz-*) associated with revolution, change, and entry, but their destination raises a linguistic eyebrow. For *vosvoiasi* ("homeward") is a pejorative adverb in the sense of belaboring someone to "go back where you came from," and with good riddance (*vozvrashchaisia tuda, otkuda ty prishel*). The editor's dismissal of the returnees is negative, but the suggestion remains in the verb that something entirely positive is also possible. Here again, the profane order serves to indicate the linguistic signs and existential symbols of the regenerative or the sacred.

For Dostoevsky, penetration of the spiritual world through the agency of earthly existence represents a return to a positive human core that is as basic to man, in his thinking, as is his depravity. A return to a morally superior self is no less than a return to one's very self. Indication of this reading is given in the second term of the expression "return home." Despite its substandard and negative ring, "homeward" (*vosvoiasi*), in the colloquial Russian Dostoevsky has his editor use dismissively, suggests motion into one's own domain, for the prefix *vo-* denotes motion inward, and *svoi* one's own possession, place, or very self. A return to one's primal essence defines humankind's inherent potential for moral goodness. This return is the polar opposite of the Biblical Fall. But it is also an integral part of our life (which includes both sin and redemption *a priori*). Again the horizontal and vertical planes meet in the editor's description, and at their juncture a most serious and authentic image of humanity takes shape, an image that partakes simultaneously of our contradictory potentials. As a consequence of these contradictions, joined with the principle of change inherent in the description of humans, no condition can be considered eternal if it does not incorporate into itself its opposite. The disgruntled officials, therefore, redeem themselves by returning to themselves. But this is only a temporary condition, a brief moment in the continual cycle of falling away, returning home to some authentic form of selfhood, then falling yet again.

Essential to the cycle of return and fall is the notion of penance. The editor's description of the dissatisfied officials' bondage to a period of service in Siberia recalls Goryanchikov's penal servitude. It is as if before receiving illumination one must serve a period of isolation, undergo despair, wander in the desert (or Siberian forest) in order to expose the petty desires and surface fascinations of material existence. Dostoevsky plots movement relative to penance along the horizontal axis. The verbal noun *perevod* ("transfer") designates motion across a threshold. Thus, when Goryanchikov's term of incarceration is over, he is transferred into town, where he lives a life that might appear to be normal. He does not, however, return to European Russia, for he is barred by the terms of his sentence from doing so. But he has apparently solved the riddle of life, not in the editor's view but in Dostoevsky's understanding of it. In this way motion along the horizontal plane simultaneously indicates, in Goryanchikov's case, motion along the vertical axis. When Goryanchikov takes up residence in semi-isolation, he has made a move from prison society to normal society (horizontal movement) which denotes a simultaneous awakening and release (vertical movement). Goryanchikov exclaims upon his release, "What a glorious moment!" (*Ekaia slavnaia minuta*!)[59] They are the final words of the text.

He appears to the editor, however, to be a complete misanthrope who shuns the company of others. Clearly, in terms of the fusion of the two axes, where the editor reads a negative trait in Goryanchikov, we are meant to perceive a "transfer" into a different category of existence. For, it can be argued, Goryanchikov hardly avoids uplifting work despite the fact that he avoids people. He teaches children, and a good number of the papers discovered by the editor are dedicated to this service. In Goryanchikov's example, therefore, we have another road which may be travelled in order to return to one's self. Disgruntled officials may leave Siberia to find temporary respite from sinfulness; Goryanchikov stays and finds himself. In other words, motion from a state of disgrace to grace is enacted within the self. Likewise, horizontal motion in the everyday world indicates a potential for the individual's eventual release in an image, in the text, of movement upward.

If Dostoevsky's language reveals an evil core to life in the prison and town environs, that language also works to restore and renew it. Life in a small Siberian town may suddenly open up as well as down. The editor suggests as much in his concluding remark about the unhappy officials who leave Siberia: "They are wrong: not only from a civil service point of view, but also from many other points of view—in Siberia one may find bliss [*blazhenstvovat'*]," a verb which derives from the

---

[59] Dostoevsky, *House of the Dead*, 361; 232.

root *blag/blazh-*.⁶⁰ This last term serves the editor's mundane description perfectly. But its root structure also suits Dostoevsky's designs as well, for implicit in man's fall is the possibility of his redemption, his return to some state of grace (*blago*, "good," "the good," and "blessing"). Goryanchikov's rebirth in a Siberian prison suggests the potential for renewal in the fallen towns of Siberia as well.

Dostoevsky's ironies, openly cued in the verb "to be blessed/to find bliss" spiritually and/or materially, increase from this moment forward in every utterance of the introductory paragraph. But the editor's concluding remarks, where Siberia is viewed in mundane terms as a utopian land of plenty, of milk and honey, are undermined by an insistent misuse of such abundance. Sensual indulgence for its own sake represents one of the forms this misuse takes. He writes: "It has an excellent climate; there are many remarkably rich and hospitable merchants and many extremely prosperous non-Russian inhabitants. The young girls bloom like roses and are chaste to the nth degree."⁶¹ In the description of the chaste young girls we are reminded of the editor's first utterance. There the word denoting limit or boundary (*krai*) appears only to find its way back into the text again in reference to *extreme* chastity or purity (*do poslednei krainosti*). In moral terms there is as much irony in this remark about pure girls as there is in the description of merchants who come to Siberia "enticed" by financial rewards and in the reference to "solving the riddle of life." For Dostoevsky, an extreme abundance places the unwary at the very edge of a precipice. Plenty blinds. One's ability to perceive an alternative to gross materialism is diminished by the security that issues from abundance of any sort in the material world. It would appear that, in Dostoevsky's conception, human beings are incapable of doing anything with paradise other than misuse it without knowing it. Therefore, young girls "chaste to the nth degree" in the Russian original are chaste "to the utter limit [*do poslednei krainosti*]."⁶² They are, in other words, on a precipice and thus

---

⁶⁰ Dostoevsky, *House of the Dead*, 1; 5 (my translation).
⁶¹ Dostoevsky, *House of the Dead*, 5–6; 1–2 (translation altered).
⁶² Goryanchikov makes a similar remark about limits in reference to prisoners: "[They] are submissive and obedient up to a point, but there is a limit [*krai*] which must not be crossed" (Dostoevsky, *House of the Dead*, 2, 16; 5–6, 14). All limits are to be challenged by the Dostoevskian protagonist. For example, Nikolai Berdyaev writes regarding *Crime and Punishment*, "Raskolnikov's fixed

in a state of readiness for a transgression of that limit, for a fall into dissipation and licentiousness, to which Dostoevsky alludes symbolically in the editor's concluding hyperbolic lines of the first paragraph: "Wild game flies about the streets and throws itself in the hunter's path. Champagne is drunk in incredible quantities. The caviar is marvelous. In some places the harvest yields fifteen hundred per cent. . . . The land in general is richly blest [*blagoslovennaia*]. One must only know how to use it. In Siberia they know how to use it."[63]

The editor's high-flown praise, with its emphasis on possession and utility rather than on care and moderation, signals the very condition from which humans suffer disgrace. If this land and its inhabitants are blessed, at the same time both are accursed by the illusions which come with material bounty. Indeed, in the very roots of the Russian word for "blessed" are *blag*, which we have already observed is poised on the border of the sacred and the profane, and *slovo* ("word"), two central concerns for the moralist Dostoevsky. In the editor's final remarks of the first paragraph Dostoevsky completes and summarizes the text's inversions: the Biblical "Word made flesh" becomes in the editor's mouth a profane "flesh made words." The philistine world's lost garden, its unreachable promised land, cannot be located in the editor's space or time despite his insistence to the contrary. It is to be found only when individuals lose themselves (on the editor's model), fall from a transcendent condition, and mistake the luminous world for nothing but a world of possessions.

It must be emphasized that Dostoevsky's subversive voice does not supersede the editor's description of his paradise. Indeed, it would be incorrect to devalue the editor's voice in favor of Dostoevsky's covert reckoning of values. Dostoevsky seeks a simultaneous reading of the surface utterance and its hidden meanings as coexistent variations on one and the same theme, one constituted of both the editor's voice and the author's. If one of the two is reduced in status, then the unified image of humanity obtained from both ceases to operate. It is, therefore, as important to perceive clearly the editor's horizontally-organized world

---

idea is to experiment with the utter limits of his own nature" (*Dostoevsky*, 96). Dostoevsky himself likened Raskolnikov to the prisoners of *House of the Dead* (V. A. Tunimanov, *Tvorchestvo Dostoevskogo: 1854–1862* [Moscow: Akademiia nauk, 1980], 7).

[63] Dostoevsky, *House of the Dead*, 5–6; 2 (translation altered).

as it is to move through it to perceive its vertical potentials. We simply cannot obtain an adequate image of humankind if we deny either our material or spiritual dimensions. Motion from one plane of existence to another (and back) is continually implied in the description. Each axis represents a mirror of the potentialities of the other. When we are fallen, we exist in a precondition necessary to any possible future recovery. When, on the other hand, we live in a state of grace, in our human weakness we are in a dangerous condition, rife with the potential for another fall. By virtue of this motion, then, the editor is redeemable. And the chaste young girls shall transgress the extreme limit of their purity and fall, like the game that flies straight into the hunter's arms.

As central symbol, Goryanchikov is located somewhere between these two poles; once fallen and then released, he is persistently reminded, by his fellows and through his own experience, of the tenuousness of humanity's condition, understanding that he can be both saved and disgraced at any moment in his life. Existence implies a series of reversals, and the image of humanity that Dostoevsky attempts to describe in the remainder of *House of the Dead* incorporates this motion as its linguistic foundation and as its most fundamental illumination.

If it is necessary to caution against the replacement of either covert or overt voice by its opposite in the editor's first paragraph, it is also essential to appreciate that the literalization of root meanings contained in the editor's speech does not correspond in any measure to the "reality" represented by the prosaic and ordinary language employed by the editor. Although the two messages cannot be equated in terms of everyday speech with its associated phenomenological order, it must be understood that Dostoevsky, like any great author, is inclined to transgress the barriers of mundane language in order to grasp its hidden potential. As the editor's initial remarks reveal, the power of Dostoevsky's language to break its own shell and to overcome its limitations is reflected elsewhere in the text. In the final analysis, Dostoevsky seeks a simultaneous reading of the surface utterance and its deeper implications as equal halves of a single, unified image of humanity envisioned in a primal duality. It may not be an image that withstands the test of time, but it is Dostoevsky's. The quest for a means to express that duality takes as its point of illumination the root essences of language as they suggest a revised, de-automatized set of referents. In regard to that duality, it is important to recall Goryanchikov's message concerning the way in which he read the first books he was allowed to examine at the end of his ordeal in prison. He attended to both "the kernel and the husk" with emphasis on sensation, not mere reason; on the plasticity of a most receptive mind, not on the brittle surface of discursive logic; and on the power of language to break the bonds of common parlance and to deliver genuine insight.

The introduction to *House of the Dead* indicates Dostoevsky's entirely new understanding of how fecund the introduction can be, how richly it can contribute to a story. Through it he teaches us how to read his troublesome novel. But more to the point, in the language of the conventionally conceived editor, a philosophy of humankind emerges to challenge two audiences—those of the 1840s whose idealism interfered with the apprehension of who we are as a species; and the young men of the 1850s and 1860s who insisted on the exclusivity of a material, phenomenal world. This Dostoevsky found not only wrong-headed, but dangerously unrealistic. For Dostoevsky, life is a never-ending pilgrimage in search of self and some impenetrable, ultimate truth, a truth in which the alternating enactments of humanity's fall and redemption are constituent parts.

It can be argued that Dostoevsky never again achieved with an introduction what he did in *House of the Dead*. Conversely, it can also be asserted that he never returned to the convention-bound insipidity of the Introductory to *Stepanchikovo*. If nothing as philosophically deep emerges in his later introductions, they still have a bearing on essential questions in the Dostoevsky oeuvre. With these thoughts in mind, we turn now to Dostoevsky's introductions of the 1860s, a period when he targeted the young generation of radical thinkers and writers whose philosophies he found as error-ridden in their own way as the editor's philistine perspective in the introduction to *House of the Dead*.

Playing with Authorial Identities

CHAPTER 3

These were exciting years for Dostoevsky. With his *Notes from the House of the Dead*, he had achieved some of the success he longed for. He was noticed again by critics and by an ever-widening audience of readers from many strata of society. Dostoevsky, however, did not settle on the production of fictional texts alone to reassert his name. In letters written in the 1840s and during his exile, Dostoevsky had discussed with his brother, Mikhail, the idea of entering the publication business. In fact, while Dostoevsky was still residing in Siberia, Mikhail submitted the paperwork to the authorities to receive permission to publish a literary journal. Permission was granted in 1858. With Fyodor and Mikhail back together within the next year, they pursued their dream and opened the "thick" journal *Time* (*Vremia*, 1861–1863). It was closed by the censor, but the journal *Epoch* (*Epokha*, 1864–1865) followed hard on its heels. These two journals created outlets for Dostoevsky's work. They are where he published *Notes from the House of the Dead*, *The Insulted and the Injured*, short stories, and the non-fiction piece *Winter Notes on Summer Impressions*, which we take up in a moment.

More than an outlet for the publication of his fiction and memoirs, *Time* allowed Dostoevsky an opportunity to enter the literary debates of the day, to foster new talent, and to learn his craft from an entirely new angle, that of editor. And even more than a means by which (using Rudy Panko's famous phrase) to "poke his nose out of his hole into the great world," it was an investment through which the brothers sought to improve their financial circumstances, Dostoevsky being the more strapped of the two.¹ He would receive payment for his publications as well as from profits derived from sales of the journal.

In the winter of 1863 Dostoevsky published his thoughts on his recent (and first) trip to Europe in the soon-to-be-extinguished *Time*. He had begun writing his notes in late 1862 and completed them in January 1863.² They appear to have offered little that was new to the public. For example, Tolstoy had published his travel notes "Lucerne" as early as 1857, and its anti-European bias rendered Dostoevsky's disparagement of revolutionary Europe's aftermath less than noteworthy.

The genre of travel notes extended well back into the eighteenth century. Not only Dostoevsky's contemporaries, but many of his predecessors in the early nineteenth century, found fit to publish their notes—not only of Europe, but of south Asia, the Caucasus, and other far-flung reaches. As a work of non-fiction, Dostoevsky's *Winter Notes* does not fall within the narrow focus of this study, but its preface forms an interesting discourse with which to compare the fiction. Consequently, we shall examine it briefly. The exercise should prove useful to us when we consider subsequently Dostoevsky's *Diary of a Writer* and the stimulus behind his use (and non-use) of introductions in his oeuvre.

I

WINTER NOTES ON SUMMER IMPRESSIONS

Winter Notes has been mined previously for what it portends about Dostoevsky's great novels and the themes they deliver up, for its biographical content (where he went, what he saw, whom he met, and how he filtered it through his consciousness)³, and for its presentation

---

[1] During Fyodor's exile, Mikhail had purchased and run a tobacco manufacturing business, much to Fyodor's dismay. For a discussion of the journal's political and social orientation, see L. P. Grossman, *Dostoevsky: His Life and Work*, trans. Mary Mackler (New York: The Bobbs-Merrill Co., 1975), 221–259; and Joseph Frank, *The Stir of Liberation, 1860–1865* (Princeton: Princeton University Press, 1986), 133–348.

[2] Dostoevskii, *PSS*, V, "Zimnie zametki o letnikh vpechatleniiakh: Istochniki teksta," 357.

[3] His meetings with Herzen and Bakunin are considered extremely valuable.

of ideas long associated with his later post-exile life and work (his nationalism, anti-westernism, moralism, and religious set of beliefs). The preface, however, permits us the opportunity to look at the work's dynamics, as an artifact bound by a moment, not by what it presages. It plunges us into direct authorial discourse (Genette's "authentic authorial" type of introduction). In this intimate form of address, where the authorial persona turns directly to readers of every stripe in the creation of an illusion of direct conversation, we are led to believe that the voice leaping off the page is Dostoevsky's.

Dostoevsky does not seem entirely comfortable with unmediated intercourse with readers. Consequently, he speaks ironically, with a glance over his shoulder, with a wink, as though what he has to say must be taken with a grain of salt. The label he uses for his preface suggests this much. It is entitled "In Place of a Foreword" ("Vmesto predisloviia"). That is, it is not a foreword, but something that stands in a foreword's stead. What it is in itself is anyone's guess. After the affixation of the self-cancelling label, the authorial persona speaks:

> For some months now, my friends, you have been urging me to hurry up and describe to you my impressions from abroad, never suspecting that your request simply has me at my wit's end. What shall I write to you? What can I say that is new, as yet unknown, that has not been said before?[4]

Dostoevsky's openers are reminiscent of two strains. On the one hand, they represent a conventional travel note apology. Karamzin, Denis Davydov, Bestuzhev-Marlinsky, and many others conformed to this type of opening.[5] On the other hand, Dostoevsky's is something of

---

[4] Fyodor Dostoevsky, *Winter Notes on Summer Impressions*, trans. David Patterson (Evanston, IL: Northwestern University Press), 46; Dostoevskii, *PSS*, V: 1.

[5] Karamzin's *Letters of a Russian Traveler* (*Pis'ma russkogo puteshestvennika*, 1797–1801) established the model for openers: "I have left you, my dears. I have left you! My heart is yours in all its tenderest feelings, but now with each moment I move farther and farther away from you" (N. N. Karamzin, *Letters of a Russian Traveler: 1789–1790*, trans. Florence Jonas [New York: Columbia University Press, 1957], 29). Bestuzhev-Marlinskii's earliest travelogues solidify the norm and reveal one of his and Karamzin's European models: "You wished— and I promised, my exacting friends [*drugi*]— / That I regale [you] / with tales / [in] the leisure of my momentary respites / And [that I] describe adventures of my travels as did Dupaty" (A. A. Bestuzhev-Marlinskii, *Vtoroe polnoe sobranie sochinenii*, II Pt. 6 [Petersburg, 1847], 3).

a Gogolian apology in that it utilizes both self-abnegation and antilogy. We read, ". . . aside from these general considerations, you no doubt know that I have nothing in particular to relate and even less to properly write because I saw nothing properly myself, and what I did see I had no time to examine."[6] Why should he publish this work if he in fact has nothing to contribute to our understanding? And why should we continue to read on?[7]

Dostoevsky sets a trap for his readers, at least for those who do not sense what he is up to. Precisely by saying he has nothing to say, we must assume that he is being coy and that something new, some riches, are to be extracted from the travelogue. In other words, through the irony of his preface's title and its first sentences, we are manipulated into a state of readiness, of expectancy. Interesting in this regard is that Dostoevsky suggests that he knows us. We are his "dear friends," he says. He asserts a claim on our intimate mutual understanding: "You will recall [!] that I drew up my itinerary beforehand, while still in Petersburg."[8] Reader beware.

Dostoevsky's preface inclines in two directions. He suggests that it is not a preface, but something undefined. And he also suggests that the preface, from the perspective of literary convention, is indeed a normal preface in that it conducts us into the world the travelogue describes. To reverse an adage about Gogol's art, Dostoevsky's preface takes with one hand and then gives back with the other. Anti-prefaces, in fact, have a rather distinguished history in letters. To step away from Russian literary exemplars for a moment, Dostoevsky enjoyed reading Pierre Carlet de Chamblain de Marivaux (1688–1763) who provided him with a model of an upside-down preface in his *La Voiture Embourbée* (1714):

> The first lines I address to my friend at the beginning of this story ought to spare me the burden of writing a preface, but a preface is necessary; a book printed and bound without a preface—is it a book? No, without doubt, it does not yet deserve the name; it is a sort of book, a book without proper authorization, a work of the same species as those that are books, an applicant, aspiring to become a book, and only when

---

[6] Dostoevsky, *Winter Notes*, 1; 46.
[7] Ingred Kleepsies argues that Dostoevsky thoroughly debunked the Karamzin model of travel notes. See her *A Nation Astray: Nomadism and National Identity in Russian Literature* (DeKalb: Northern Illinois University Press, 2012), 23–46.
[8] Dostoevsky, *Winter Notes*, 1; 46.

vested with this last formality is it worthy to truly bear that name. Only then is it complete: whether it be dull, mediocre, good or bad, with its preface it bears the name of book wherever it goes . . . And so, dear Reader, since a preface is necessary, here is one.[9]

Marivaux concludes his rambling anti-preface (which I have expurgated to spare my dear readers) with a delightful *non sequitur*: "Thank God, now I am released from a great burden, and I am still laughing at the part I would have played had I been obliged to go through with my preface. Farewell. I infinitely prefer stopping short [of] boring you by going on at too great a length. Let's move on to the work."[10]

More than a century later, Balzac commented sarcastically on the convention of prefaces by means of the very title he affixed to his in *Vicaire des Ardennes* (1822): "A Preface That One Will Read If One Can." As mentioned earlier, Walter Scott played the game, too. He entitled the last chapter of *Waverley* "A Postscript, Which Should Have Been a Preface." Acknowledging that readers "rarely read prefaces" and "begin reading at the tale's end" to find out what happens before even beginning page one, his postscript thus "serves as a preface."[11] How playful introductions can be.

Through its growing set of ironies, Dostoevsky's lightheartedness, however, turns more serious. He turns away from the ostensible object of his focus—his travels in Europe—towards the subject, that is, himself. "I had never been abroad. I had longed to go almost since my earliest childhood, from the time when I spent long winter evenings, before I could read, listening open-mouthed, paralyzed with ecstasy and terror, as my parents read to me the novels of Radcliffe at bedtime; then I would rave deliriously about them in my sleep."[12]

This sudden shift in focus to the subject-as-child creates a new aura around the text. Readers are asked to join child-listeners to comprise the audience encountering enchanting texts. We are welcomed into the magic circle of childhood story-telling and are thus asked to step back from our expectations of something new from the author's travel notes and to move in the direction of something as old as the first story told

---

[9] Cited in Genette, *Paratexts*, 231–232.
[10] Cited in Genette, *Paratexts*, 232.
[11] Scott, *Prefaces to the Waverley Novels*, 172.
[12] Dostoevsky, *Winter Notes*, 1–2; 46.

and the mysterious capacity of narrative to engage our full and wide-eyed attention.

Once welcomed into the domestic setting Dostoevsky evokes, readers are confronted with a challenge. Having drawn us into his world (through our decoding his irony and by our identification with a story-ready child), Dostoevsky begins to complicate author-reader relations. He collapses the narrative enterprise, even of the non-fictional variety, claiming that he can provide little of what is normally expected of travelogues, for even when attempting to deliver up an account of his experiences—the people and the places—he is forced to deceive the reader. Not because he is, as he puts it, "a liar," but because objective narrative discourse that is adequate to the object is an impossibility, first because the thing in itself is impenetrable, but also because readers necessarily filter their experiences and are thus suspect in their capacity to complete the cycle of communication competently.[13] If the first point is philosophical, the second is personal, self-analytic, and self-conscious in an Underground-Man sense. The center does not hold; the self and its perceptual faculties operate poorly: ". . . if I begin to depict and describe even a single panorama, then I am bound to lie, not because I am a traveler but simply because in my circumstances it is impossible not to lie."[14] Dostoevsky goes on from this remark to illustrate the subjectivity of his perceptual apparatus, his biases, his imperfect skills as a writer. He refers here to his response to Germany, specifically to Berlin and Cologne:

> Judge for yourselves: Berlin, for instance, produced in me the most bitter impression, and I spent all of one day there. I know now that I am guilty before Berlin and that I would not dare to positively assert that it produces a bitter impression. Well, maybe bittersweet at any rate, but not just bitter. And what did my pernicious error result from? Surely from the fact that I, a sick man suffering from a liver ailment, bounced along the railway for two days through rain and fog to Berlin; once

---

[13] For comments on the Russian poetic tradition that subscribes to the ineffability of the Real, see Sofya Khagi, "Silence and the Rest: The Inexpressible from Batiushkov to Tiutchev," *Slavic and East European Journal* 48 (2004): 41–61. On lying in relation to the fabrication of literary fictions, see Deborah A. Martinsen, *Surprised by Shame: Dostoevsky's Liars and Narrative Exposure* (Columbus: The Ohio State University Press, 2003), 18–51.

[14] Dostoevsky, *Winter Notes*, 47; 2.

> arriving there, having gone without sleep, wan, tired, and worn out, I suddenly noticed at a glance that Berlin resembled Petersburg to an incredible degree.... "Oh, my God," I thought to myself. "Was it worth wearing myself out for two days in a train car just to see the same thing I left behind?" I did not even like the linden trees ...[15]

Dostoevsky lifts his description of the motive for his bile from out of his travelogue and plants a variant of it squarely in the first utterances of his Underground Man: "I am a sick man ... I am a wicked man ... I think my liver hurts."[16] The move from the psychological and emotional to the physiological has its roots in Lermontov's *A Hero of Our Time* where Pechorin explains away an emotional outburst (breaking down in tears when his horse dies as he vainly pursues his departing lover, Vera), asserting, "... it pleases me that I am capable of weeping. It may have been due, however, to upset nerves, to a sleepless night, to a couple of minutes spent facing the muzzle of a pistol, and to an empty stomach."[17] So, it is Dostoevsky's liver that predisposes him to a calloused opinion of Berlin and of Germany.

False national pride and its hidden twin, a ready self-defensiveness, also pollute Dostoevsky's capacity to render his travels objectively. They cause him to flee Germany:

> The second circumstance which infuriated me and made me unfair [in my views of Germany] was the new Cologne bridge. The bridge, of course, is magnificent, and the city has a right to be proud of it, but I felt that it was too proud. Needless to say, I immediately became angry about this. Besides, the penny collector at the entrance to the wondrous bridge had absolutely no right to take from me that reasonable toll, looking at me as if he were collecting a fine for some unknown offense I had committed. I do not know, but it seemed to me that this German was throwing his weight around. "He probably guessed that I am a foreigner and a Russian at that," I thought. His eyes, at least, were all but declaring, "You see our bridge, miserable Russian; well, you are a worm before our bridge and before every German because you do not have such a bridge."[18]

---

[15] Dostoevsky, *Winter Notes*, 47; 2.
[16] Fyodor Dostoevsky, *Notes from Underground*, trans. Richard Pevear and Larissa Volokhonsky (New York: Vintage Books, 1994), 3; Dostoevskii, *PSS*, V: 99.
[17] Lermontov, *Hero*, 176; 308.
[18] Dostoevsky, *Winter Notes*, 48; 4.

Dostoevsky's self-criticism expands beyond defensiveness to a level of comic absurdity that is darkly entertaining:

> You will agree that [the toll collector's remark] is offensive. *The German, of course, never said any such thing, and perhaps it never entered his mind, but that does not matter*: at the time I was so certain that this was precisely what he meant to say that I finally flew into a rage. "The devil take you," *I thought*. "We invented the samovar too ... we have journals ... we do things officers do ... we have ..." In a word, I was infuriated and, after buying a bottle of *eau de cologne* (which I could not avoid), I immediately skipped off to Paris, hoping that the French would be much nicer and more entertaining.[19]

They were not.

It is amusing that Dostoevsky depicts his flying into a rage as an interior event. The a-logism ("I flew into a rage" versus "I thought") is deepened by the fact that the German, too, says nothing ascribed to his voice. In fact, the entire scene does not take place at the level of social performance. It is entirely fabricated by Dostoevsky's subjectivity, based as it is on an abiding sense of inferiority. But, it becomes clear, this in fact is hardly Dostoevsky's subjectivity—it is his alter ego's. Another way to put it, the conscious self that writes up *Winter Notes* is different from the self that had experienced the summer events. The first is the "narrating-I," and the second the "experiencing-I." Neither represents Dostoevsky, the historical figure. The two identities belong to two authorial projections.

What can be said about Dostoevsky's introduction to *Winter Notes on Summer Impressions* is that even in a non-fictional context, Dostoevsky's preface presents a voice other than that of the author. This is not to say that we must draw an entirely predictable conclusion about his prefatorial discourse for non-fiction—that the voice speaking to us is not that of the historical personage of the writer. Rather, it is to say that within this paradigm we are asked to identify ever more refined divisions within voice. We cannot merely distinguish between writer and narrator and character utterances. In *Winter Notes* there emerges a new pattern to be discerned in Dostoevsky's oeuvre, specifically, free indirect speech. This form of discourse represents utterance that glides from one person's voice to another then back again, most

---

[19] Dostoevsky, *Winter Notes*, 48–49; 4 (Dostoevsky's ellipses; my emphases).

commonly from the narrator's to that of a character, but without quotation marks.[20]

In the introduction to *Winter Notes*, Dostoevsky, the author, pens the text's first words as an interplay between his authorial persona (with its twenty-twenty vision of hindsight) and Dostoevsky the dramatis persona who has traveled recently to Europe. For Dostoevsky the author, the text becomes an act of ventriloquism, but with a variety of marionettes. When they seem most to represent Dostoevsky, as they often do, for example, in his non-fiction, journalism, and opinion-pieces, we learn to be wary. *Winter Notes* cautions us to be careful when we think we have a direct view of the authentic authorial person. This is also the case in *Notes from the Underground*, the first work of fiction to be published after *Winter Notes*. In both texts, an authentic authorial preface seems to be at hand. Yet in both instances, a chorus of voices suggests otherwise.

II

NOTES FROM THE UNDERGROUND

The footnoted introduction to *Notes from the Underground* is signed by "Fëdor Dostoevskii," the name affixed at the end of the prologue, not by the Underground Man, whose two-part account (a monologue followed by a narrative) makes up the text's narrative, nor by Fyodor Dostoevsky, the author of the work.[21] In the footnote introducing *Underground*, the Underground Man enters literary history in one hundred and seven remarkably deceptive words:

> Both the author of the notes and the *Notes* themselves are, it goes without saying [*razumeetsia*], fictional. Nevertheless, such persons as the writer of such notes not only may but even must [*dolzhno*] exist in our society, taking into consideration the circumstances under which

---

[20] See Roy Pascal, *The Dual Voice (Free Indirect Speech and its functioning in the nineteenth-century European novel)* (Manchester: Manchester University Press, 1977), 136–137.

[21] I utilize here an alternate system of transliteration in order to point toward a signatory other than the historical figure Fyodor Dostoevsky.

our society has generally been formed [*skladyvalos'*]. I wished to bring before the face of the public, a bit more conspicuously than usual [*povidnee obyknovennogo*], one of the characters of a time recently passed. He is one representative of a generation that is still living out its life [*dozhivaiushchego pokoleniia*]. In this fragment, entitled "Underground" [i.e., Part One], this person introduces himself, his outlook, and seeks, as it were [*kak by*], to elucidate the reasons why he appeared and had [*dolzhno*] to appear among us. In the subsequent fragments will come this person's actual "notes" about certain events in his life [i.e., Part Two]. Thus, the first fragment [Part One] should [*dolzhno*] be considered sort of [*kak by*] an introductory [*vstuplenie*] to the whole book, almost [*pochti*] a foreword [*predislovie*].[22]

Dostoevsky's footnote has been mined for its content as it relates to the Underground Man's speech mannerisms, his unique consciousness, and his literary and socio-historical roots. But the form and language in which the introduction is cast have, in the main, suffered inattention. On the rare occasion when the *Underground*'s prologue is referenced in the critical literature, it is most often assumed to represent Dostoevsky's voice, not an implied or projected author's. Critics have long assumed we are dealing with an authentic authorial preface, that is, one cast in the author's own voice. After all, he signed it.

The critical literature has focused on the *what*, not the *how*, of Dostoevsky's introduction. Critics assume that the author's brief framing of the Underground Man's narrative is a sufficient means of contextualizing the narrative in historical, psychological, philosophical, and ethical terms. For example, in his discussion of the conclusion of the Underground Man's narrative, Robert Louis Jackson perceives a brief, overt coincidence of the author's intent with the Underground Man's utterance that links that utterance to the author of the introduction:

---

[22] Fedor Dostoevskii, *Zapiski iz podpol'ia*, *Epokha*, nos. 1–2 (1864): 498. See also *PSS*, V: 99 and Fyodor Dostoevsky, *Notes from Underground*, trans. Richard Pevear and Larissa Volokhonsky (New York: Vintage Books, 1993), 3. The thirty-volume collection uses the revised footnote of 1866 when the work appeared in full for the first time. It excludes the final sentence of the original. That sentence was expunged from later editions because the work no longer appeared in the serial form that called for it. The 1866 (canonical) text also revised the penultimate sentence's "in the following fragments" ("v sleduiushchikh otryvkakh") to the singular in order to reflect final changes in the work's actual design.

The last paragraph of *Notes from the Underground*, beginning with the words "Even now, after all these years, it is with a particularly *bad feeling* that I recall all this," almost has the character of a detached chorus. Here the disillusioned idealist looks back on his encounter with Liza through sixteen years of remorse and suffering with a crime on his conscience: "never, never shall I recall that moment indifferently." The words of the Underground Man are now devoid of pun or paradox. He distances himself from the events described and places his own tragedy in a general broadly cultural and social light. He defines himself as an antihero. His tone seems to approach the calm objectivity *of Dostoevsky's footnote-preface*, or prologue, to *Notes from the Underground*.[23]

Ralph Matlaw also presents the prologue as belonging to Dostoevsky. In asserting that Apollon, the Underground Man's servant, is cut from the same cloth as his master, Matlaw remarks: "If the narrator's report can be trusted, the portrait of Apollon indicates, beneath the mask of human dignity, the same malicious, sadistic traits characteristic of the narrator . . . He is thus an extension of the narrator's personality, a proof, as it were, of his ubiquity in the modern world, and once more refers the reader to *Dostoevsky's footnote*."[24]

Like Jackson, Gary Saul Morson discusses the closing words of the narrative in light of the footnoted introduction, both of which he associates with the implied Dostoevsky's voice: "Just as he has the first word, the author also has the last."[25] James Scanlan makes a similar assumption: ". . . Dostoevsky used *Notes from Underground* to create [the Underground Man] as part of an attack on the then-fashionable conception of egoism advanced by the Rational Egoists. This interpretation is consistent with *Dostoevsky's enigmatic annotation* [i.e., the footnoted introduction] in which he wrote that people such as his Underground Man 'not only can but even must exist in our society, considering the circumstances under which it has generally been formed.'"[26]

---

[23] Jackson, *The Art of Dostoevsky*, 183–184 (my emphases).
[24] Ralph Matlaw, "Structure and Integration in *Notes from Underground*," in *Notes from Underground*, ed. Robert G. Durgy (Washington, DC: University Press of America, 1969), 193 (my emphasis).
[25] Gary Saul Morson, *Narrative and Freedom: The Shadows of Time* (New Haven: Yale University Press, 1994), 37.
[26] James P. Scanlan, *Dostoevsky the Thinker* (Ithaca: Cornell University Press, 2002), 62 (my emphasis).

The notion is repeated by Joseph Frank: "... the Underground Man is not only a moral-psychological type whose egoism Dostoevsky wishes to expose; he is also a social-ideological one, whose psychology must be seen as intimately interconnected with the ideas he accepts and by which he tries to live.... *Dostoevsky*, it seems to me, *overtly pointed to this aspect of the character in the footnote appended to the title of the novella . . . Dostoevsky's footnote* . . . attempted to alert his audience to the satirical and parodistic nature of his conception; but it was too oblique to serve its purpose."[27]

John Jones' understanding of Dostoevsky's signature ("a device like any other") goes against this tradition and has roots as far back as Nikolai Strakhov. He provides a valuable clue to the potential for polyphony in the introduction. Unlike Jackson and Morson, Jones views the voices at the beginning and conclusion of the narrative as distinct from one another:

> The introductory note seems to forebode an editorial role like that of the finder of the tatty manuscript in *The Notes of the Dead House*. In fact "Fedor Dostoevsky" never moves [into the body of the narrative]. And not only does he keep out, he disappears ... He melts into a "we" which is how the book is brought to a stop. The underground man who has been showing no sign of flagging suddenly says he has had enough, and his discourse breaks off. Another voice informs us "However this isn't yet the end of the *Notes* of this paradoxist. He failed to keep to his resolve and went on writing. But it seems to us, too, that we may well stop here." And that really is the end of the novel, and yet . . . a dubious "really" since the underground man is carrying on without his readers.[28]

If the signature is a device, as Jones calls it, and the voice of the ending something of a ruse of collectivity that creates the illusion of a completely framed narrative, then perhaps the utterances that belong to "Fëdor Dostoevskii," the prologue's signatory, might also be a ruse. Who, in fact, speaks in the footnoted introduction to *Underground*?

Assayed against Dostoevsky's preceding introductions, *Notes from the Underground* stands out. It bears no formal label (e.g., introduction, prologue, etc.) and appears in a manner not encountered in Dostoevsky's

---

[27] Frank, *Stir of Liberation*, 314–316 (my emphasis).
[28] John Jones, *Dostoevsky* (Oxford: Clarendon Press, 1983), 178–179.

writing of the period—as a footnote. Footnoted introductions are broadly attested in the journals of the day, including in the Dostoevsky brothers' journal, *Time*. In issues preceding the publication of *Underground* (which was to appear in *Time* until it was shut down, only to appear subsequently in the first issue of their next journalistic enterprise, *Epoch*) there is ample evidence of its use.[29] Occurring with some regularity as brief notes that introduce the work of others, footnotes of the *Underground* variety accompany reports, translations, non-fictional articles of a social and political nature, works of fiction by authors other than Dostoevsky, as well as articles by one of the key contributors to the journal, Nikolai Strakhov.[30] These footnoted introductions are uniformly explanatory and utilize a direct form of address that in no manner is meant to complicate, retard, or make strange one's apprehension of the subsequent discourse. On occasion they caution the reader about the point of view taken in the piece. For example, the editor, who is most likely Dostoevsky, introduces a report entitled "From a Doctor's File" ("Iz portfelia doktora") with a footnote that reads: "A few years ago this article was read before the Society of Lovers of Russian Literature in Kazan'. The manuscript was given the title 'On the Benefits of Medicine.' 'The Great Fire' which the author references on the first pages was the conflagration of 1842 when almost all of Kazan' burned down."[31] Notes of this matter-of-fact nature are often used to provide justification for including a specific article in an issue of *Time*.

In another variant of this single-function type of footnoted introduction, when Dostoevsky shifted the serial publication of his *House of the Dead* from the rather obscure journal *The Russian World* (*Russkii mir*) to the first issues of *Time*, he appended the following in a footnote affixed to the work's title: "We reprint from *The Russian World* these

---

[29] *Underground* came out in the first issue of *Epoch* (spring 1864), the journal Mikhail and Fyodor received permission to publish after *Time* was closed by the censor in the fall of 1863. *Time* provides extensive models of footnoted introductions (as do other journals of the period). For extensive publication details, see V. S. Nechaeva's *Zhurnal M. M. i F. M. Dostoevskikh 'Vremia' 1861–1863* (Moscow: Khudlit, 1974) and *Zhurnal M. M. i F. M. Dostoevskikh 'Epokha' 1864–1865* (Moscow: Khudlit, 1975).

[30] Frank discusses Strakhov's dissatisfaction with Dostoevsky for appending introductions to his, Strakhov's, articles (*Stir of Liberation*, 107 and *passim*).

[31] *Vremia*, no. 8, 1861, 453, (my translation).

four chapters which serve as a form of introduction to *Notes from the House of the Dead* for those readers who are not acquainted with it. We will take up the *Notes*' continuation upon our completion of the novel *The Insulted and The Injured*."[32]

Apropos an article of translated literary criticism, "Sketches on the Latest Literary Development in France" ("Ocherki poslednego literaturnogo dvizheniia vo Frantsii") with which he did not wholly agree, the editor of *Time*, most likely Dostoevsky, added the following footnote: "This article in large measure has been taken by us from public lectures by William Raymond that he read in 1861 in Berlin, subsequently published under the title 'Études sur la littérature du second Empire français depuis le coup-d-État du deux Décembre.' The author's perspectives on many contemporary phenomena of literature are French-oriented and therefore do not accord with [the perspectives of] our Russian criticism. None the less the article is of value and therefore we submit it to the judgment of our readers."[33]

Because it can be assessed against these norms, the footnoted introduction to *Underground* holds a special place in Dostoevsky's immediate post-exile publications, not just because of its argument—the usual focus of the critical literature—but because of its appearance as a footnote, as something markedly unique in Dostoevsky's fictional oeuvre. It possesses, too, a notable feature that distinguishes it from others, specifically, Dostoevsky's "signature." As John Jones indicates, even here we have reasons to be careful in assuming that this indeed represents Dostoevsky's authorial persona. There are three reasons for caution. First, prior examples in Dostoevsky's work from the immediate post-exile period suggest the likelihood of a voice other than the author's. Second, the tradition of fictional introductions itself recommends the exercise of some restraint. And third, Dostoevsky raises a red flag about the way in which his signature is affixed to the introduction. Specifically, he calls attention to his "signature" *qua* object.

Whenever Dostoevsky flags something linguistically or stylistically in his writing, there is usually good reason for it. His name, as one would expect, is printed at the conclusion of the footnote. But four features mark it. First, that it appears at all is unusual, for most of the

---

[32] *Vremia*, no. 4, 1861, 1 (my translation).
[33] *Vremia*, no. 3, 1862, 149 (my translation).

footnoted introductions preceding it in *Time* bear no authorial mark of provenance whatsoever. Second, when authorship appears at the end of a footnote, what is affixed is always a function—editor (*red*.), not a personal name.[34] Third, Dostoevsky's "signature" is set apart on a separate line and justified to the right (that is, it is not continuous with the final line of the note, as it is in almost all other examples where the label "editor" appears). Fourth, it is printed in a font distinct from the one used in the body of the footnoted text and it is italicized. Both of these last two features are not attested elsewhere in *Time* or in the first volume of *Epoch*. Perhaps these are merely coincidental signs, but I think not. Dostoevsky was a stickler for details both in his editorial capacities for *Time* and as an author.[35]

Although applied to the circumstance of frame narratives, not to brief introductions of the type addressed here, Charles Isenberg provides valuable insight into their significance. He remarks that "one defining feature of frame narratives is that they assign more or less distinguishable domains to narrative situation and to plot, the former being most prominent in the frame, the latter in the embedded part."[36] Furthermore, "[f]rame narration would [appear] to objectify a fundamental process of all narrative acts: *every* story at least implies a frame, in that it marks off one chunk of discourse from this world of language and experience."[37] Isenberg's description may be applied fruitfully to Dostoevsky's introductions, which uniformly provide a framing function, if in miniature, similar to the frame narratives Isenberg discusses in his study. In *Underground*, Dostoevsky's prologue serves to identify a narrating situation outside the Underground Man's chronotope. It encloses that narrative within an overarching design (the Underground Man as a social-historical and psychological type), motivates the monologue that forms Part One, and anticipates the confessional discourse of Part Two that appears in a later edition of *Epoch*.[38]

---

[34] An exception is Apollon Grigoriev, Dostoevsky's friend and colleague. When he attached an introduction to his articles, he affixed his signature. His introductions, however, never appeared in footnoted form.
[35] Frank, *Stir of Liberation*, 64–75.
[36] Isenberg, *Telling Silence*, 9.
[37] Isenberg, *Telling Silence*, 9.
[38] Dostoevsky had not started to write Part Two when he consigned Part One to print. He certainly had a rough idea of the form the second part would take: "In the subsequent fragments will come this person's actual 'notes' about certain

There are several reasons for considering Dostoevsky's introductions, and *Underground*'s specifically, as a special category of discourse. The frequency of their use in Dostoevsky's immediate post-exile period makes them unique in his oeuvre in general. Furthermore, as we have already noted, they call attention to themselves through a set of labels that differ one from the other. The way introductions are represented on the page (e.g., as a sustained presentation at the outset of a work, as, for example, in *House of the Dead*, or as a footnote) also distinguish them from each other. In addition, they engage the reader in a framing context that is differentiated from the narrative. In this last instance, the framing context of *Underground* itself requires reexamination, for it has been assumed to represent a chronotope belonging to Dostoevsky. There are voices in the introduction that suggest otherwise.

The introduction's formal elements call attention to it as a self-conscious literary device that points in a direction that is yet to emerge. Deterministic claims made in the footnote provide insight into that direction. They occur twice in the introduction. The second sentence of the note reads: "Nevertheless, such persons as the writer of such notes not only may *but even must [dolzhno] exist in our society*, taking into consideration the circumstances under which our society has generally been formed."[39] Socio-historical determinism of this type appears again in the fifth sentence: "In this fragment, entitled 'Underground,' this person introduces himself, his outlook, and seeks, as it were [*kak by*], to elucidate the reasons why he appeared and *had [dolzhno] to appear among us*."[40]

There is an overt conflict between the prologue's acceptance of historical determinism and the alternative position held in varying

---

events in his life." But the idea proved to be only partially correct—only one additional fragment appeared subsequently.

[39] Dostoevsky, *Notes from Underground*, 3; 99 (my emphasis).

[40] Dostoevsky, *Notes from Underground*, 3; 99 (my emphasis). *Dolzhno* occurs again in the seventh sentence of the magazine text, but in an alternate sense: "Thus, the first fragment [Part One] should [*dolzhno*] be considered sort of a prologue/introductory to the whole book, almost a foreword." The triple repetition of this lexical element in the introduction provides another formal clue for taking an interest in the introduction as a conscious device. We are being asked, in effect, to notice repetition and, therefore, to seek its source—whose voice is using it?

degrees by both Dostoevsky and his Underground Man. It hardly bears repeating—Dostoevsky was taking on the radicals of the 1860s, not, as Frank indicates pointedly, for personal reasons or merely to correct the error of their ways as young idealists (with whom Dostoevsky could identify, in part, on the basis of his own beliefs of the 1840s), but for their unquestioned acceptance of the deterministic argument that came as baggage with their adherence to materialism, empiricism, positivism, and a philosophy of rational egoism.[41] The Underground Man, like the radicals, now accepts the inevitability of determinism, then, like their opponents, rails against that inevitability (he calls it "the wall"). He is incapable of mounting a substantive *reasoned* assault on it, and is consequently forced to rely on two weapons Dostoevsky makes available to him—aggressive, if self-defeating, irrationalism that is conscious of itself, and a discourse that performs his independence, his free will, in holding firmly to any position absolutely.[42] This is the vantage point from which the Underground Man can argue with conviction that "two times two is five is sometimes also a most charming little thing" and alternately submit to the inevitability of "two plus two is four."[43]

Dostoevsky, on the other hand, was disturbed by the naïve literary representation of determinism, and not only in Chernyshevsky's *What is to be Done?*, which he parodies in *Underground*. He stood firmly behind his Underground Man's attempt to discredit it. As Scanlan notes, "Dostoevsky repeatedly voiced his disagreement with [any] deterministic view of human action."[44] But he did not fully accept or attempt to reject determinism in the way his Underground Man does. Nor, as a result, would he appeal to irrational argument alone to challenge it. After all, he had the power of fiction at his disposal, and his *Underground* in particular.[45]

The epistemological problem "determinism versus free will" is far from being resolved any time soon. Dostoevsky in *Underground*

---

[41] Frank, *Stir of Liberation*, 323–324.
[42] In Gene Fitzgerald's words, "The Underground Man defeats determinism, not because he says he is against it, or because he has free will, but because his discourse illustrates it" (personal communication).
[43] Dostoevsky, *Notes from Underground*, 34; 119.
[44] Scanlan, *Dostoevsky the Thinker*, 73.
[45] And not only fiction. There was his incipient, and growing, faith as well as his interest in paranormal phenomena and the supernatural.

simply does his part to incorporate the vexed and prolonged debate surrounding the topic. He uses two methods to advance a fictionalized position. First, he shifts the problem from the philosophical to the narratological plane. The latter, as Scanlan argues, is where Dostoevsky best demonstrates his strength as a thinker.[46] Second, Dostoevsky moves from an abstract to a pragmatic level of discourse. Scanlan writes:

> There is no doubt that Dostoevsky shared the Underground Man's opposition to psychological egoism (the descriptive side of Rational Egoism). Psychological egoism as advanced by Chernyshevsky and Pisarev rested on a denial of free will, whereas Dostoevsky repeatedly voiced his disagreement with [such a] deterministic view of human action. . . . The characters who people Dostoevsky's stories are notoriously either ignorant of their own interests and motives, or hopelessly ambivalent, or captious, or prone to spiteful and malicious acts from which they expect no benefit to themselves—all situations that cannot be accommodated by psychological egoism.[47]

Dostoevsky provides a pragmatic response to the idealistic thinking underlying the radicals' utilitarian proposition, and he does so from a principle of psychological ambiguity rather than reason (ambiguity in that the individual cannot always be cognizant of what constitutes his or her interests).[48]

The picture, in fact, is rather more complex. There is ample evidence in the Underground Man's narrative to suggest that a deterministic model is something Dostoevsky was not willing to relinquish entirely. Despite his protestations, the Underground Man periodically submits to a deterministic model of human action (and lives with the consequences of that

---

[46] Scanlan, *Dostoevsky the Thinker*, 1–4. See also, V. Kirpotin, *Dostoevskii v shestidesiatye gody* (Moscow: Khudlit, 1966), 483.
[47] Scanlan, *Dostoevsky the Thinker*, 73.
[48] Scanlan puts it as follows: "[Dostoevsky] is concerned . . . to show what egoistic action really consists in, and he is convinced that it is not simply a matter of responding mechanically to perceived interests. True egoism is something quite different from that, he believes, and from the very first lines of *Notes from Underground* he is engaged in demonstrating that people do not always (or even typically) take action for the sake of promoting what they themselves believe to be their own best interest (except in the case of one very peculiar 'interest' not anticipated by the Rational egoists [i.e., freedom of choice, free will])" (Scanlan, *Dostoevsky the Thinker*, 68).

submission), at least until he can reject it behaviorally, in irrational, or self-defeating, (in)action. What is worse for him, however, as Morson points out, is that the footnoted introduction itself encloses the Underground Man within a deterministic model:

> ... [I]t is Dostoevsky who establishes the hero's lack of freedom most conclusively. In his role as "editor" of the Underground Man's text, Dostoevsky appends an "explanation" to the title of part I, "Underground." The Underground Man claims full freedom to define himself or to leave himself altogether undefined, but he does not have the first word. Before we hear from the Underground Man's self-characterization, we hear him characterized by another, who is inaccessible to him: "The author of these notes, *not only may, but positively must*, exist in our society, considering those circumstances under which our society was in general formed." Ironically enough, it would seem that the Underground Man's very polemic on behalf of freedom was inevitable.
>   ... Here Dostoevsky makes shrewd use of metaliterary devices. For all of his struggles to be free, the Underground Man is doubly determined, not only from within the narrative world but also from without; not only by the iron logic of spite governing his actions but also by the fact that he is the creation of someone who has plotted all his actions in advance. His world is not just deterministic but overdeterministic. What Dostoevsky has done here is to make the very fact that the story is a story, that it has a structure and *has already been written*, a sign of failed choice and futile self-assertion.[49]

At this level, it can be argued that Dostoevsky, in his authorial role, is a determinist. This condition, however, applies to many a nineteenth-century author. But can it be that Dostoevsky holds a deterministic view beyond his authorial role and beyond the limitations he seems to have set for himself within the introduction and the larger text? Is this the text's secret message arising, as Isenberg argues in regard to frame narratives, in the interaction between frame (introduction plus concluding words) and insert tale? But this would negate two of the tenets (free will and the personal responsibility for one's behavior that flows from it) that he is supposedly hard pressed to assert through the

---

[49] Morson, *Freedom and Narrative*, 36–37 (Morson's emphases).

medium of his art. To forestall this conundrum momentarily, it may be worthwhile to examine the language of the footnoted introduction to review how Dostoevsky's deterministic stance is articulated in the introduction, at which levels of discourse, and in what context it is given room for play.

The first sentence is a reminder, as if one were needed, that *Underground* is a work of fiction: "Both the author of the notes and the *Notes* themselves are, it goes without saying [*razumeetsia*], fictional." This proviso sets up Dostoevsky's next argument, to wit, notwithstanding the fact that Part One of the text, titled "Underground," represents fictional discourse, it is relevant to contemporary life in general and to the appearance of the Underground Man specifically: "Nevertheless, such persons as the writer of such notes not only may but even *must exist in our society* taking into consideration the circumstances under which our society has generally been formed."[50] The assertion of inevitability hinges on the reader's willingness to accede to the qualifier "the circumstances under which our society has been formed."

It is important to note the sequencing of the argument in the second utterance. First, the speaker imagines a community of like-minded people (emphasis here is both on "our" and "society"). Second, there is only allusion to, rather than explication of, the conditions (*obstoiatel'stva*) that made the Underground Man's presence a necessary historical event.[51] And third, a historical process is encapsulated in the phrase "generally been formed" (*skladyvalos'*), thus giving broad, if minor, illumination to the point about the conditions that inevitably produced the Underground type. There are no specifics given; that is the job of Parts One and Two. But we at least know that the Underground Man is not a happenstance. The historical situation that produced him evolved from out of the 1840s, when German Idealism held sway in Russia, and

---

[50] My emphasis.
[51] Frank states, "Dostoevsky here is obviously talking about the formation of Russian ('our') society, which, as he could expect all readers of *Epoch* to know—had he not explained this endlessly in his articles in *Time*, most recently and explicitly in *Winter Notes?*—had been formed by the successive waves of European influence that had washed over Russia since the time of Peter the Great" (*Stir of Liberation*, 314).

emerged in the period when the radical intelligentsia of the 1850s and 1860s commanded center stage.[52]

If one assumes that the voice in the introduction is the implied author's (not Dostoevsky's direct voice, as some suggest), and if it utilizes a deterministic argument to situate the text's antihero, then the voice stands in opposition to Dostoevsky's position as Scanlan, among others, have defined it. Clearly, something has to give. That something is the assumption that we encounter a unified implied author's voice in the introduction.

An initial chink in the armor of a unified-voice theory can be represented graphically:

Identity: Fictional Editor **Tone: Matter-of-fact**	*Identity: Determinist* **Tone: Insistent, decisive**
Both the author of the notes and the *Notes* themselves are, of course, fictional. Nevertheless, such persons as the writer of such notes not only may	
	but even must exist in our society,
taking into consideration the circumstances under which our society has generally been formed	
In this fragment, entitled "Underground," this person introduces himself, his outlook	
	and seeks, as it were, to elucidate the reasons why he appeared and had to appear among us.

Once we are willing to perceive two distinct voices operating in the first two sentences of the introduction, we can ask ourselves whether additional tones are present elsewhere. We read again from the beginning (as many a Dostoevsky fictional opening asks us to), attempting to hear new intonations, citations, or allusions to other authors and their texts.[53] The first sentence suddenly appears

---

[52] See Frank, *Stir of Liberation*, 327.
[53] See a most recent example in Robert L. Belknap, "The *Siuzhet* of Part 1 of *Crime and Punishment*," in *Dostoevsky on the Threshold of Other Worlds (Essays in Honour of Malcolm V Jones)*, ed. Sarah Young and Lesley Milne (Ilkeston: Bramcote Press, 2006), 153–156; and V. N. Toporov, "On Dostoevsky's Poetics and Archaic Patterns of Mythological Thought," *New Literary History* 9 (1978): 333–352. Morson cautions us about re-reading and the deterministic interpre-

quite altered. It contains a likely nod in Gogol's direction, and even practices the Underground Man's equivocating style itself. This first sentence, clarifying that this is indeed a piece of fiction, seems direct enough. But why say it if it goes without saying? It is a red herring and, harkening back to Gogol's openings, serves multiple functions, of which parody and satire are prominent components.

Re-examining the introduction's utterances from the first sentence forward, we find that things are not as stable as they originally appeared. Such an acknowledgement forces us to pay attention to each word, each phrase, each speech tick. For example, the turn in the fourth sentence, "He is one representative of a generation that is still living out its life," appears mocking, suggesting that we might have done better in "our [current] society" without that generation. The phrasing "as it were" in the fifth sentence, too, seems odd: "In this fragment, entitled 'Underground' this person introduces himself, his outlook, and seeks, *as it were*, to elucidate the reasons why he appeared and had to appear among us."[54] We detect a sarcastic note lurking behind what in other contexts might appear to be a matter-of-fact reference to the difficulties the Underground Man encounters in his attempt to make sense of himself. It isn't that he *wants* to explain himself, but *as if* he wants to do so. This "as it were/as if" (*kak by*) in turn throws a back light on the first sentence's use of "it goes without saying." Cued by these speech oddities, we consider it plausible that a third voice (alternating between sarcastic, ironic, and satiric tones) appears in the introduction, expanding its vocal potentials beyond those uncovered in the first two sentences:

---

tations that often derive from it (*Prosaics and Other Provocations: Empathy, Open Time, and the Novel* [Boston: Academic Studies Press, 2013], 46–49). I am determined to disregard that caution for the moment.

[54] Dostoevsky, *Notes from Underground*, 3; 99 (my emphasis).

Playing with Authorial Identities 83

Identity: Fictional Editor **Tone: Matter-of-fact**	**Identity: Determinist** **Tone: Insistent, decisive**	**Identity: Parodist** **Tone: Equivocating**
Both the author of the notes and the *Notes* themselves are, it goes without saying, fictional. Nevertheless, such persons as the writer of such notes not only may		Both the author of the notes and the *Notes* themselves are, it goes without saying, fictional.
taking into consideration the circumstances under which our society has generally been formed	but even must exist in our society, taking into consideration the circumstances under which our society has generally been formed.	
I wished to bring before the face of the public, a bit more conspicuously than usual, one of the characters of a time recently passed. He is one representative of a generation that is still living out its life.		that is still living out its life.
In this fragment, entitled "Underground," [i.e., Part One], this person introduces himself, his outlook,	and seeks, as it were, to elucidate the reasons why he appeared and had to appear among us.	and seeks, as it were,

Under this illumination, the third sentence comes into new focus. It, too, combines the tones of a fictional editor, a satirist, and a determinist. They, respectively, provide stage directions, wink at the audience, or hold forth pompously. For example, anticipating the response of an hypothetical reader who wishes to obtain more detail pertinent to the claims made by the prologue's narrator(s) about the appearance of the Underground type "in our midst," the fictional editor responds, "I wished to bring [*vyvesti*] before the face of the public, a bit more conspicuously than usual [*povidnee obyknovennogo*], one of the characters of a time recently passed." The verb *vyvesti* signals a new tactic. To be literal about the components of this verb, the speaker will "bring/ *lead out* before the reading public, more conspicuously than is usually done, one of the characters of our most recent past."[55] Alternatives to

---

[55] My emphasis.

vyvesti are entirely plausible. The narrator might have "introduced" (*predstavit'*) or "described" (*opisat'*) his character. However, the verb of motion's (*vyvesti*'s) metaphoric qualities are realized, wrenched out of their automatized speech condition to set the Underground Man before us as on a stage. As the Russian verb suggests, he has been led out before us to perform.

What are we to make of the remark "a bit more conspicuously than usual" (*povidnee obyknovennogo*)? To what level of discourse does it belong? It may belong to the fictional narrator. Alternatively, it may issue from the pen of the implied author, Dostoevsky. If it is Dostoevsky's literary persona, then a fourth voice appears at this point in the introduction—the implied author's (the one who seems to have signed the footnote).[56]

With the Underground Man now positioned on the soap box from which his tumultuous confession overwhelms us, the editor-narrator goes on to describe him, as before, in general terms: "He is one representative of a generation that is still living out its life." The disparaging "still living out its life" aside, it is important to note that the Underground Man is introduced here as one of a set, reinforcing the notion that he is not only typical, in the special sense that Dostoevsky gives this word in his art, but that he is a being who realizes, through *reductio ad absurdum*, the logical, and extreme, consequences of a way of thought then holding sway in contemporary society. The Underground Man's individuality, of which he is vehemently conscious, is thus subsumed within a larger group (of which he might not be aware). This renders him, paradoxically, representative—typical and decidedly not unique. If there is strength in numbers, then the fictional editor-narrator of the introduction elicits that strength through making the Underground Man merely one of a larger body of these so-called individuals.[57] The irony should be apparent to us, as well as the double-voicing that produces it.

Having established the Underground Man's appearance within society as a type, the narrator immediately returns to the theme of that type's inevitable appearance "in our midst": "In this fragment,

---

[56] This is one of two fairly overt moments when a "Fëdor Dostoevskii" appears in the introduction. All other utterances issue from the lips of the fictional editor-narrator, the determinist, or the satirist/ironist.

[57] For a detailed description of the Underground Man as a literary type, see V. Kirpotin, *Dostoevskii v shestidesiatye gody* (Moscow: Khudlit, 1966), 471–481.

entitled 'Underground' [i.e., Part One], this person introduces himself, his outlook, and seeks, as it were [*kak by*], to elucidate the reasons why he appeared and had [*dolzhno*] to appear among us." By-passing the Gogolian allusion in "as it were," the repetition of *dolzhno* reinforces the voice of historical determinism at work in the footnote. But it also emphasizes the notion that the Underground Man will speak for himself and his views (the Underground Man's task), and he will do so in an attempt to make clear why he "must have come into existence" in society (Dostoevsky's task).[58] The fictional editor-narrator of the footnote is stating here that the narrative that follows (Part One for readers first encountering the text in the April 1864 edition) gives the floor to a contemporary type who will perform his identity for us as a process through which he clarifies his origins, if not to himself, then to readers.

The final sentences of the introduction wrap up the ventriloquist's act: "In the subsequent fragments will come this person's actual 'notes' about certain events in his life." This penultimate comment prepares the reader of the first edition of *Epoch* for what comes two months later in June 1864. The fictional editor follows up this remark in a determinist vein: "Thus, the first fragment should [*dolzhno*] be considered sort of an introductory [*vstuplenie*] to the whole book, almost [*pochti*] a foreword [*predislovie*]."[59] We note a shift in the meaning of *dolzhno*. Here it belongs to quotidian rather than philosophical discourse. That is, the homonym marks a semantic shift from the speech category of modal imperative (*dolzhno* as "must/have to") to the discourse of pragmatic deontics (*dolzhno* as "should").[60] All manner of instability operates in

---

[58] Dostoevsky's letters to brother Mikhail indicate how much he struggled to formulate the Underground type. The letters also describe his anxieties about how the Underground Man and *Notes from Underground* would be received. See Frank, *Stir of Liberation*, 294, 347. One identifies with Dostoevsky, for it is not Part One that explicates why the Underground Man came into existence. It has been the task of critics, using extraliterary materials, to do so.

[59] The narrator's reference to Part One as an "introductory" or "foreword" to Part Two supports Isenberg's thesis that *Underground* is a frame narrative (*Telling Silence*, 17). I consider it a doubly framed narrative, seeing the footnoted introduction as a small frame of the larger one Isenberg views as the entirety of Part One.

[60] James Forrester, *Why You Should: The Pragmatics of Deontic Speech* (Hanover, NH: University Press of New England for Brown University Press, 1989). Dostoevsky could have used *mozhno* or *sleduet* for the deontic use of *dolzhno*, but did not.

the introduction. In this way it duplicates the Underground Man's own discourse, particularly in Part One.

The demotion of abstract discourse to the mundane is reinforced here (as elsewhere in the prologue) by a repetition of the qualifier "as if/sort of" (*kak by*) and its semantic second cousin "almost" (*pochti*): what we are presented in the footnote is "sort of an introductory to the whole book, almost a foreword." What is clarified by these qualifiers? Or, more to the point, what is obfuscated? Complicating matters even further, what is the difference between an "introductory" and a "foreword"? Again, a destabilizing voice announces its presence.

It seems judicious to view the footnote, signed in a self-conscious way by a Fëdor Dostoevskii, as a set of sometimes overlapping voices that perform multiple functions. Viewed from this perspective, the prologue enters fully into the vocal qualities of *Underground*. It is part and parcel of the work's entirety, rather than mere appendage. Just as much as the philosophical and confessional discourses that form Part One are joined with the more traditional storytelling qualities of Part Two to form the whole of *Underground*, the footnoted introduction may also be accorded the privilege of conceptual unification with the body to which it belongs.[61] The introduction is consonant with the larger text as governed by its parodic intent and its use of multiple voices.

If the introduction participates in the larger narrative's satiric thrust, then it is important to ask what the object of its parody might be. Parody, of course, is a method by which the satirized object is exposed from within, through its own discourse, speech habits, and verbal ticks. This seems to be the operative principle of the introduction as well as the larger text. It parodies the voices which constitute it. If it is deeply ironic, it is also instructive, for it encapsulates in miniature the features of voice play that inhere in Part One and to a lesser extent in Part Two. The prologue prepares readers to read the following inset tale with a questioning mind and an ear sensitive to shifts in tone and voice.

To summarize, the introduction breaks into four distinct voices. We have a fictionalized editor-narrator whose normative editorial voice is distinct from the other three: the radical's (a determinist),

---

[61] Robert Louis Jackson, "Aristotelian Movement and Design in Part Two of *Notes from Underground*," in *Dostoevsky: New Perspectives*, ed. Robert Louis Jackson (Englewood Cliffs: Prentice Hall, 1984), 66–68.

Playing with Authorial Identities 87

the feuilletonist-satirist's (an ironist), and the implied author's, the signatory, Fëdor Dostoevskii. We have first the fictional editor who presents information Dostoevsky deems necessary to frame his tale in some manner. His voice is matter-of-fact. The second voice is the determinist's. His is insistent, pseudo-syllogistic, and dogmatic. The determinist is the object of the third voice's satire. In it, as in the Underground Man's speech, there is a prevaricating tone, an allusion to a possible loophole, a glance backward, a wink in the reader's direction, all of which undermine the determinist's stance. The fourth voice is the implied author's. His remarks overlap in part with the fictional editor-narrator's, but suggest a position outside the fictional structure, a level of which the fictional editor cannot be cognizant:

Identity: Fictional Editor **Tone: Matter-of-fact**	**Identity: Determinist** **Tone: Insistent**	**Identity: Satirist** **Tone: Equivocating**	**Identity: Implied Author** **Tone: Soto Voce**
Both the author of the notes and the *Notes* themselves are, of course, fictional. Nevertheless, such persons as the writer of such notes not only may but even must exist in our society,	*may but even must exist in our society,*	Both the author of the notes and the *Notes* themselves are, of course, fictional	
taking into consideration the circumstances under which our society has generally been formed.			
I wished to bring before the face of the public, a bit more conspicuously than usual, one of the characters of a time recently passed. He is one representative of a generation that is still living out its life.		*a generation that is still living out its life.*	*a bit more conspicuously than usual,*
In this fragment, entitled "Underground," this person introduces himself, his outlook, and seeks, as it were, to elucidate the reasons why he appeared and had to appear among us.	*as it were, to elucidate the reasons why he appeared and had to appear among us.*	*as it were,* *and had to appear among us.*	
In the subsequent fragments will come this person's actual "notes" about certain events in his life. Thus, the first fragment should be considered sort of a prologue/introductory to the whole book, almost a foreword.		*sort of a prologue to the whole book, almost a foreword.*	Thus, the first fragment should be considered *sort of a prologue to the whole book, almost a foreword.*

The normative reading of the footnoted introduction has previously produced an assumption of a unified voice, that of the implied author, even of Fyodor Dostoevsky himself. But "Dostoevsky's" voice, as we see here, fragments into discrete voice-positions. The deterministic elements, although serving Dostoevsky's purposes conveniently, do not accord with the author's, for whom determinism is to be refuted, if not completely, than certainly as it relates to the question of free will and moral responsibility. It is for this personage that the satire of a facile and clumsy determinism works perfectly well. There is present, too, the normative voice of an omniscient narrator who provides building blocks and motivates the narrative in matter-of-fact terms. This voice overlaps with the implied author's, but only on the neutral ground on which the narrative scaffolding stands. Nothing much is on the line in these remarks. They perform their perfunctory duty as do unburdened introductions *per se*. The final sentence, however, can be performed with different tones, with the implied author's, with the fictional editor's (who performs the duty on behalf of the implied author), but also with the satirist's, whose word-feints destabilize the consciousness underlying the utterance. It cannot be that Part One is to be read as "sort of an introduction" or "almost as a foreword." It either is or isn't to be read this or that way. Equivocations like these—Gogolian suggestions of something distinct that, upon consideration, dissolve—lead the reader into a dead end. But the equivocations may possess the dual purpose of destabilizing utterance and, at the same time, of calling attention to less dramatized forms of prevarication elsewhere in the note.

The staging of potential voices in the footnote suggests that there are multiple ways to read it, combining and recombining elements across the four voice-positions I have outlined. These utterances can be seen as a set of the author's doubles who serve his purposes—not philosophically, but in terms of expedience. What, then, is the purpose of the prologue? Is it merely "pedagogical" in that it trains the reader to be aware (and wary) of multiple voices in the text?

The critical literature indicates that the prologue can be viewed from a variety of angles. On the one hand, it can be seen as an entry point into Dostoevsky's conception of his reader as social radical for whom the logic of determinism would be welcomed (and the irony either missed or registered with disdain). As an example of inverted irony, the footnote can be read along with the rest of the narrative as a parody of the radical's position.[62] On the other hand, because Dostoevsky had only thought through his narrative in general terms and had not in fact completed it when he published Part One, the introduction can also be seen, in Morson's words, as "processual." That is, it projects a pathway into narrative without closing options or directions for the author as he draws forth his text through a series of open choices.[63]

From another perspective, the introduction might be viewed as a preliminary statement of Dostoevsky's acceptance of determinism merely as a *modus operandi* within distinct spheres of cognition. From yet another, it reveals his dissatisfaction with determinism as the deliverer of the final word in the matter of ethics. Like many intellectuals of his day and ours, Dostoevsky held to deterministic models for the physical universe, biology, social evolution, aspects of history, and cultural manifestations of the same.[64] The introduction may also represent what Michael Holquist has called a "dueling relationship" between speaker/narrator and reader. A dueling relationship in the footnote would mean that in yet another way the prologue models the tone and approach of Part One.[65] Conversely, the introduction may merely serve a formal function, as Matlaw argues, in that it marks the Underground Man "as a new phenomenon in literature."[66]

Given multiple possibilities for describing the purposes to which the multiple and overlapping voices of the introduction are put, perhaps it is

---

[62] Frank, *Stir of Liberation*, 322.
[63] Morson states: "Narrative structure was . . . deeply disturbing to Dostoevsky, and he sought yet another way around it. He tried to find a literary form that would not implicitly endorse the wrong theology and the wrong view of life. In short, he needed to find an alternative to structure. . . . His idea was this: what if the author did not plan the work in advance, but instead created rich situations and let the work proceed as it would? Something I have referred to elsewhere as 'algorithmic' creation or as 'creation by potential.' Would that not be close to life? Would such a method not refuse both the consolation and the threat to freedom implicit in an over-arching design?" ("Conclusion: Reading Dostoevskii," in *The Cambridge Companion to Dostoevskii*, ed. W. J. Leatherbarrow [Cambridge: Cambridge University Press, 2002], 224–225).
[64] Frank provides examples of each in *The Stir of Liberation*, 300, 307–308, 323–324, 334, 372.
[65] Michael Holquist, *Dostoevsky and the Novel* (Princeton: Princeton University Press, 1971), 64.
[66] Matlaw, "Structure and Integration," 183.

useful to ask what would become of *Underground* were it to lack the footnote altogether?[67] Would the text be altered irreparably? Would Dostoevsky's argument, his reason for laying before the reader the underground in the first place, be in some manner damaged? These questions return us to our starting point—the period when Dostoevsky utilized introductions with some regularity.

As Dostoevsky set out on a new, post-exile path in society—as novelist, social commentator, literary critic, publisher, editor, and figure of growing social renown, even disrepute—it was important to him that his narrative style be unique and, in its uniqueness, associated most clearly with his person. It was important for Dostoevsky to have his name figured in the text, and not merely on the title page and in *Epoch*'s table of contents. Despite the capacity of the introduction to prepare the reader to engage the text (as polyphonic, inverted irony, satiric parody, or new word) and to get readers practiced at tackling his unique style, for Dostoevsky there was more to it than that. He wanted to be in the mix, to have his name associated with the text (flagged as it is at the end of the footnote), not only as author, not merely as disembodied voice framing Part One, but as someone with a decided stake in the matters undertaken in the body of the narrative.

In *Underground*, Dostoevsky reexamines both national and personal pasts, the idealism (*his* idealism) of the 1840s, the contented quietude of philosophic inaction, the banality (*poshlost'*) of imagined romantic heroic sacrifice, and the dangers inherent in a philosophy of rational egoism. He was willing, therefore, to fragment the voice in the introduction and speak with a backward glance about his complex position on the most pressing issues of the day. But he spoke only provisionally, through a ventriloquist's act of multiple voicing, through apocryphal authorial address. One rather doubts that he was perturbed in the least by his dissolution of the determinist argument through the self-conscious and parodic asides of the satiric voice that dominates the prologue. This allowed him merely to *seem* to explain the appearance of the Underground Man in the 1860s. Thus, the introduction's removal would constitute a loss, for there would be no multi-voiced trickster's performance for us to encounter in the *Underground*'s first words, a performance that foreshadows so very much to come in Dostoevsky's art.

---

[67] Isenberg suggests we ask this question of frame narratives (*Telling Silence*, 33, 48).

Monsters Roam the Text

CHAPTER 4

I

DEMONS

Dostoevsky's post-exile fiction up to the publication of *Demons* (1871–1872) provides for distinct experiences of the texts' first words. Except for *Underground*'s apocryphal authorial prologue, Dostoevsky's are uniformly fictional allographic introductions, the texts' initial utterances (other than title and epigraph) coming from a fictional editor, author, or narrator. Despite the uniformity, Dostoevsky nonetheless delivers up a wide variety of forms just as he assigns a wide variety of labels to identify them. In *Demons*, he returns to the formal design he utilized in *The Village of Stepanchikovo and its Inhabitants*, if with an altered label for it. In both novels, the narrator's first chapter serves explicitly as an introduction (it is called one). Both novels represent chronicles presented through the fictional author-narrator's perspective. In each novel the narrator plays two roles, one as chronicler of recent events (the "narrating I"), and the other as actor, if secondary, in the action that takes place (the "experiencing I"). *Stepanchikovo* and *Demons*, too, are comic novels, the first a low comedy, the second an "evil" one.[1]

As in *Stepanchikovo*, in *Demons* Dostoevsky has his narrator provide a preface, or it seems he does. In a Gogolian manner he gives us an

---

[1] This is Richard Pope's label in his "Peter Verkhovensky and the Banality of Evil," in *Dostoevsky and the Twentieth Century: The Ljubljana Papers*, ed. Malcolm

introduction with one hand, but takes it away with the other. Here is how it is laid out at the novel's opening:

> Chapter One (*Glava pervaia*)
> Instead of an Introduction (*Vmesto Vvedeniia*)
> A Few Details from the Biography of the Much-Esteemed Stepan Trofimovich Verkhovensky[2]

Dostoevsky merges Chapter One with the introduction, acknowledging it as an irregular one in that it does not stand alone as a pretextual conveyance that carts us from one level of discourse to another, from one chronotope to another, from a device of framing to its insert narrative, or from one narrator to another. Because of its ambiguous status, he labels it an introduction that simultaneously is not one: "Instead of an Introduction" is also a "Chapter One." As a preface, it is to be viewed as distinct and in some measure separate from the following narrative, but as the following narrative's first chapter, it is linked to its discourse, plot, and characters.

The only other time in his fiction that Dostoevsky merged his first chapter with an introduction was, of course, in *Stepanchikovo*. Given the strong elements of farce and satire in *Demons*, it is almost as though Dostoevsky is doing his damnedest to reinvent his early failed novel, to elevate *Demons* to a level of profundity *Stepanchikovo* lacked. If, however, *Stepanchikovo* cannot be rescued, *Demons* itself achieves a frightening level of gravitas, suffused as it is with disaster, lies, manipulation, stupidity, madness, murder, suicide, and horror, as well as moments of tenderness, honesty, soulful reflection, and spiritual recovery, not to mention scenes of carnival laughter, painful exposure, outright farce, buffoonery, comic twists, and sudden reversals.[3]

V. Jones (Nottingham: Astra, 1993), 39–47. In comparing *Stepanchikovo* and *Demons*, we should also note Foma Opiskin's and Stepan Trofimovich's literary pretensions, respectively, and each narrator's satiric response to his character's lame attempts at creative writing.

[2] Dostoevskii, *PSS*, X: 7; Fyodor Dostoevsky, *Demons*, trans. Richard Pevear and Larissa Volokhonsky (New York: Vintage Classics, 1994), 7.

[3] Most critics note both the novel's "demonic" themes and their counterpoint in sincere human connection and empathy. Rima Iakubova addresses the comic elements in her "Dostoevsky's Novel *Demons* and the Russian Balagan," in *The New Russian Dostoevsky*, ed. Carol Apollonio (Bloomington: Slavica, 2010), 189–216. She connects the *balagan* (puppet) tradition to the tragic as much as

These disparate elements of *Demons* represent to Kate Holland the Dostoevsky novel in the throes of re-formation. In her study, Holland treats Dostoevsky's work (both fiction and journalism) of the 1870s, that is, in the post-Reform period when the consequences of failed policies, and not only those relating to the emancipation of the serfs, had become acute a decade after their implementation. She argues that Dostoevsky sought a new approach to fiction that would be equal to the task of representing social disintegration in an integrated aesthetic manner. In her words, Dostoevsky sought "to represent on a formal level the sense of disintegration and atomization that is fundamental to the experience of modernity. [He] assumes that the world is radically contingent and seeks to replicate this contingency with as open and unfinished a structure as possible . . . This fragmentation impulse is countered by an opposing impulse toward formal unity. [Dostoevsky's] approach seeks to reintegrate the fragments of a world shattered by modernity . . . [and] strives toward narrative totality."[4]

Dostoevsky's quest for a form that would allow him to integrate the theme of disintegration and fragmentation into the novel's discourse without tearing it apart aesthetically led to a wide number of solutions many of which continue to confound readers. The overlapping of Chapter One and the "Instead of an Introduction" is the least of the worries. The person of the narrator, Anton Lavrentievich, G-v, has elicited a wide number of treatments in the literature, not only because he is the self-proclaimed "chronicler" of the events that unfold in *Demons*, but because he is also an actor (if peripheral, it would seem) who interacts with the key players in the drama.[5] Anton Lavrentievich (not the implied author), is the one who selects the work's epigraph from The Book of Luke. He subscribes to many roles in the text: chronicler of the tale's events, actor in the drama (even one of its dupes), author of the text we read as an aesthetic object

---

to the text's vaudeville elements.
[4] Kate Holland, *The Novel in the Age of Disintegration: Dostoevsky and the Problem of Genre in the 1870s* (Evanston: Northwestern University Press, 2013), 5.
[5] What we come to know about Anton Lavrentievich G-v grows over the course of the novel. Malcolm Jones catalogues much of what we know in "The Narrator and Narrative Technique in Dostoevsky's *The Devils*," in *New Essays on Dostoyevsky*, ed. Malcolm V. Jones and Garth M. Terry (Cambridge: Cambridge University Press, 1983), 100–101.

(including the novel's frame structure and its epitextual features), confidant to one of the key protagonists (Stepan Trofimovich Verkhovensky), satirist, and even, as one critic argues, leftist radical actively covering his involvement in the intrigue by penning the tale.[6] We shall have more to say about this last point later in our discussion.

Because the text is freighted with such weighty matters, it appears that introductions take a hit at this stage in Dostoevsky's career. We note that the tendency of his novels' first words to indicate what genre we are about to read, or to instruct readers on how to attend to the narrated word (cautiously, attentive to who is speaking at any given moment in the chorus of voices), or even to mislead (and thus instruct us how to read only belatedly) does not persist in *Demons*. In contradistinction to the works we have already examined, the novel's title may carry more weight than the preface. In addition, epigraphs from Pushkin and The Book of Luke guide our response to the text even more than the introduction. The "Instead of an Introduction" undergoes transformation, both in name and function, becoming something of an anti-introduction akin to *Underground*'s prologue .

This is not to say that the preface to *Demons* no longer has any stature as a coding device. The text's first words still signify:

> In setting out to describe the recent and very strange events that took place in our town, hitherto not remarkable for anything, I am forced, for want of skill, to begin somewhat far back—namely, with some biographical details concerning the talented and much esteemed Stepan Trofimovich Verkhovensky. Let these details serve merely as an introduction [*vvedenie*] to the chronicle presented here, while the story itself, which I am intending to relate, still lies ahead.[7]

Where the implied author labels his foreword "Instead of an Introduction," Anton Lavrentievich G-v labels his an "introduction." This is an aside to readers that they may best approach the text at two discursive levels simultaneously, keeping authorial audience identity (the community shared by implied author and implied readers) separate

---

[6] Most critics are apologists of the narrator, arguing that he was not complicit in the left-radical plot of destruction in the provincial capital where the action is located. Adam Weiner argues to the contrary in his *By Authors Possessed* (Evanston: Northwestern University Press, 1998), 93–137.

[7] Dostoevsky, *Demons*, 7; 7.

from narrative audience identity (Anton Lavrentievich, his townspeople, and perhaps the investigating authorities). More on this later.

Anton Lavrentievich provides us with his introduction in order, as he claims, to set up his narrative adequately. He begins at a temporal remove from "the story . . . which still lies ahead." He introduces his tale in order to frame it. His design and Dostoevsky's coalesce here. He delivers up something of a biography of his mentor, Stepan Trofimovich Verkhovensky. It is not a laudatory one. It highlights a "man of the 1840s," a cultural construct of import for the depiction of the "men of the 1860s," i.e., the radicals who wreak havoc on the provincial capital. As Gene Fitzgerald has noted, the "narrator G-v," beginning with his introduction, represents a narrating consciousness to be differentiated from the "character/actor G-v," who was involved in the events of catastrophe that struck his home town only recently.[8] The "experiencing I" versus the "narrating I" stand in discrete psychological and chronotopic positions relative to each other. The first Anton Lavrentievich G-v is depicted by the second Anton Lavrentievich as someone who might have been duped by the radicals. At the time of his writing, he knows that he has been fooled. He builds his narrative as something of a cover. He bases it on four elements: interviews with the principles who remain alive after the disaster; his conjectures about meetings between principles in which he was not in attendance; rumors he has heard; and his own peculiar form of hindsight. He knows where he is taking his narrative when he begins it in the introduction. This means that he knows *how* he wishes to depict his mentor, once beloved, now the object alternately of his scorn and of melancholy attachment. The second paragraph encodes this complex of responses:

> I will say straight off: Stepan Trofimovich constantly played a certain special and, so to speak, civic role among us, and loved this role to the point of passion—so much so that it even seems to me he would have been unable to live without it. Not that I equate him with a stage

---

[8] Gene D. Fitzgerald, "Anton Lavrent'evic G-v: The Narrator as Recreator in Dostoevsky's *The Possessed*," in *New Perspectives on Nineteenth-century Russian Prose*, ed. G. J. Gutsche and L. G. Leighton (Columbus: Slavica, 1982), 121–134. Slobodanka B. Vladiv makes the same case, indicating how the first sentence of the novel points in two directions, first at the events to be narrated, and second at the narrator's evaluative position (*Narrative Principles in Dostoevskij's Besy: A Structural Analysis* [Bern: Peter Lang, 1979], 117).

actor: God forbid, particularly as I happen to respect him. It could all have been a matter of habit, or, better, of a ceaseless and noble disposition, from childhood on, towards a pleasant dream of his beautiful civic stance. He was, for example, greatly enamored of his position as a "persecuted" man and, so to speak, an "exile." There is a sort of classical luster to these two little words that seduced him once and for all, and, later raising him gradually in his own estimation over the course of so many years, brought him finally to some sort of pedestal, rather lofty and gratifying to his vanity.[9]

Damned by faint praise. The narrator's verbal ticks ("so to speak," "sort of") alone reveal his ambivalence about the man he has long respected. In case we have missed the point, Anton Lavrentievich continues his description, likening Stepan Trofimovich to Gulliver among the Lilliputians, where neither Stepan nor his protégés come off well.[10]

At every turn in his introduction the narrator subverts claims he makes on behalf of Stepan Trofimovich's "vanity" (*samoliubie*). Indicating his dual role as actor (in the past) and narrator (in the "present"), Anton Lavrentievich states, "*Just the other day* I learned, to my great surprise, but now with perfect certainty, that Stepan Trofimovich had lived among us, in our province, not only not in exile, *as we used to think*, but that he had never even been under surveillance. Such, then, is the power of one's own imagination!"[11]

As Anton Lavrentievich takes Stepan Trofimovich down, his ambivalent feelings toward the man form a leitmotif:

> He himself sincerely believed all his life that he was a cause of constant apprehension in certain spheres, that his steps were ceaselessly known and numbered, and that each of the three governors who succeeded one another over the past twenty years, in coming to rule our province, brought along a certain special and worrisome idea of him, inspired from above and before all, upon taking over the province.

---

[9] Dostoevsky, *Demons*, 7; 7.

[10] This is the first of a host of references to European and Russian literature that Russell Scott Valentino catalogues in his *Vicissitudes of Genre in the Russian Novel* (New York: Peter Lang, Middlebury Studies in Russian Languages and Literature, 2001), 123–124. Reinforcing Kate Holland's argument about Dostoevsky's search for new means by which to narrate, Valentino focuses on Dostoevsky's attempt to discredit the "tendentious novel" of the 1860s and 1870s by fusing allegory and satire (87–125).

[11] Dostoevsky, *Demons*, 8; 8 (my emphases).

> Had someone then convinced the most honest Stepan Trofimovich, on irrefutable evidence, that he had nothing at all to fear, he would no doubt have been offended. And yet he was such an intelligent man, such a gifted man, even, so to speak, a scholar—though as a scholar, however . . . well, in a word, he did very little as a scholar, nothing at all, apparently. But with scholars here in Russia that is ever and always the case.[12]

Even Anton Lavrentievich's attempts to salvage something positive from his description of Stepan Trofimovich fall flat, as in the satiric remark about Russian scholars, itself an old saw of the publishing intelligentsia that does nothing to provide Stepan Trofimovich cover.

Sequestered in the narrator's remarks we find self-referential comments, perhaps unwitting ones, that hint at the way we might best approach his chronicle. When he notes, "Had someone then convinced the most honest Stepan Trofimovich, on irrefutable evidence, that he had nothing at all to fear, he would no doubt have been offended," we find ourselves in something of a bind in regard to Anton Lavrentievich's own discourse. He often appeals to evidence that is questionable, if not refutable. It is difficult, after all, for readers to reject reported facts for which they rely on the narrator alone. They can only be questioned. There are few certainties.

Tunimanov identifies three narrative strategies used by Anton Lavrentievich: cataloguing is his method when playing fully the chronicler's role; paraphrasing recurs in the description of scenes where Anton Lavrentievich is present; describing without explanation or comment ("stage directions," in Tunimanov's words) occurs in those scenes where the narrator is conspicuously absent.[13] To this we add dialogue, whether overheard by the narrator, reconstructed

---

[12] Dostoevsky, *Demons*, 8–9; 8. Gene M. Moore finds this pattern productive in the chronicler-narrator's discourse: "With the introduction of Stepan Trofimovich the reader is . . . introduced to the narrator's characteristic technique of oscillating suggestion or chronic *epanorthosis*, which consists in first making an assertion, then qualifying it, then contradicting it directly, then re-qualifying it back in the other direction . . ." ("The Voice of Legion: The Narrator in *The Possessed*," *Dostoevsky Studies* 6 [1985]: 53). If not to the same degree, the narrator shares this rhetorical device with the Underground Man.

[13] V. A. Tunimanov, "Rasskazchik v 'Besakh' Dostoevskogo," in *Issledovanie po poetike i stilistike: sbornik statei*, ed. V. V. Vinogradov (Leningrad: Nauka, 1972), 87–162.

on the basis of evidence he claims to have gathered from unidentified source(s), or fabricated based on intuition.[14] In her exhaustive study, Vladiv lists thirty-nine scenes from which the narrator was physically absent, but for which the narrator recreates dialogue, setting, and even gesture.[15] They appear in Parts Two and Three of the novel and represent some of the most problematic (in terms of the criterion of verisimilitude in the realist text) for their being so entirely ambiguous as sources of reliable information. It is significant that the narrator cautions us beforehand about them. Because they so thoroughly destabilize narrative, they may represent, in fact, the most avant-garde element in Dostoevsky's experiment with narrative discourse in *Demons*: "*I do not know if it is true*," the narrator recounts later in his introduction, "but *it was also asserted* that in Petersburg at the same time they unearthed a vast anti-natural, anti-state society of some thirteen members which all but shook the foundation. *It was said* that they *supposedly* intended to translate Fourier himself."[16]

Anton Lavrentievich is noted for being a rumor-monger, as we see in the citation here. More significant, I believe, is the degree to which the unknown and unknowable figure in Anton Lavrentievich's discourse. It is not just rumors, and the overt reconstruction of scenes on their basis, that is the problem. It is, to use Kate Holland's term, Dostoevsky's attempt to discover adequate means for expressing in formal, aesthetic terms the phenomena of disintegration within society.[17] Contrary to Ivan Karamazov's opinion, facts seem not to matter, especially when one has suspect motives for controlling a narrative.

---

[14] Fitzgerald argues that the chronicler-narrator is an artist who uses his imagination to provide complete and detailed dialogue even for scenes in which he did not participate ("Anton Lavrent'evic G-v," 127–128).

[15] Vladiv, *Narrative Principles*, 170–172. For a discussion of these scenes, which Dostoevsky calls "tête-à-tête" (*sam drug*) in his notebooks for the novel, see V. A. Tunimanov, "Rasskazchik v 'Besakh,'" 168–170.

[16] Dostoevsky, *Demons*, 9; 9 (my emphases).

[17] In his notebooks for *Demons*, Dostoevsky himself says that these fabricated, or recreated, or imagined scenes are nonetheless "true": "Either I have positive facts, or I am perhaps *inventing* them myself, but in any case, I can assure you that everything is true," Dostoevsky writes in his narrator's voice (Dostoevskii, *PSS*, XI: 92). Dostoevsky's remarks indicate just how aware he was of his narrative's experimental nature.

What we take away from the first part of Chapter One/"Instead of an Introduction" is the simpering ineffectuality, weak-kneed liberalism, verbose emptiness, lofty dreaming, and romantic posing of Anton Lavrentievich's mentor, Stepan Trofimovich. And we learn it from a narrator who once felt the very opposite about him, who once worshipped him, hung on his every lofty word, and saw him through the "recent and very strange events that took place in our town." It turns out, in keeping with the narrator's distorting discourse in the introduction, that the descriptors "recent and strange" can hardly capture the disaster that befalls the town, that deals death blows to so many of its inhabitants, and that challenges the very foundations of the narrator's apprehension of reality. As suggested by continuous hints in the "Instead of an Introduction," this is a tale of deep disillusionment, a fall from grace both for the object of the narrator's initial focus (Stepan Trofimovich) and for Anton Lavrentievich himself, fooled as he has been by empty dreaming, led astray by naïveté, and oblivious when murder and mayhem were being planned and executed under his nose. This is an essential point to which we will return later.[18]

We have dealt only with the narrative dynamics found in the first two paragraphs of the lengthy introduction (one of the longest in all of Dostoevsky's works).[19] Because it is also labeled a Chapter One, it is not surprising that it goes into much greater detail about Stepan Trofimovich, whom we must consider (incorrectly, it turns out) on first read the central character of the tale. In fact, there is much we cannot glean from the introduction without acquiring an overview of the entire text; we must read the introduction a second time both to mine any riches that lie within it and to understand how it might have trained

---

[18] Malcolm Jones puts it bluntly in stating that Anton Lavrentievich is trying in his chronicle "to understand why and how his whole intellectual, spiritual, and social world has collapsed around him, sweeping away his friends and acquaintances, his social superiors, and people who have trusted him with their confidences, with one of whom (Liza [Tushina]) he has even briefly been in love, leaving the stage littered with corpses of people whose company he has regularly kept and whose personalities and views have fascinated him, and to try to reorientate himself after the wreckage" ("The Narrator," 109–110). We must wonder whether this is how Anton Lavrentievich wishes us to view him. Can he be trusted?

[19] The "Instead of an Introduction" comprises more than five percent of the entire text. The only other introduction that is longer occurs in *Stepanchikovo*.

us to deal with Dostoevsky's quixotic chronicler-narrator. Then again, this kind of retrospection seems to be required of us in dealing with any Dostoevsky preface.

The "Instead of an Introduction" more clearly becomes a Chapter One as it progresses, that is, as it provides background information that initiates conventional storytelling. In the second through ninth subchapters of the introduction, the narrator flushes out Stepan Trofimovich's current living arrangements and supplies extensive biographical information—he has been a "hanger-on" for twenty years in the household of Varvara Petrovna Stavrogina at her estate, Skvoreshniki. He has only twice seen his son in those two decades. He has been married twice. After his second wife died, Varvara Petrovna invited him to become her son's tutor.[20] He has served as tutor and mentor as well to many other young people in the provincial capital, both women and men, including, of course, our narrator, Anton Lavrentievich. The roles of teacher and mentor are thus inscribed early in the text. The theme of the disillusioned pupil and misguided instructor is repeated in two of Stepan's students—Nikolai Stavrogin and Peter Verkhovensky. Each of these three so-called leaders falls from the pedestal on which others have placed them. Thus, it is not only Anton Lavrentievich's disillusionment that is enacted in the drama, but Peter Verkhovensky's, Shatov's, and Kirillov's in relation to Nikolai Stavrogin, and the five political conspirators' in relation to Peter Verkhovensky. Any primary, secondary, or tertiary character who is not disillusioned by the end of the novel is either dead, in prison, or in full flight from the Investigating Committee convened to look into the conspiracy.[21]

The remainder of Chapter One describes the tragi-comic ups-and-downs in Stepan Trofimovich's relations with Varvara Petrovna, their travels, their own disappointments (in each other, in their reception

---

[20] Nikolai Vsevolodovich Stavrogin is the novel's central figure, which we cannot know at this point in a first reading of the novel.

[21] It is no trivial matter that Anton Lavrentievich rushes to get his "chronicle" of the disaster into his community's hands before the Investigating Commission can publish its findings. Note: Shatov is murdered; Kirillov and Nikolai Stavrogin kill themselves; Stepan Trofimovich dies on the road; and Peter Verkhovensky flees abroad. With a few exceptions, Anton Lavrientievich G-v is the last man standing.

in urban society), and their backwardness. Through what Vladiv calls the narrator's "summarizing" narrative mode, we gather that Stepan Trofimovich is a rather quaint representative of the 1840s, which seems harmless enough until his pupils enter the scene: "It was a peculiar time; something new was beginning, quite unlike the former tranquility, something quite strange, but felt everywhere, even in Skvoreshniki. Various rumors arrived."[22] With this remark, the introductory narrative shifts from anecdote and scandal scene toward the more ominous. It, therefore, foreshadows the brief months in time that make up the plot of heinous, if madcap, intrigue masking as revolution.

The narrator knows what has occurred when he describes this moment of change in the provincial capital, but he withholds information to build suspense, as would a novelist: "Various rumors arrived. The facts were *generally more or less* known, but it was obvious that, besides the facts, *certain accompanying ideas* also appeared, and, what's more, in exceeding numbers. That was what was bewildering: there was no way to adapt and find out just exactly what these ideas meant."[23] The novelist *cum* chronicler-narrator then goes on to introduce various members of Stepan Trofimovich's entourage, those pupils who once gathered about him to discuss liberal ideas. Most of them fall into the son's, Peter Verkhovensky's, hands. He misuses them terribly. Their appearance in the introduction, therefore, is an entirely conventional plot move. Chapter One/"Instead of an Introduction" comes to a close with the mysterious Shatov (the character Peter Verkhovensky murders) declaiming on two topics dear to Dostoevsky—*pochvenni-chestvo* (Russian native soil philosophy) and Slavophilism, both ridiculed by the chronicler. Twenty years of ideological evolution are thus summarized in the introduction, from the 1840s to the "current" moment in the 1860s.

---

[22] Dostoevsky, *Demons*, 21; 20.
[23] Dostoevsky, *Demons*, 21; 20 (my emphases). On the convention of the narrator's non-disclosure of information, David Stromberg writes, "there are many details that he knows at the time of the telling that he did not know at the time of the events—allowing him to narrate 'knowingly.' In *Demons*, however, this convention has a second effect; it allows G-v to stealthily pass on the reins of narrative agency to other characters only to pick them up again while seeming merely to 'report' an event as it happened" ("The Enigmantic G-v: A Defense of the Narrator-Chronicler in Dostoevsky's *Demons*," *The Russian Review* 71 [2012]: 472).

II

FRAME NARRATIVE

There is every indication that *Demons* might productively be viewed as a frame narrative, one where the front and back sections (introduction and conclusion) meet to contain the central portions of the text. But it's a bit tricky to define the parameters of the frame in *Demons*. The novel begins with the biography of Stepan Trofimovich Verkhovensky. The novel's final chapter completes his tale (his enlightenment and demise). The novel's introduction would, therefore, seem to represent the first half of a frame narrative. The first and last chapters together seem to frame the text perfectly. But there is one wrinkle in the design. The novel also contains a Conclusion, which follows the final chapter treating Stepan Trofimovich. The Conclusion summarizes the fates of many of the dramatis personae. Furthermore, the dramatic closure of the novel centers on the depiction of Nikolai Stavrogin's suicide. This would seem to nullify the framing capacity of the final chapter.

Typical of the opening games Dostoevsky often plays in his fiction, and as we have seen in the several titles to the opening chapter/introduction to *Demons*, Dostoevsky alters the parameters of the frame. He doubles them. There are in fact two introductory and two concluding chapters. The first two chapters of the novel's Part One, "Instead of an Introduction" and "Prince Harry. Matchmaking," treat, in the largest measure, Stepan Verkhovensky and Nikolai Stavrogin, respectively. The novel's last two chapters, "The Last Peregrination of Stepan Trofimovich" and the "Conclusion," treat the same two characters in the same order. They enter and exit the text twinned. Chapter Two of Part One opens with both characters presented together: "There was one other person on earth to whom Varvara Petrovna was attached no less than to Stepan Trofimovich—her only son, Nikolai Vsevolodovich Stavrogin. It was for him that Stepan Trofimovich had been invited as a tutor."[24]

Drawing the two chapters together even further, Chapter Two is no less comic than Chapter One. Both Stepan Verkhovensky and Nikolai Stavrogin appear to be buffoons, play actors, and innocuous

---

[24] Dostoevsky, *Demons*, 40; 34.

wordsmiths. Stavrogin bites people, pulls a distinguished gentleman around by the nose, and in general behaves in a manner that leaves all the characters baffled, the chronicler-narrator included. And it leaves the reader laughing, if uncomfortably, for we sense the riveting edge of chaos about to impinge on the tale.

The conclusion of Chapter Two brings the narrative to the moment when the "recent and strange events" of the work's first sentence begin to occur. This makes the related chapters unified as an introductory, or opening, frame. The counterpoised generations figured by Stepan Trofimovich and Nikolai Stavrogin (clearly in response to Turgenev's *Fathers and Sons* of 1862), are brought before the reader in a temporal setting distinct in two ways from the events that overtake the town. First, they take place in the past. Second, they both set the stage for the intrigue to come.

Frame narratives have a history in Russia going back at least to the late eighteenth century. Nikolai Karamzin's "Poor Liza" (1792), for example, and Ivan Turgenev's "First Love" (1860) bookend the tradition Dostoevsky inherited. As we have seen already, in Charles Isenberg's conception, frame narratives render a variety of services to the author and to the fictional enterprise itself. They occur "any time one speech event contextualizes another, that is, frames it . . . [in such a way as to create] a product, a complete text, where the frame-and-insert structure is relevant to the entire work."[25] What he means by "frame-and-insert structure" refers to the introductory and any concluding material that make up the frame versus the storyline proper that is presented within it. Although Isenberg's discussion addresses short stories and novellas only, his remarks have relevance to our discussion of *Demons*' frame structure.[26]

Isenberg points out that the mere presence of an inserted narrative (say, "Captain Kopeikin" in Gogol's *Dead Souls*) is insufficient evidence for establishing the presence of a frame narrative for the remainder (and the bulk) of the text. Rather, "we are dealing with a frame narrative whenever we are aware of the frame as a frame; that is, whenever we

---

[25] Isenberg, *Telling Silence*, 1.
[26] Isenberg does not insist on a closure to the frame. It can be implied (*Telling Silence*, 1–21). He also restricts his treatment of frame narratives to tales of "renunciation," as his book's title states, a theme to which *Demons*, in its way, also adheres.

can speak of at least two separable stories rather than a simple reminiscence in which a narrator speaks directly to the reader about events in the past."[27] Isenberg's definition has relevance to *Demons* in that ". . . there must be a tension between the speech event and the narrated event such that the former, losing its degree-zero transparency, calls attention to itself, developing into a kind of parallel plot of its own."[28] Which is to say that in Dostoevsky's novel, and in its Chapter One/"Instead of an Introduction," we are made aware of the narrator's speech as a discursive event that occupies a separate temporal field than does the insert story about the generations. As we have seen already, the first two utterances of the novel are made up of a discourse that calls attention to itself.

Isenberg finds, too, that frame closures often do not accord with frame openings, that a variety of narratological events take place at a tale's end that represent shifts of a great variety. As he puts it, ". . . even in our most 'traditional' frame narrative, Turgenev's 'First Love,' . . . such stories always involve hazards to storytelling, albeit more obviously in the narrative situation (here the relations between tellers and listeners) than within the inner stories themselves."[29] There is something of value here that we might bring to the issue of inconsistency in Dostoevsky's narrative form that has been noted by critics. *Demons* begins with a *skaz*-like voice, then shifts to an omniscient-sounding narrative voice of matter-of-fact discourse. The satiric voice of the initial frame of Chapter One/"Instead of an Introduction" gives way to a reportage that better houses the novel's many acts of violence. The narrator's mocking tone is overwhelmed by the insert story's sheer negativity. A new voice appears that replaces the one in the opening frame. "Instead of an Introduction" leads to a quasi-omniscient-sounding narrator who stands, so to speak, "Instead of our Original Narrator." Isenberg states that this type of shift is normative in frame narratives.[30] In the final chapter of the novel and its conclusion, the narrative voice shares more with the insert story than with the introductory framing voice of Anton Lavrentievich. In any case, the front and back of the narrative together frame both Parts Two and Three, which contain the insert novel of intrigue.

---

[27] Isenberg, *Telling Silence*, 2.
[28] Isenberg, *Telling Silence*, 2.
[29] Isenberg, *Telling Silence*, 7.
[30] Isenberg, *Telling Silence*, 12.

More important than the fact that *Demons* represents frame narrative, if in a unique way, we encounter what Isenberg calls the frame tale's "third story": "The double action brought about by the juxtaposition of frame and insert is a way of making two stories tell a third."[31] The two stories combine to deliver up another, synthetic tale that Dostoevsky was deeply committed to and that extraliterary materials (letters, notebooks) support. This third story is the heart of his narrative and accounts for the reason that it took him a good long time to shape (to paraphrase Kate Holland again) an aesthetically coherent novel about a fragmented time. The composition of this story is the result of the combination of the frame narrative and the insert novel—what seeds the 1840s sowed were harvested in the 1860s.

In the final chapter (preceding both Stepan Trofimovich's and Stavrogin's deaths), Stepan Trofimovich makes explicit the connection between the frame and insert narratives, putting it, of course, in his own unique language (and as reported by Anton Lavrentievich, who was not in attendance, yet again). In Stepan Trofimovich's account, a Bible seller, Sofya Matveevna, reads him the passage on demons inhabiting swine that then plunge into the sea; this Gospel verse, the narrator says, "I have placed as the epigraph of my chronicle."[32] Stepan Trofimovich responds to Sofya Matveevna's reading:

> "My friend," Stepan Trofimovich said in great excitement, "*savez-vous* this wonderful and . . . extraordinary passage has been a stumbling block for me all my life . . . *dans ce livre* . . . so that I have remembered this passage ever since childhood. And now a thought has occurred to me; *une comparaison.* Terribly many thoughts occur to me now; you see, it's exactly like our Russia. These demons who come out of a sick man and enter into swine—it's all the sores, all the miasmas, all the uncleanness, all the big and little demons accumulated in our great and dear sick man, in our Russia, for centuries, for centuries! *Oui, cette Russie que j'aimais toujours.* But a great will and a great thought will descend to her from on high, as upon that insane demoniac, and out will come all these demons, all the uncleanness, all the abomination that is festering on the surface . . . and they will beg of themselves to enter into swine. And perhaps they already have! It is us, us and them, and Petrusha

---

[31] Isenberg, *Telling Silence*, 10.
[32] Luke 8: 32–36; Dostoevsky, *Demons*, 654; 498.

[his son, chief conspirator, and amoralist] . . . *et les autres avec lui*, and I, perhaps, down into the sea, and all be drowned, and good riddance to us, because that's the most we're fit for. But the sick man will be healed and 'sit at the feet of Jesus' . . . and everyone will look in amazement . . . Dear, *vous comprendrez après*, but it excites me very much now . . . *Vous comprendrez après . . . Nous comprendrons ensemble*."[33]

In thrusting the voice of his narrator into the foreground ("the epigraph to my chronicle") in the final pages of the novel, and in providing a retrospective view of his tale's paratextual phenomena (title, epigraph, and introductions) Dostoevsky reinvented the preface, providing a new rationale for it.[34] In this way he composed a form unique to him—a framed novel.

III

THE THIRD TALE

We may locate the novel's secret heart in the sole figure who occupies both frame and insert tale and survives to write about it—Anton Lavrentievich. As noted already, his preface is anything but conventional in that it is both Chapter One and something that simultaneously claims to be and claims not to be an introduction. Furthermore, it is only the first part of a twinned introduction that also includes the novel's second chapter. If this sounds rather Sternian or Gogolian in its toying with formal literary categories, we mustn't be surprised, for buffoonery, slaying satire, and oblivion play decisive roles in the chronicler-narrator's depiction of most every character and many a comic scene in *Demons*. The very subtitle to Chapter One/"Instead of an Introduction" echoes chapter titles of the eighteenth century and should surely be taken in jest. But a jest with serious import, for the comments that form the non-introduction pertain, as

---

[33] Dostoevsky, *Demons*, 655; 499 (ellipses in the original).
[34] At one point in time in the 1870s, as he attempted to find a shape for his novel, Dostoevsky began writing it backwards from the end, working in reverse so that he eventually might be able to work his way forward. He eventually dispensed with this practice, but it suggests that he was aware early on that the novel would end with Stepan Trofimovich's final pilgrimage and death and Stavrogin's suicide (Frank, *The Miraculous Years*, 430).

we have seen, to Dostoevsky's theme of the generations, specifically, how the men of the 1840s deformed their offspring. The *Fathers and Sons* theme is laid out with a powerful Dostoevskian twist toward dark, conspiratorial, nihilistic meaninglessness.[35] In *Demons*, the world is viewed as an imminent void, a theme that surpasses the troubling negativity of Gogol's work.[36] But it is a view of reality that the narrator generates with decided intent. The third story lurks in his motives for overwhelming us with his tragi-comic vision.

The point is not that Dostoevsky had gone to school on Nikolai Gogol. Dostoevsky himself initiated that cliché, truthful as it is about his early work. Instead, we see in Anton Lavrentievich's remarks in the novel's first words that he, too, had been brought up on Gogol.[37] There is something curious about a narrator who was born between the two generations (1840s and 1860s) that populate *Demons*. We are forced to consider which generation he belongs to.[38] There is something decidedly suspicious, too, about a narrator who turns to Gogol as a discursive source, not in imitation of Gogol as much as with the intention of turning readers' attention toward matters that are of less relevance than the secret purposes of his controlling, even deceptive, discourse.

As critics often acknowledge, the narrator's secret about his text may be related to Dostoevsky's interpretation of his own youth, exile, and recovery from delusional thinking. Like Stepan Trofmovich Verkhovensky, he had been an idealistic lad of the 1840s, reared on Western socialist ideas. He was a staunch defender of the little man, proponent of the emancipation of the serfs, in other words, a Westernized liberal. By the 1860s, idealists had become radicals, then nihilists, and,

---

[35] Dostoevsky was keenly aware that he was creating a corrective to Turgenev's rather sanguine novel of the generations and of emerging nihilism. For a discussion of this topic, see Frank, *The Miraculous Years*, 430–431.

[36] The connection is made by Elizabeth Welt Trahan, "*The Possessed* as Dostoevskij's Homage to Gogol': An Essay in Traditional Criticism," *Russian Literature* XXIX (1996): 397–418.

[37] As we have seen earlier, both Fitzgerald ("Anton Lavrent'evic G-v," 122) and Alexandrov argue that Anton Lavrentievich wishes to become an author in his own right. There are reasons for this other than his vanity. V. E. Alexandrov, "The Narrator as Author in Dostoevskij's *Besy*," *Russian Literature* 15 (1984): 243–254.

[38] See Martinsen, *Surprised by Shame*, 117.

by the 1870s, terrorists and murderers. *Demons* was originally meant to be a political pamphlet, the intention of which was to rout the thinking of these new young men and women, people willing to deny others' freedoms and to take others' lives in order to secure a fantasy of the greater good. But Dostoevsky's pamphlet evolved into fiction, and then into the most disturbing of his many soul-wrenching and mind-bending novels.

Dostoevsky has Anton Lavrentievich draw the connection between the generations by tracing Stepan Trofimovich's biography, bits of it certainly based on Dostoevsky's life. The fourth paragraph of Chapter One/"Instead of an Introduction," continuing in Gogolian fashion, presents Anton Lavrentievich's scathing attitude toward his, and his generation's, former naïveté:

> [Stepan Trofimovich] returned from abroad and shone *briefly* as a lecturer at the university back at the end of the forties. But he managed to give *only a few lectures*, apparently on the Arabians; he also managed to defend a brilliant thesis on the nearly emerged civic and Hanseatic importance of the German town of Hanau, in the period between 1413 and 1428, together with *the peculiar and vague reasons why that importance never took place*. This thesis cleverly and painfully needled the Slavophils' of the day, and instantly gained him numerous and infuriated enemies among them. Later—*though by then he had already lost his lectureship*—he managed to publish (in revenge, *so to speak*, and to show them just whom they had lost), in a monthly and progressive journal, which translated Dickens and preached George Sand, the *beginning of a most profound study*—having to do, *apparently*, with the reasons for the remarkable moral nobility of *some* knights in *some* epoch, *or something of that sort*. At any rate, *some lofty and remarkably noble idea was upheld in it*. Afterwards *it was said* that the sequel of the study was promptly forbidden, and that the progressive journal even suffered for having printed the first part. *That could very well have happened, because what did not happen back then?* But in the present case *it is more likely that nothing happened*, and that the author himself *was too lazy to finish the study*. And he stopped his lectures on the Arabians because *someone evidently from among his retrograde enemies somehow* intercepted a letter to *someone* giving an account of *some "circumstances,"* as a result of which *someone demanded some explanations from him. I do not know if it is true*, but *it was also asserted* that in Petersburg at the same time they unearthed a vast anti-natural, anti-state society

of some thirteen members which all but shook the foundations. *It was said* that they *supposedly* intended to translate Fourier himself. *As if by design*, at the same time in Moscow they seized a poem by Stepan Trofimovich, written six year earlier in Berlin, in his first youth, which circulated in manuscript *among two amateurs and one student*. This poem is now also sitting in my desk drawer; I received it just last year, in a quite recent copy, handwritten by Stepan Trofimovich himself, with his inscription, and bound in magnificent red morocco. *Incidentally*, it is not lacking in poetry, or even in *a certain* talent; it is a strange piece, but in those days (that is, more precisely, in the thirties) that kind of thing was not uncommon.[39]

The narrator then attempts to describe the "dangerous" poem's contents, but cannot. It is completely beyond his ken because it is allegorical in nature, cast in a metaphoric language that has no place in his, Anton Lavrentievich's, conceptual framework.[40] Might this be because the narrator is in part a man of the 1860s, too, who has bought into the idea that boots are of greater value than poetry? It is in Anton Lavrentievch, who spans both generations, that the third story emerges.

It is almost impossible for our analysis to remain within the confines of the introduction, for the introduction opens out into the text itself, becoming an integrated part of it. Hence its curious double title: "Instead of an Introduction" and Chapter One. Heretofore Dostoevsky's prefaces perform useful functions in terms of preparing readers for what they are about to encounter in the following narrative. We are given an idea of the work's genre, are presented with the type of discourse we will eventually have to contend with in the text, or are presented an opportunity to preview some of the character relations or plot dynamics we soon encounter in the text. Whether the fictional author/editor's foreword to *House of the Dead* or Dostoevsky's hybrid, footnoted prologue to *Underground*, the introductory material has been presented in such a way as to separate it from the fictional narrative. Like the beasts illuminated on the pages of *Marvels of the East* that are contained within the imagery of the frame, they form a coherent whole unto themselves. They work suggestively in relation to the text, their relevance deriving from the accompanying discourse. But in *Demons*,

---

[39] Dostoevsky, *Demons*, 9–10; 8–9 (my emphases).
[40] Anton Lavrentievich is unaware, of course, that his narrative represents Dostoevsky's allegory.

we might say that the metaphor of the beast is realized. Monsters roam the pages of the novel and devour everyone and everything in sight.[41] Here the introduction to the novel suggests the imagery of the broken frame in *Marvels of the East*. The frame is rent, and the brute wanders the page unrestrained. In *Demons*, the narrator stalks the pages of his chronicle. He is ubiquitous. He has burst out of the introduction's container and moves everywhere, even, paradoxically, where he is not.[42] As a consequence, to locate the third story of *Demons*, we are forced to roam the text with Anton Lavrentievich, emerging from the confines of the frame (Chapters One and Two) to inhabit the whole.

In Chapter One/"Instead of an Introduction," we are introduced to our narrator, of course, to the object of his focus, Stepan Trofimovich, and to the "Club" that has gathered around him. The members include Shatov, Liputin, Virginsky, Lebyadkin, Lyamshin, and Anton Lavrentievich G-v. By the tale's end, Shatov and Lebyadkin are murdered. Liputin, Virginsky and Lyamshin are arrested because of their involvement in Peter Stepanovich's terrorist plotting. Stepan Trofimovich dies on the road (in the closing frame narrative). Shatov is killed by Stepan's son, Peter. Lebyadkin is killed, along with his wife Marya Timofeevna Lebyadkina and Marya's servant, by Fedka, murderer for hire, formerly Stepan Trofimovich's serf. Fedka himself is murdered. Virginsky's sister and sister-in-law as well as another plotter and dolt, Tolkachenko, are also arrested. From here things don't get any better.

Although the buffoon governor, Andrei Antonovich von Lembke, dies while attempting to save others' lives in a conflagration planned by Peter Stepanovich (a wooden beam falls on von Lembke's wooden head), others die in more dramatic or melodramatic ways. Marya Shatova and her newborn die from complications related to childbirth, but Alexei Kirillov and Nikolai Stavrogin, two of the main characters in the apocalyptic thematics of the novel, commit suicide, if for entirely different reasons: the first to prove he is god; the other because he is the opposite—a void. The mysterious and quirky radical, Shigalev (the one

---

[41] For example, the murderer Peter Stepanovich Verkhovensky is described as a serpent; Fedka the convict kills for money; Nikolai Stavrogin sanctions murder.

[42] This occult point would explain why he can report on events, meetings, and dialogue where he was absent.

who announces the topsy-turvy logic of the movement)[43], disappears from the pages of the text without mention. His end may be the most frightening of all.[44]

Discarding from consideration the sundry tertiary characters, we are confronted with the fact that the last person standing in town is the chronicler-narrator, Anton Lavrentievich G-v. He is, perhaps, the most clever devil of the lot, first, because he is the most literary (he wishes to be a writer, as proven by the text we read and his many references to this aspiration within its pages). His point of view predominates. In fact, Anton Lavrentievich may even be more deceptive, in his way, than Peter Stepanovich.[45] We know that Peter Verkhovensky is guilty. We cannot know that about the narrator, and he is the reason for our unknowing.

As we observe at the tale's outset, in its initial frame piece, Chapter One/"Instead of an Introduction," Anton Lavrentievich maintains close proximity both to the principle parties of the older generation and to the young instigators of chaos. He also maintains a rather dispassionate narrative position *vis-à-vis* events and dramatis personae, including those with whom he is most close (e.g., Stepan Trofimovich). He claims that he aims toward objectivity in his chronicle, which explains a good deal of the *feeling* of omniscience, after the conclusion of Part One, that overtakes his now objective-sounding, now *skaz*-like discourse. But his objectivity is questionable, as he proves in the text's first words.

Anton Lavrentievich's omniscience rests on his capacity to create an illusion of it. As Alexandrov argues, ". . . the narrator in *Besy* might perhaps be best seen as a self-conscious *author* figure, one who, moreover, himself employs novelistic techniques analogous to those Dostoevskij used in writing the novel."[46] In his analysis, Alexandrov "takes into account the *metaliterary dimension* of the novel's narrative strategy," to wit, his deflating *skaz*-like approach as it occurs

---

[43] "Starting from unlimited freedom, I conclude with unlimited despotism" (Dostoevsky, *Demons*, 402; 311).
[44] For an argument on behalf of Shigalev's centrality to the themes of demonic possession and literary pretension, see Weiner, *By Authors Possessed*, 101–106.
[45] On this point, see Weiner, *By Authors Possessed*, 108–123.
[46] Alexandrov, "The Narrator as Author," 244. See also Fitzgerald, "Anton Lavrent'evic G-v," 122; and Frank, *The Miraculous Years*, 474.

overtly and in its most condensed form in Chapter One/"Instead of an Introduction," where the pattern is laid down (in good prefatorial style), and, most importantly, "in practically all the scenes that the narrator did *not* witness" directly.[47] Most of the tête-à-tête scenes between the principle plotters or bearers of the ideological and metaphysical messages (Stavrogin, Shatov, Kirillov) are, by definition, not available to Anton Lavrentievich other than through indirect information. They are, in Alexandrov's term, "probable fictions" that can hardly be rationalized, as the narrator attempts to do, by labeling his narrative a chronicle.[48]

In his reports of scenes where he was absent, Anton Lavrentievich uses qualifiers of the type "I think," "I imagine," "through my guesses," and "I believe I can say positively." They perform two functions. They create the illusion of his objectivity, sincerity, and seeming omniscience. At the same time, they indicate just how lacking in objectivity and omniscience he in fact is. As Fitzgerald and Alexandrov argue, the narrator is more than a self-proclaimed "chronicler" of the events he recounts, a label Weiner discounts entirely.[49] He is also the text's author. That is, he fabricates, invents, recreates. But this opinion may be too generous.

We are forced to ask if the scenes that are *not* witnessed by Anton Lavrentievich are truly a result of information supplied by others (e.g., by Stepan Trofimovich) or whether they are fabricated by Anton Lavrentievich on the basis of his retrospective knowledge of the plot and understanding of the dramatis personae's personalities? Alexandrov submits a third possibility—the narrator intentionally writes himself out of scenes at which he was present because he does not wish the reader to know he was in fact in attendance.[50] Why would Anton Lavrentievich expunge himself from key scenes?

Alexandrov suggests that the chronicler-narrator manipulates the scene in this way "so that the reader [is] drawn into the novel as a participant."[51] This, too, is generous. We must ask ourselves as readers to what extent we have been played by the narrator, to what degree we

---

[47] Alexandrov, "The Narrator as Author," 244–245.
[48] Alexandrov, "The Narrator as Author," 244–245.
[49] Weiner, *By Authors Possessed*, 120.
[50] Alexandrov, "The Narrator as Author," 250.
[51] Alexandrov, "The Narrator as Author," 251.

have been manipulated by a discourse which may in fact be intended to lull us into a sense of security about Anton Lavrentievich's capacities as narrator *throughout* the narrative and across his diverse narratological roles (called "legion" by Gene Moore).[52] The introduction and most of Part One amount, then, to a public relations campaign to put readers to sleep. Through the narrator's personality, his trustworthiness, and his facile ability to identify with characters and simultaneously to distance himself from them, readers form a contract of trust with him on which he builds the remainder of his narrative.

Gene Fitzgerald's formulation of the chronology of the novel, painstakingly reorganized out of the chaos of Anton Lavrentievich's non-linear form of chronicling, allows us to do what is virtually impossible upon first reading, to wit, to gain perspective on what transpires in the novel by placing the plot in chronological order, something we might expect Anton Lavrentievich in the role of chronicler to have done in the first place.[53] If he has distorted chronology (and he clearly has), but avoided misrepresentation (which he might have), then he cannot be accused of self-serving fabrication. Similarly, if he reports verbatim scenes at which he was not present, readers might likewise assume that he continues to avoid fabrication or outright lying for the sake of the tale's veracity. Can we remain sanguine about such a reading? Doubt impels us to ask: What can we say of his involvement in the conspiracy he "chronicles" for us readers? Can he be trusted in the depiction of his role as mere witness?

Adam Weiner argues that Anton Lavrentievich G-v is at the heart of the novel's darkness. Like so many characters of both generations

---

[52] Gene M. Moore, "The Voices of Legion: The Narrator of the Possessed," *Dostoevsky Studies* 6 (1985): 51–65. Weiner makes the same point as I: "G-v intentionally deceives and beguiles readers, using the scenes between himself and Stepan Trofimovich to enhance his credibility as chronicler of events he has witnessed with the goal of taking us into his confidence so that we accept him as a reliable chronicler of scenes he has not witnessed—especially those with Stavrogin and Peter, whom it is G-v's intention to deck out as the two great 'devils' of the novel" (*By Authors Possessed*, 121).

[53] Gene Fitzgerald restores the plot chronology, establishing it out of the complex mixture of temporal clues provided throughout the text by the narrator ("The Chronology of F. M. Dostoevskij's *The Possessed*," *Slavic and East European Journal* 27, no. 2 [1983]: 19–46).

in *Demons*, the narrator, too, has been seduced or possessed by evil.[54] This is true not simply because our chronicler stands on the periphery of events as mere witness, or because he plays the role of guide through the narrative maze he himself creates, but because his heart, too, has beat in the darkness of conspiracy. As the novel concludes, the fools and dupes are either living in exile, languishing in prison, or lying in their graves. Anton Lavrentievich is a sole survivor who does not wish to join any of them in their respective fates.[55]

The genre of *Demons* might best be reconsidered at this moment. It is not simply a crime novel. Nor is it a novel of political intrigue alone. It is too comic and the principle conspirators too inept for that. Nor is it a mere satire, nor only an allegory. It may be more akin to the genre Dostoevsky so often put to use in his work—the confession. But it is a confession of a different order, not as we encounter in Rousseau, say, or in Pechorin's journal in *Hero of Our Time*. As a socio-political genre it appears to be a political confession very much akin to the extensive police confessions of the Decembrists of 1825–1826. Those against whom the evidence of guilt was overwhelming, who played a leadership role, or whose statements in response to the investigating commission were boldly self-indicting, were hanged. Others, who used the confessional genre in a way to balance the evidence against them with a clever rhetoric by which to cloak the full nature of their commitment to the cause, were either exiled or sent to fight in the Caucasus, sometimes consigned to a rather severe form of isolation.[56] Anton Lavrentievich may in fact come to us in this mold. Unlike the Decembrists, however, there is no evidence against him. This is because he is our sole source. He may have tampered with the facts.

---

[54] Weiner, *By Authors Possessed*, 121.

[55] Some critics, but not many, admit the possibility that Anton Lavrentievich is culpable. See Craig Cravens, "The Strange Relationship of Stavrogin and Stepan Trofimovich as Told by Anton Lavrent'evich G-v," *Slavic Review* 59, no. 4 (2000): 801. Note: The radical youth, Erkel', and Shigalev survive, if only because their fates go unmentioned.

[56] I have Bestuzhev-Marlinsky and two of his brothers in mind. See my *Alexander Bestuzhev-Marlinsky and Russian Byronism* (University Park: Pennsylvania State University Press, 1995), especially the chapters "Incarceration" and "Siberian Exile," 170–236. Bestuzhev's friend and colleague, the poet Kondraty Ryleev, was one of the five conspirators hanged for his offense.

In addition to the Decembrists we also have the case of the Petrashevtsy, the conspirators among whom we find Fyodor Dostoevsky. He was a radical of the 1840s and, like the Decembrists before him, did his best to disguise his role before the investigating commission as much as he could while also rendering up his *mea culpa* in a manner that would satisfy his interrogators enough to allow him to remain silent about even more condemning information concerning his involvement.[57] Dostoevsky was familiar with the genre of "police confession" as half truth, half deception.

Critics have argued strongly, if not vehemently, against any notion of Anton Lavrentievich's complicity in the crimes committed in *Demons*. V. A. Tunimanov states categorically in his thorough study of the narrator that Anton Lavrentievich G-v, is innocent of any crime: "As a character the chronicler is a passive puppet-like figure, and although he often bustles about, in essence he takes almost no part in the action; what he hears and sees is important and significantly less important is what he says and does during events."[58] Slobodanka Vladiv's analysis of *Demons* provides most compelling evidence, too. She fills in gaps in Tunimanov's argument about what precisely our narrator-chronicle knows outright, knows by hearsay, or reconstitutes through guesswork. As she and Tunimanov see it, Anton Lavrentievich is thoroughly in the camp of the older generation, the one represented by Stepan Trofimovich Verkhovensky, Varvara Petrovna Stavrogina, the writer Karmazinov, and the mayor and his wife, the von Lembkes. He is of the same socio-economic class, is educated "classically" (as the conspirator Liputin puts it condescendingly), speaks the same language (Vladiv's analysis is strong here), and holds Stepan Trofimovich closely to his heart despite his disillusionment with him.[59] Anton Lavrentievich, in fact, begins and ends his chronicle with Stepan Trofimovich, as we have seen, framing the narrative with

---

[57] For a full treatment of what Dostoevsky had to hide, see Frank, *Seeds of Revolt: 1821–1849*, 239–291, and *The Years of Ordeal: 1850–1859*, 3–66.

[58] Tunimanov, "Rasskazchik v 'Besakh,'" 167–168.

[59] David Stromberg presents a counterargument to Weiner's charge that the narrator is complicit in the crimes. His argument rests almost entirely on the "narrative faith" Anton Lavrentievich elicits from his readers. See "The Enigmatic G-v: A Defense of the Narrator-Chronicler in Dostoevsky's *Demons*," *The Russian Review* 71 (2012): 481. Cf. Nadine Natov, "Rol' filosofskogo podteksta v romane 'Besy,'" *Zapiski russkoi akademicheskoi gruppy v SShA* 14 (1981): 79.

the novel's first words about this gentleman idealist of the 1840s and closing the final chapter (before the Conclusion) with his lonely death. But he is also Stepan's greatest critic, more critical than even Varvara Petrovna Stavrogina, whose accusations and rants amount more to low comedy than deep disillusionment. She is, after all, his greatest fan as well, at least until she, too, is blinded by the plotters.

In Varvara Petrovna and the von Lembkes, the text offers examples of idealists of the 1840s who are drawn into the radical fringes of the 1860s. Superficial though they may be—for example, Julia, the mayor's wife (who courts the radicals as a fashion statement but also because Peter manipulates her into their camp)—it is suggested that sympathy for contemporary radical causes was not unusual.[60]

It seems plausible, given that our narrator-chronicler is the silhouetted figure on a burning street, that during the initial official inquiry Anton Lavrentievich would have been asked about his knowledge of the conspirators, their organization, their plans, and of any ancillary parties of interest. As he wraps up his narrative/confession in the form of his novel *Demons*, he maintains full attention on everyone but himself. He summarizes the characters' fates, describes Stepan Trofimovich's demise, and records Nikolai Stavrogin's suicide. He says nothing about himself. The two chapters of the closing frame, in which the characters' fates are summarized, do not contain him.

As Isenberg argues in his study of frame narratives, it is important to consider the space or setting in which the framing takes place. Where does it occur? From out of what physical location does the narrative issue? The frame and insert story have distinct locations, the first belonging to narrating time, the insert to narrated time. *Demons* conforms to Isenberg's model. But the setting in both is the same—we are in a provincial capital and on one of its nearby estates. The narrator moves between the two, town and estate, with the same alacrity that he moves from one of his guises to another—chronicler, satirist, novelist—from one discursive mode to another, and with the same facility that he moves temporally between narrated and narrating time. But where is he as he pens his novel, his confession, his narrative response to the

---

[60] Dostoevsky saw Ivan Turgenev in this light. His satiric portrait of Turgenev in the character Karmazinov is infamous. For a discussion of Peter's manipulation of Julia von Lembke, among others, see Martinsen, *Surprised by Shame*, 120–124.

authorities and to the town's surely flummoxed, if unnamed citizens and survivors?

Given the point of view we have, it is improbable that we can draw reasonable conclusions about Anton Lavrentievich's involvement (or lack thereof) in the intrigue. But there is psychological evidence to suggest one cause for the narrator's impulse to recount the "recent and very strange events that took place in our town." First we must consider the guilt of the survivor.[61] As the only one of the primary and secondary characters to remain in the aftermath of the chaos, he must surely be suffering from more than mere disillusionment with his mentor. He has been privy to the goings-on about town and at Skvoreshniki for months, but suspects nothing until too late. He can forestall nothing, proving himself to be an ineffectual provincial bureaucrat duped first by Stepan Trofimovich (a twenty-year delusion) and by the sundry bearers of the word from elsewhere who have only recently arrived in town.[62]

Furthermore, Anton may be in the throes of the same self-aggrandizing despair that Stepan Trofimovich undergoes at the end of his days and during his wandering without aim or direction. Believe him or not, Stepan overtly expresses responsibility for his part in creating the monsters who have come out from under the desks of his classroom. Although Anton Lavrentievich seems not to understand, or, like Julia Mikhailovna von Lemkbe, to believe Stepan's turn toward an absolute solution (God), he can understand Stepan Trofimovich's impulse to somehow assuage his guilt and to attend to his shame. Anton Lavrentievich writes to assuage his guilt while doing his utmost to hide the truth of his involvement, if only as witness, in the disasters that have befallen his town.

Like the solutions advanced by others in regard to the narrator's culpability, my conjecture cannot be proven, of course, but it remains one of the logical possibilities the text's frame structure allows us to elucidate: Anton Lavrentievich's composition is an act of atonement,

---

[61] Weiner ascribes Anton Lavrentievich's entire narrative to the desire to get revenge on Peter Verkhovensky and Nikolai Stavrogin for seducing Liza Tushina. This motivation is hardly convincing. The weight of supposition is in favor of the narrator's innocence and against his being one of the text's monsters. The narrative structure, however, forces us to ask about his complicity.
[62] Anne S. Lounsbery, "Dostoevsky's Geography: Centers, Peripheries, and Networks in *Demons*," *Slavic Review* 66, no. 2 (2007): 213.

an apology offered to his townspeople, a hermeneutic exercise through which he might comprehend the terrible events that make up his tale, and a clever attempt to hide any sense of guilt he may bear, any shame he may feel, even if he was not a member of the conspiratorial group.

In *Demons* the introduction is anything but an unnecessary or whimsical appendage with odd labels attached to it. But it loses its former sovereignty in comparison to the works we have treated already. First, Chapter One/"Instead of an Introduction" does not stand alone. It joins with Chapter Two to form a more complete preface. And it also links up with the final two chapters of the novel to form a frame narrative. Therefore, its potential for bestowing meaning on the text, if in retrospect, is shared with the text's final chapter and Conclusion. Because of these complications in the design of the introduction, its heft is diminished. Other elements of the paratext come into play, specifically, the novel's title and epigraphs, which point more directly at the author's themes than the covert operations out of which the frame's third tale emerges. Nevertheless, in the introduction to *Demons*, Dostoevsky dramatizes the preface's capacities to rend introductory frames asunder in order that they might stalk the entirety of the text. The foreword alone suffices in representing in miniature the aesthetically coherent, formally unified narrative means through which Dostoevsky depicted all-encompassing contingency and complete chaos.

Re-Contextualizing Introductions

CHAPTER 5

Dostoevsky wrote and published *The Diary of a Writer* (*Dnevnik pisatelia*) in 1873, then terminated the series to write a second novel-experiment, *The Adolescent* (*Podrostok*, 1875).[1] Upon that novel's completion, he took up *The Diary* again for the years 1876 and 1877, put it aside yet again to write *The Brothers Karamazov*, and returned to *The Diary* for only occasional publications in 1880 and 1881.[2] There are very few fictional offspring birthed in *The Diary*, but cousins crop up regularly. Morson labels these kin semi-fictions. They include reportage that drifts in and out of imaginings that, in some measure, constitute fictionalized narratives. Consequently, an immediate complication in studying introductions in *The Diary of a Writer* is that it is difficult to tell what is an introduction and what is not. This may seem to overstate the case when dealing exclusively with the prefaces to Dostoevsky's prose fiction. But in the context of the *The Diary*, a prefatorial aura surrounds each of the overt prefaces that accompany the stories Dostoevsky created for *The Diary* as well as the fiction that lacks a preface proper. Robert Louis Jackson summarizes the interaction of texts, pre-texts, and post-texts,

---

[1] The first novel-experiment being *Demons* (Holland, *The Novel in the Age of Disintegration*, 101–130).

[2] These final two years of *The Diary* contain no fiction. *The Diary* presents, among its extensive journalistic entries, feuilletons, physiological sketches, and other narrative forms that represent something between fiction proper and overt imaginative excursions of a quasi-fictional nature (Gary Saul Morson, "Introductory Study: Dostoevsky's Great Experiment," in Fyodor Dostoevsky, *A Writer's Diary* I, trans. and ed. Kenneth Lantz [Evanston: Northwestern University Press, 1994], 1–117).

referencing one example that can be applied fairly to each of the three instances we treat here:

> ["The Boy at Christ's Christmas Party"] appears in Dostoevsky's *Diary of a Writer*, January 1876, chapter two. It is bracketed by two other sketches devoted to the plight of poor, homeless street boys. The first extremely brief sketch, "A Boy with his Hand Outstretched for Alms" ["Mal'chik s ruchkoi"], forms a kind of prologue to "A Boy at Christ's Christmas Party" ["Mal'chik u Khrista na elke"]. The third sketch in the trio, "A Settlement for Juvenile Delinquents" ["Koloniia maloletnikh prestupnikov"], is given over to a description of a reform institution and the problem of the "conversion of wanton souls into virtuous ones."[3]

There are three ways in which Dostoevsky's *Diary* prefaces interact with the fiction that appears therein. First, as Morson argues, the prefaces are absorbed into the text they introduce, forming a part of those texts rather than standing outside their discursive umbrella. Second, any preface may be correlated or integrated with other prefaces appearing within the *The Diary*. They may be assessed in relation to the discourse of both non-fictional and semi-fictional introductions. And third, the Dostoevsky prefaces that immediately precede *The Diary*'s fiction can be viewed within the overall pattern of the entire set of texts that make up all of *The Diary of a Writer*.

Dostoevsky uses prefaces frequently in *The Diary*. They are not fictional. There are occasions when a non-fictional entry becomes, or emerges in the process of Dostoevsky's writing, as an introduction to one of his occasional fictional pieces. In many respects, the context of meta-utopian discourse swallows them into a hole of generic ambiguity. It would be inadmissible, Morson argues, to separate Dostoevsky's fictional pieces in *The Diary* from the overarching conception of its entirety, an entirety or integrated whole, it must be added, that emerges and evolves with each issue. Just as much as "meta-utopia runs the risks of its genre: namely, that its heterogeneity will be perceived as chaos, that its multiple points of view will be seen as incoherence or reduced to singularity, and that the network of allusions and repetitions which link its parts will be taken as no more than recurrent concerns," so the fictional works housed in *The Diary* and their prefaces

---

[3] Jackson, *The Art of Dostoevsky*, 260–261.

might best be viewed for their part across the entire series.[4] When we examine Dostoevsky's introductions to the short stories that appear in *The Diary*, we can view them either as discrete objects of the type we have encountered up to this point in his fiction, or as part of a unified design (e.g., meta-utopian discourse). The stories, then, stand alone as individual works whose context(s) are created out of the writing enterprise itself, and simultaneously as integral parts of the meta-utopian genre in which the stories' own generic impulses represent individual instantiations of the whole.[5]

This complex interaction across generic boundaries forces us to acknowledge something we have not had to previously. Were we to continue to isolate Dostoevsky's prefaces to the fiction as we have to this point—permitting them to speak from out of the context fictional discourse relies upon and reifies at each of its instances—we might distort their place within the aesthetics of their containing discourse and within their overriding boundary-genre structure. We proceed, therefore, with caution.

I

"BOBOK"

If the force of Morson's argument is strong enough to be taken to heart in the treatment of the whole of *The Diary* and its fictions, it may not be necessarily binding for Dostoevsky's fiction in *The Diary*'s inaugural year, that is, long before the overarching design of the entire project became more clear to him or, alternatively, before the impulses

---

[4] Morson, *Boundaries of Genre*, 175.
[5] Morson writes: "Like its generic relatives, the *Diary* invites interpretation as a 'dialogue of the mind with itself,' an 'adventure of the soul among Utopian inquiries.'" And further, "The antitheses of metaliterary play and dogmatic assertion [in the *Diary*] produce meta-utopian ambivalence—that is, not a synthesis, but an intensified dialectic of utopian 'pro' and anti-utopian 'contra.' That dialectic is, in turn, the reflection of Dostoevsky's deepest ambivalence toward what he regarded as the most fundamental moral, religious, and political issues" (*Boundaries of Genre*, 177).

of his spontaneous writings developed into that design over time.⁶ In the 1873 series of *The Diary*, only one fictional piece appears for the entire year. Most entries consist of Dostoevsky's rebuttals to criticism, anecdotes, feuilletons, physiological sketches, and explicitly noted semi-fictions. It is worth mentioning that in this last instance Dostoevsky clearly engages the techniques of fictional discourse, but he does so overtly, informing the reader at each step that he is extrapolating upon what strikes his eye as he walks the streets of St. Petersburg, spinning tales he subsequently writes down, but without attempting to create an illusion of some discursive reality that invites readers to suspend disbelief. This practice includes "Bobok," that sole piece of fiction for 1873.⁷

Dostoevsky prefaces this crazy fiction—a dialogue of the dead overheard by someone in a cemetery who is most likely sleeping off a drunk—with the briefest foreword we meet in Dostoevsky's corpus: "On this occasion I shall include 'The Notes of a Certain Person.' That person is not I, but someone else entirely. I think no further foreword is needed."⁸

Our focus is first on the function of the preface. As we have seen repeatedly, Dostoevsky's forewords usually fulfill some combination of three functions. They identify the genre of the work, introduce the central character or characters, and deliver up an explanatory note (explicitly or covertly) on the often unreliable narrator's manner of speech as it represents his point of view. These functions, shared across all the prefaces we have examined, are matched by an important set of differences. As we have seen, Dostoevsky continually shifts the source of information from one work to another. In *The Village of Stepanchikovo*, we have a fictional authorial (and somewhat actorial) narrator who introduces his narrative. In *Notes from the House of the Dead*, we hear first from a fictional editor who has purloined the text he presents. In *Notes from the Underground*, Dostoevsky's signature suggests an authentic authorial introduction, but the Underground

---

⁶ It is widely understood that Dostoevsky did not retain his original intent and that *The Diary* altered after 1873.

⁷ "Bobok" is most often left without translation. It has an absurd ring to it. In Russian it sounds like "little bean," but its referent is detached from the signifier.

⁸ Dostoevskii, *PSS*, XXI: 41; Fyodor Dostoevsky, "Bobok," in *A Writer's Diary*, trans. Kenneth Lantz (Evanston: Northwestern University Press, 1994), I: 170.

Man's speech intrudes and we surmise that we have before us two voices in dialogue with each other, which creates a hybrid form of fictional actorial and authorial utterance.

It is difficult to fix the parameters of fictionality, authoritativeness, and reliability in Dostoevsky's introductions, for they are alternately paradoxical, self-nullifying, or simply illogical. Each ultimately forces readers to shift focus from the ostensible object of depiction to the subject whose voice delivers up character and event, scene and dialogue.[9] Consequently, discourse is raised to the level of covert theme, thereby encouraging readers to engage the ensuing narrative as a charged form of expressive language. This approach to introductions, however, is destabilized in the prefaces to the fiction of *The Diary* where Dostoevsky appears to speak directly on his own behalf and in his own voice to the reader, as he seemed to do in *Winter Notes on Summer Impressions*.

"Bobok" follows Dostoevsky's initial four entries for 1873. Each of them is dedicated to a single topic: Belinsky; jury trials; Chernyshevsky; and Nekrasov's poem "Vlas." After these essays and feuilletons, the reader encounters the allegory, "Bobok," with its remarkable caution: "[The narrator] is not I, but someone else entirely." That "not I" commences to recount his grave experience, the fantastic nature of which is explained away in the narrator's first line of the tale: "The other day Semyon Ardalonovich up and said to me, 'Ivan Ivanych, tell me, for Heaven's sake, will there ever be a day when you'll be sober?'"[10] Rather than seeing pink elephants, Ivan Ivanych hears the dead speak. "Bobok" is a travesty on human foibles and pettiness—we apparently carry them to the grave with us for safe keeping.

Dostoevsky hardly need forewarn us that he is not the besotted Ivan Ivanovich. But because the previous (and initial) entries to *The Diary* have all come from the implied author's voice, Dostoevsky may have felt it necessary to indicate that he was altering the pattern

---

[9] In his treatment of "A Gentle Creature," for example, Michael Holquist examines the distinction between subject and object, in particular "the structural resistance the tale offers to its own apparent theme, the way the fact of the narrator's monologue, his *own* voice, undercuts his stated desire for harmony, *more* than one voice" (*Dostoevsky and the Novel* [Princeton: Princeton University Press, 1971], 148).

[10] Dostoevsky, *A Writer's Diary*, 170; 41.

and providing readers with a fiction recounted from the position of another person. But what reader couldn't surmise that without the caution? Only the most naïve, who would then have to presume that Dostoevsky qua narrator is the drunk Semyon Ardalonovich. Joke aside, Dostoevsky establishes a hierarchy of readers here. He draws those who perceive the joke into a network of the like-minded; and he ridicules other, less adept readers who, quoting Lermontov again, "fail to understand irony."

Throughout *The Diary* Dostoevsky plays with the notion of readership, projecting different capacities on different types of reader. What is significant in the introduction to "Bobok," however, is that Dostoevsky lays bare the device that he has used to this point in his fiction—all the prefaced texts we have examined are narrated by someone "not Dostoevsky." The introduction to "Bobok" provides belatedly an invariant governing Dostoevsky's prefaces from the beginning.

II

"THE BOY AT CHRIST'S CHRISTMAS PARTY"

The second piece of fiction Dostoevsky delivers up appears three years later in the January issue of the renewed *Diary* for 1876. "The Boy at Christ's Christmas Party" contains two authorial introductions, one preceding the text and the second embedded covertly within it. They reveal Dostoevsky in the process of inventing a story, moving from what he has observed in the streets of St. Petersburg to mental wanderings about the plight of people he has encountered *en masse* to then imagining them all reduced to a single, representative figure, the little boy of the story's title. In the first introduction, the entry titled "A Boy with His Hand Outstretched for Alms," we encounter a feuilleton *cum* physiological sketch: "Children are a strange lot; I dream of them and see them in my [imagination]. In the days before Christmas and on Christmas Eve itself I kept meeting on a certain street corner a little urchin who could have been no more than seven."[11] Dostoevsky

---

[11] Dostoevsky, *A Writer's Diary*, I: 309; Dostoevskii, *PSS*, XXII: 13.

goes on to describe the child, the Dickensian background of the child's begging (to support "a band of dodgers' drinking habits"), the boy's techniques for securing a few kopecks from passers-by, and the likelihood of a life of crime and misery. Dostoevsky concludes his remarks with a clear idea in his mind as to where his sketch is leading him: "A wild creature such as this sometimes knows nothing at all—neither where he lives, nor what nation he comes from; whether God exists, or the tsar. There are even stories about them that are hard to believe, yet they are facts."[12]

Dostoevsky tells one such story and transitions to it in two steps, shucking his authorial persona in the process. First he maintains his authorial stance: "But I am a novelist and one 'story,' it seems, I made up myself. Why do I say 'it seems' when I know very well that I made it up? Yet I keep imagining that it really happened somewhere, sometime, and happened precisely on Christmas Eve in *a certain* huge city during a terrible cold spell."[13] Then he shifts from direct authorial voice to the voice position intermediate between authorial persona and omniscient narrator: "I dreamed there was a boy—still very small, about six or even younger—who awoke one morning in the damp and cold cellar where he lived. He was wearing a wretched wrapper of some sort and he was trembling . . . he was very hungry."[14] In a third move, the omniscient narrator takes over and the tale commences: "Several times that morning he had approached the bed on which his sick mother lay on a mattress as thin as a pancake, a bundle beneath her head to serve as a pillow. How did she come to be here?"[15] The narrator flushes out his characters, their abject condition, and the boy's heart-wrenching death behind a woodpile where he has crawled after having viewed through a window the grandeur and sumptuousness of St. Petersburg high society at celebratory play.

Dostoevsky's brief introduction to "The Boy at Christ's Christmas Party" represents the first half of a frame that the omniscient narrator closes at the story's end. He shifts back to a position somewhere between his authorial persona and his narrator's voice. In this guise he delivers a sermon about the place Christ has set for the boy at His

---

[12] Dostoevsky, *A Writer's Diary*, 310; 14.
[13] Dostoevsky, *A Writer's Diary*, 310; 14.
[14] Dostoevsky, *A Writer's Diary*, 310; 14.
[15] Dostoevsky, *A Writer's Diary*, 310; 14.

celestial Christmas celebration. In "God's Heaven," the boy meets his mother, who "had died even before him."[16] Dostoevsky's authorial persona then returns fully to complete the narrative's symmetry:

> So why did I make up a story like that, so little in keeping with the usual spirit of a sober-minded diary, and a writer's diary at that? All the more since I promised stories preeminently about actual events! But that's just the point: I keep imagining that all this could really have happened—I mean the things that happened in the cellar, and behind the woodpile; as for Christ's Christmas party—well, I really don't know what to say: could that have happened? That's just why I'm a novelist—to invent things.[17]

The narrative framing that structures "The Boy at Christ's Christmas Party" represents an order of discourse quite distinct from the frame narratives of the second half of the nineteenth century in general and from the instances we have discussed previously in regard to Dostoevsky's earlier work. It was normative to develop a frame tale where the opening bit (the frame) is fictional, like the embedded or inserted tale contained within it. We think of Turgenev's "First Love" (1860) as exemplar, or, later in time, Chekhov's trilogy "The Man in a Case," "Gooseberries," and "About Love" (1898). But Dostoevsky's opener is not fictional. Consequently, it deprives the fictional discourse of the riches that accrue from framed narratives. There is no third story to be manufactured out of the interaction between the frame and insert tale. Indeed, Dostoevsky's tendentiousness is so overt in "The Boy at Christ's Christmas Party" that "The Boy" may provide indirect insight into why it is that Dostoevsky is most often inclined to speak in another's voice when building a narrative. When speaking on his own behalf Dostoevsky finds himself prone to provide the moral of his narrative in no uncertain terms. He removes alternate interpretations from the field of play and utters the text's final word. Such is not the case when Dostoevsky uses fictional introductions.

---

[16] Dostoevsky, *A Writer's Diary*, 314; 17.
[17] Dostoevsky, *A Writer's Diary*, 314; 17.

III

"THE PEASANT MAREI"

The following month, in the February issue's first entry for 1876, Dostoevsky improved upon "The Boy." Not that he gave up on sounding a sentimental note. In "The Peasant Marei," both the appeal to the reader's heart and the use of a an authentic authorial voice are reminiscent of "The Boy." Dostoevsky, however, made the narrative context more complex and, thus, satisfying. "Marei" is preceded by one of Dostoevsky's editorials, titled "On Love of the People. An Essential Contract with the People" ("O liubvi k narodu. Neobkhodimyi kontrakt s narodom").[18] It sets the theme of the brief story, providing in the character Marei an exemplar of what Dostoevsky had addressed in abstract terms in his pre-foreword, "On Love of the People."

Dostoevsky doubles the complexity of relations between the tale's frame and the tale itself. After the preparatory "On Love of the People," "The Peasant Marei" presents a brief introduction in the author's voice, followed by a frame narrative that is autobiographical in nature and within which the insert story about the author and Marei occurs. It's a room full of mirrors from which a more deepened sense of what Dostoevsky is up to in *The Diary* can be gleaned.

Having been primed about one of Dostoevsky's criticisms of his homeland (the separation of the upper classes and intelligentsia from the common Russian), readers are provided evidence for the benefit to be derived from renewing ties with the folk. Proof comes by way of the peasant Marei. Dostoevsky begins in amusing fashion (critiquing his own piece on "The People"), then turns to furnishing his proof by way of narrative:

> But reading all these *professions de foi* is a bore, I think, and so I'll tell you a story [*anekdot*]; actually, it's not even a story, but only a reminiscence

---

[18] In keeping with an emerging structure that more and more often presents frames within frames, "On Love of the People" itself is introduced by yet another article: "On the Fact That We Are All Good People. How Russian Society Resembles Marshall MacMahon" ("O tom, chto my khoroshie liudi. Skhodstvo russkogo obshchestva s marshalom Mak-Magonom"). See Dostoevsky, *A Writer's Diary*, 343–355; 39–49.

[*vospominanie*] of something that happened long ago and that, for some reason, I would very much like to recount here and now, as a conclusion to our treaties on the People. At the time I was only nine years old.... But no, I'd best begin with the time I was twenty nine.[19]

This is a fairly matter-of-fact utterance through which Dostoevsky's diary persona turns readers' attention to something more palatable than his rant about what's wrong with the country and how to mend its ways. He shifts toward storytelling. Not once, but twice. First he recounts an autobiographical sketch from his time in prison. His memory goes back to 1850 when he first entered the prison stockade. The frame narrative shifts next to the insert story that moves the temporal setting back yet again, this time to 1830. The motion, like so much of Dostoevsky's fiction, shifts backward in time in order to recreate the current historical moment.[20] "It was the second day of Easter Week.... I was wandering behind the prison barracks, examining and counting off the pales in the sturdy prison stockade, but I had lost even the desire to count, although such was my habit."[21] The prisoner Dostoevsky is confronted by all manner of depravity during the festivities: "Disgraceful, hideous songs; card games; ... convicts already beaten half to death by sentence of their comrades ... ; knives had already been drawn ... all this, in two days of holiday, had worn me out to the point of illness."[22]

Here Dostoevsky sets up a fundamental contrast, addressed already in his preparatory article on "The People," that serves his larger argument. This depravity represents the "husk" of the Russian peasant. Beneath it lies the glorious fruit. As he puts it in "On Love for the People," "One must know how to segregate the beauty in the Russian peasant from the layers of barbarity that have accumulated over it."[23] Dostoevsky fleshes out some of the barbarity as he, in a continual state of shock, encountered it upon entering prison. He suppresses the awful

---

[19] Dostoevsky, *A Writer's Diary*, 351; 42 (Dostoevsky's ellipsis).
[20] We think of Raskolnikov's dreams, for example, or the first two chapters of Part One of *Demons*, not to mention the setting of *The Brothers Karamazov* (fifteen years prior to the moment of narration).
[21] Dostoevsky, *A Writer's Diary*, 351; 42.
[22] Dostoevsky, *A Writer's Diary*, 351; 42.
[23] Dostoevsky, *A Writer's Diary*, 347; 43.

image of humankind by climbing onto his bunk and closing off his senses to the madness surrounding him:

> I liked to lie like that: a sleeping man was left alone, while at the same time one could daydream and think. . . . Little by little I lost myself in reverie and imperceptibly sank into memories of the past. All through my four years in prison I continually thought of all my past days, and I think I relived the whole of my former life in my memories. These memories arose in my mind of themselves; rarely did I summon them up consciously.[24]

At this moment in the frame narrative, Dostoevsky recalls one specific memory and how it acted upon his heightened sensitivities at the time. The front frame (the prison scene) closes and the memory of the peasant Marei begins.

It is an idyllic time and setting—the countryside in late summer with nature's beauty surrounding the nine-year-old Fyodor as he explores the family property looking for bugs, beetles, lizards, mushrooms, berries, birds, hedgehogs, and squirrels. The idyll is broken when he hears someone shout "Wolf!" Frightened to death, he runs to a peasant mowing the field adjacent to the thicket where he had been playing. We encounter with the narrator the beauty below the husk of the peasant: "'What do you mean, lad? There's no wolf; you're just hearing [things,' he said], reassuring me. But I was all a-tremble and clung to his coat even more tightly; I suppose I was very pale as well. He looked at me with an uneasy smile, evidently concerned and alarmed for me."[25]

The central pieces of Dostoevsky's evidence then come forth. Marei touches the child thrice, each time indicating either a maternal gesture or a priestly blessing:

First, "he stretched out his hand and suddenly stroked my cheek." After delivering more reassuring words of comfort, Marei "quietly stretched out a thick, earth-soiled finger with a black nail and gently touched it to my trembling lips." The boy calms down and Marei says, "Well, Christ be with you, off you go," and makes "the sign of the cross over me, and crossed himself. I set off."[26] The child returns home with a look and wave back to Marei. The insert story then ends.

---

[24] Dostoevsky, *A Writer's Diary*, 347; 43.
[25] Dostoevsky, *A Writer's Diary*, 354; 48.
[26] Dostoevsky, *A Writer's Diary*, 354; 48.

The frame is taken back up and we return to Dostoevsky's depiction of his twenty-nine-year-old self in prison on his bunk surrounded by a topsy-turvy world of depravity. But the rank behavior of the inmates cannot touch him any longer: "I recalled the tender, maternal smile of a poor serf, the way he crossed me and shook his head: 'Well you did take a fright now didn't you, lad!' And I especially remember his thick finger, soiled with dirt, that he touched quietly and with shy tenderness to my trembling lips."[27] Marei is the wheat and the chaff, the skin and the fruit: "Of course, anyone would try to reassure a child, but here in this solitary encounter something quite different had happened, and had I been his very own son he could not have looked at me with a glance that radiated more pure love, and who had prompted him to do that?"[28] Here is Dostoevsky's evidence: the rough, dirtied hand; the touch of love and succor; the blessing. "Our encounter was solitary, in an open field, and only God, perhaps, looking down saw what deep and enlightened human feeling and what delicate, almost feminine tenderness could fill the heart of a coarse, bestially ignorant Russian serf who at the time did not expect or even dream of his freedom."[29]

With his memory of Marei fresh in mind, Dostoevsky can now view "these unfortunate [prisoners] in an entirely different way and ... suddenly, through some sort of miracle, the former hatred and anger in my heart vanished."[30] Dostoevsky's epiphany is complete and the frame tale ends. Readers, of course, are meant to duplicate Dostoevsky's insight and rest assured that the common people are indeed beautiful and capable of everything he has advanced in his argument in the preceding two journal entries.

As with "The Boy at Christ's Christmas Party," we are narrated into an emotional, perhaps even ideological corner.[31] The Dostoevsky

---

[27] Dostoevsky, *A Writer's Diary*, 355; 49.
[28] Dostoevsky, *A Writer's Diary*, 355; 49.
[29] Dostoevsky, *A Writer's Diary*, 355; 49.
[30] Dostoevsky, *A Writer's Diary*, 355; 49.
[31] The ideology being "nativeness" or "national/ethnic identity" (*pochvennichestvo*), which is indicated symbolically in Marei's blackened fingernails and soiled hands. See Wayne Dowler, *Dostoevsky, Grigor'ev, and Native-Soil Conservatism* (Toronto: University of Toronto Press, 1982); Robert Louis Jackson, *Dostoevsky's Quest for Form: A Study of His Philosophy of Art* (New Haven: Yale University Press, 1966), 71–91; *Dialogues with Dostoevsky: The Overwhelming Questions* (Stanford: Stanford University Press, 1993), 237–241;

who appears to speak in his own voice again attempts to reduce reader response to one option. Whether or not we readers submit to the response Dostoevsky seeks from us is beside the point. What matters here is that the authentic authorial preface in Dostoevsky's hands uniformly inclines in a monologic direction. The frame and insert narratives do not interact except as a motivational device linking the state of separation from the common people with a reunion with them. Other than that, the frame and insert tales do not mingle in such a way as to create a third tale, a covert story behind the crust of surface narrative. As touching as "The Peasant Marei" might be, it does not open out into dialogic possibilities. The impulse, as in "The Boy," is all in one direction—toward the implied author's position.

Sensing something out of place, or knowing that it is, Dostoevsky does not return to the practice of monologism again. But in the penultimate piece of prose fiction in the *The Diary*, "A Gentle Creature" ("Krotkaia"), he nevertheless engages direct authorial address again in his foreword. This time, rather than providing us with a sentimental tale of injustice, or a moving memory of contact with a good heart, and then telling us how to interpret it, in "A Gentle Creature" Dostoevsky returns to the techniques of his previous fictional introductions. In the story, Dostoevsky produces a multi-functional and densely encoded preface that he labels "From the Author" ("Ot avtora"). In it, Dostoevsky's discourse reflects the notion that language can create meaning in the process of actively seeking it. For this, something more complex than a graveyard allegory, an outworn sentimental tale, or a memory of a kind peasant is required.

IV

"A GENTLE CREATURE"

By utilizing the distinctive sign "From the Author," Dostoevsky forces a separation of previous diary entries from this one, if only in a formal sense. For we know that *The Diary*'s entries always come "from the

---

and *Close Encounters: Essays on Russian Literature* (Boston: Academic Studies Press, 2013), 211–225.

author." What the foreword's title indicates is that a change is afoot—he is about to tell a story. Not just any story, but one that differs from his previous attempts. The author's intent appears to have altered, and his design for the narrative with it, for he begins the November issue of *The Diary* with this story, not with an article preceding it that might be configured into a frame structure that in some manner anticipates the narrative and in some manner shapes it.

After begging his reader's indulgence for including a piece of fiction in his diary entry (a rather shopworn opening), Dostoevsky immediately turns to two literary matters that concern him greatly—the often fantastic nature of reality and associated problems of depicting it plausibly in fiction: "Now a few words about the story itself. I called it 'fantastic,' even though I consider it to be realistic in the highest degree [*v vysshei stepeni real'nym*]."[32] Dostoevsky does not wish to clarify his self-contradictory statement too quickly, seeking instead to draw readers into the text at this early moment by creating and sustaining a level of cognitive dissonance.

It must be observed that Dostoevsky's use of this seeming paradox at the outset not only hooks his readers intellectually in the discourse, it duplicates the very type of speech readers soon encounter in the pawnbroker-narrator's monologue. As Dostoevsky himself puts it later in the introduction when characterizing his fictional narrator: "Despite the apparent coherence of his speech, [the pawnbroker-narrator] contradicts himself several times, both logically and emotionally."[33] This can be said, too, of the implied author of the preface. There are affinities, in other words, between the narrator's utterances in the story and Dostoevsky's discourse in the introduction. This affinity is not only a matter of logic, or the lack of it, but of feelings as well. To sort out the contradiction that the author finds superficial, Dostoevsky attempts twice, in the third and fourth paragraphs of the introduction, to explain himself: "But [the story] truly does contain something fantastic, which is the form of the story itself, and it is this which I find necessary to explain beforehand."[34]

Having promised now to give his readers an explanation of an apparent paradox, Dostoevsky does not present us with a syllogism,

---

[32] Dostoevsky, *A Writer's Diary*, I: 677; Dostoevskii, *PSS*, XXIV: 5.
[33] Dostoevsky, *A Writer's Diary*, 677; 5.
[34] Dostoevsky, *A Writer's Diary*, 677; 5.

let us say, or a series of rational arguments to support his assertion.[35] Rather, he sets before the reader a scene, a character, and a problem of interpretation. In other words, in the third paragraph of the introduction Dostoevsky turns from the problem of genre (the fantastic vs. the realistic) to the question of narrative technique, outlining his story and then presenting readers with information both about his narrator and his peculiarities of speech. Delaying any discussion of the generic problem until the final (fourth) paragraph of the introduction, Dostoevsky at this moment focuses reader attention on the problem of language and utterance. In this way the third paragraph becomes central to any appreciation of Dostoevsky's language as an object. That language, below the surface level of normative speech, is pregnant with covert meaning. Dostoevsky and his narrator utilize language as a medium of inquiry and as a repository of potential meaning. Readers are meant to absorb both simultaneously. In "A Gentle Creature" we are dealing with a process through which the implied author and the narrator are thematized as seekers of a truth contained in the expressive, de-automatized capacities of language.[36]

Readers are asked to join the author and narrator in terms of their understanding of plot and character. One level shared by them is temporal in nature and has to do with a primary opposition at work in text: before/after. In thematic and plot terms, the pawnbroker discovers *after* his wife's suicide that he had ample *fore*warning of the impending tragedy. At the auctorial level, Dostoevsky *pre*pares his reader both generically, thematically, and in terms of discourse, for what *follows* the introduction. Depending upon readers' sensitivity to the text, their experience either duplicates the one toward which Dostoevsky gestures in his introduction or toward that of the pawnbroker. If readers take Dostoevsky's cues, they find themselves amply prepared *in advance* for the narrator's monologue with all its psychological and dialogical complexity. If they do not, after the conclusion

---

[35] V. A. Sidorov long ago argued that we should not expect to find forms of logical argument in *The Diary*. He sees, and correctly so, that *The Diary* is a work of art above all else ("O *Dnevnike pisatelia*," in *Dostoevskii: Stat'i i materialy: sbornik statei* 2, ed. A. S. Dolinin [Leningrad-Moscow: Mysl', 1924], 109–116).

[36] Isenberg raises the question of whether language can perform this service either for the narrator or for Dostoevsky. He argues that the role of silence in the story is hermeneutically significant (*Telling Silence*, 68–76). I advance the argument that de-automatized utterance speaks volumes.

of the story they are called upon to duplicate the narrator's quest for understanding and to ferret out the myriad details of plot and character psychology that confound the narrator himself, and to seek belatedly the truth the narrator attempts to discover.

The temporal opposition between *before* and *after* is insinuated into the text in Dostoevsky's introduction: "[The story] truly does contain something fantastic, which is the form of the story itself, and it is this which I find necessary to explain *beforehand*." This innocuous temporal adverb is anything but, for, in the narrator's mind, everything hinges on his understanding of the causes of his wife's suicide. Had the narrator of the tale been able to decode the cues of his wife's approaching leap, icon in hand, from a window, as he tells us in self delusion later, the tragedy could have been averted.[37] In like manner, if readers decode the temporal and spatial clues embedded in the introduction (which the narrator, of course, is not privy to), they become better equipped than the narrator to comprehend the tragedy.

The narrator ruminates beside his deceased wife who "only a few hours earlier has killed herself by jumping out a window."[38] He attempts to understand why his wife, the Gentle Creature, has died by suicide. By introducing the issue of causality in the introduction, Dostoevsky involves readers in the interpretation of the problem even before the monologue begins. In effect, the narrator and his readers attempt to interpret what has happened together, even simultaneously. Consequently, subject/object relations become blurred and deep affinities are created between author, narrator, and reader.

Repetition plays an important role in the introduction, the most blatant form represented by the expression "to gather [one's] thoughts into a point" (*sobrat' mysli v tochku*). It occurs on three occasions within the third paragraph of the introduction, each time in a different form. First it occurs in the implied Dostoevsky's own voice under the imprint of the genitive of negation: "He is in a state of bewilderment and still has not managed to collect his thoughts" (*On v smiatenii i eshche ne uspel sobrat' svoikh myslei*).[39] In the next two remarks, Dostoevsky presents the idea within quotation marks. This signals a movement away from Dostoevsky's speech position toward that of the

---

[37] Dostoevsky, *A Writer's Diary*, 714; 33–34.
[38] Dostoevsky, *A Writer's Diary*, 677; 5.
[39] Dostoevsky, *A Writer's Diary*, 677; 5.

pawnbroker-narrator. First Dostoevsky defines just what he means by the phrase: "He paces through his apartment, trying to make sense out of what has happened, to 'focus his thoughts.'"[40] By setting the expression off as quoted speech, Dostoevsky in effect cites the pawnbroker who, in the first chapter, utilizes the phrase himself an additional three times.[41] By repeating the pawnbroker's own expression, Dostoevsky reverses the reader's temporal encounter with the text, signaling again the opposition before/after. In calling forth the pawnbroker's speech before it occurs in the text, Dostoevsky engages in a temporally complex form of double-voiced speech.[42] Writer and narrator are again linked to each other.

In the third use of the phrase, Dostoevsky foretells what occurs in the narrator's quest for the truth: "Little by little he really does *make the matter clear* to himself and gather 'his thoughts into a point.'"[43] The phrase is repeated here in yet a third variant. This time the verb is not enclosed in quotation marks but the rest is. This consigns the verb "to gather" (*sobrat'*) to Dostoevsky's voice and its direct object to the narrator's. In sum, the verb occurs three times in the introduction, twice within the technical confines of Dostoevsky's own speech. From this perspective it is possible to join the verb of "gathering" or "collecting" not only with the narrator's personal search for the truth, but with Dostoevsky's search for a means by which to encapsulate the narrator's search. Both quests implicate readers, drawing them into a similar effort to comprehend the coincident truths of the narrative. Three processes of interpretation are themselves gathered into a point—the pawnbroker's struggle to comprehend what has happened, Dostoevsky's struggle to encode the pawnbroker's quest, and readers' attempts to render the two comprehensible, if not meaningful.

---

[40] Dostoevsky, *A Writer's Diary*, 677; 5.
[41] Dostoevsky, *A Writer's Diary*, 678–683; 6–10.
[42] Bakhtin would call this the "active" form of double-voiced speech, which he defines as "discourse with an orientation toward someone else's discourse." The active variety denotes "hidden internal polemic," "any discourse with a sideward glance at someone else's word [*ogliadka na chuzhoe slovo*]," a "rejoinder," "hidden dialogue" (*Problems of Dostoevsky's Poetics*, trans. Caryl Emerson [Minneapolis: University of Minnesota Press, 1984], 197–199; M. M. Bakhtin, *Sobranie sochinenii v semi tomakh*, 2 [Moscow: Russkie slovari, 2000], 220–223).
[43] Dostoevsky, *A Writer's Diary*, 677; 5 (author's emphases; translation modified).

In the overlapping forms that link encoding and decoding, matters of interpretation and interpenetration play central roles in the discourse. Dostoevsky signals the value of these hermeneutic principles twice in the third paragraph, both times through a repetition of the verb "to clarify" (*uiasnit'*). To call our attention to the verb's importance, Dostoevsky italicizes it each time it is used. It is like a flag waving from off the page. The only other lexical item to receive attention in this manner is the noun "truth" (*pravda*). The thematic, psychological, and intellectual links between the process of comprehension and the noun that constitutes its goal ("truth") should be clear enough. There is a third use of the verb's root (with alternate prefixation) that links Dostoevsky's commentary to that of the narrator's story. We have cited the passage already: "But [the story] truly does contain something fantastic, which is the form of the story itself, and it is this which I find it necessary to explain [*poiasnit'*] beforehand."[44]

The semantic difference between "to explain" (*po* + *jasn-* + *it'*) and "to clarify" (*u* + *jasn-* + *it'*) is rather well marked in terms of the opposition between author and narrator. The first is synonymous with the verb "to explain" (the alternately-prefixed verb *ob* + *jasn-* + *it'*). The latter, with the prefix *u-*, refers to an individual's effort to render something comprehensible to himself or herself and to others. "To clarify" belongs to the pawnbroker's speech in that it encapsulates his quest to understand himself and what has happened to him and his wife, and also to explain himself before imagined interlocutors.

"To explain" (*pojasnit'*), on the other hand, belongs to Dostoevsky's authorial persona. Despite the difference between the two meanings of the verbs that share a common root (*-jasn-*), Dostoevsky suggests an affinity between his and his narrator's tasks and between their imagined interlocutors (Dostoevsky's implied readers and the narrator's imagined "ladies and gentlemen"). The narrator conceives of his implied interlocutors as judges. He attempts to "clarify" for himself what has happened to him and the Gentle Creature, and thus to justify himself before his projected conscience. Dostoevsky also stands before an audience, his readers, who have the capacity to judge his text as an aesthetic object. As readers of their shared texts, we are meant to assess both of the encoders at two distinct rhetorical levels. Author, narrator, and reader

---

[44] Dostoevsky, *A Writer's Diary*, 677; 5.

meet in the communication paradigm, each with discretely defined roles specified within the text and its pre-text "From the Author."

I have already mentioned that repetition functions in the introduction as a clue to the reader on how to proceed with the ensuing text. We have also seen that there are elements in the introduction which recur in the story as well, specifically the phrase "to gather into a point." There is yet another repeating form, morphological in this instance, which is of significance for the interpretations writer, narrator, and readers impose on or make of the text. That morphological form is opposed to the theme of *gathering* versus *collecting*. As noted, the centripetal idea "gather one's thoughts into a point" (or "to collect one's thoughts") is crucial to the tale's encoding and decoding. But no less important is its contrary—centrifugal motion. The verb that most dramatically encapsulates this opposition is "to jump out of" (*vybrosit'sia*). Needless to say, this verb plays a crucial role in the tale. It describes the event that precipitates the narrator's monologue. To put it in causal terms (and remembering the narrator's quest for a causal understanding of the tragedy), his wife's suicide brings him to reflect on his behavior, his identity, and his past. We note, of course, that motion in this instance is not toward a center, but away from it. In raw spatial terms, "to jump out of" is the riddle the narrator attempts to decipher. Just as much as there is a temporal opposition before/after at work in the text, there is a complementary spatial conflict between motion *inward* and *outward*.

The tension created by the opposition in/out is presented in physical as well as metaphorical terms. The pawnbroker understands that when he brings the Gentle Creature into his home, she will not leave it: "The fact is, she did not have the right to leave [*vykhodit'*] the apartment."[45] Her dramatic exit through the window, a symbolically rich threshold that places the Gentle Creature somewhere between heaven and earth (at least for a moment), brings an absolute halt to the conflict between them (which the pawnbroker has caused), that in turn animates the temporal opposition before/after.

The spatial opposition at work, inward/outward, is embedded in the two verbs (and their prefixes) "to gather" and "to exit." The first is prefixed by *so-*, which indicates, among other meanings, motion toward a center. The second, "to exit out of" is prefixed by *vy-*, which

---

[45] Dostoevsky, *A Writer's Diary*, 694; 17.

indicates motion from within outward. The narrator attempts to "gather his thoughts into a point" in order to understand the Gentle Creature's suicide which comes by her throwing herself out the window of their apartment. Centrifugal force represents the challenge to any possible unity the narrator's vain centripetal forcefulness might bring to the quest. In the opposition inward/outward, fragmentation clashes with the desire for unified understanding. The two motions are contrary. They are nonetheless causally related. His unforgiveable behavior causes her suicide; and her suicide (exit) causes him to gather his thoughts together and, perhaps, to work his way toward an understanding of his complicity in her death.

But nowhere is the significance of "outward" indicated more strongly than in the narrative's fifth chapter ("The Gentle Creature Rebels") where verbs of motion occur with the prefix *vy-* seventy-four percent of the time. We recall that in this chapter the Gentle Creature challenges the pawnbroker to face up to a previous act of cowardice. In the exchange between them, the pawnbroker deliberately avoids using the verbs of motion that the Gentle Creature prefixes with *vy-*:

> "Tell me, is it true they drove you out [*vygnali*] of the regiment because you were too cowardly to fight a duel [*na duel' vyiti*]?" she asked me suddenly, right out of the blue, her eyes flashing.
> "It's true. By decision of the officers I was asked to leave the regiment, though I had sent in my resignation even before that." [The narrator avoids repeating the verbs prefixed by *vy-* in his response.]
> "They kicked you out [*vygnali*] as a coward?"
> "Yes, the verdict was that I was a coward." [Again he avoids her verb and its prefix.][46]

In this dialogue, the literal and metaphoric stand in conflict. The Gentle Creature calls it like it is—his fellow officers drove him out of the regiment for failing to uphold its and their honor. The pawnbroker substitutes alternate descriptions, rather bookish and proper in form. His denial of her descriptors encapsulates the problem of the monologue where the narrator would like to substitute the truth of her accusation with an obfuscation. It is interesting that the pawnbroker's ambivalent movement toward the truth (as Dostoevsky describes it in the introduction) is forestalled by the centrifugal force of *vy-*, which

---

[46] Dostoevsky, *A Writer's Diary*, 695; 18 (translation altered).

he studiously avoids repeating.⁴⁷ It creeps into his defensive speech in the second rejoinder to the Gentle Creature's accusation: "'I refused the duel not as a coward but because I didn't want to submit to their tyrannical decree and challenge [*vyzyvat'*] a man who, in my view, had caused me no offense. You must realize,' I couldn't resist adding, 'that standing up to that sort of tyranny and accepting all the consequences meant showing [*vykazat'*] far more courage than fighting in a duel' . . . She laughed spitefully."⁴⁸

In this text, the power of *vy-* (exit) is superior to the power of *so-* (gathering in). But the hope that issues from the tortuous monologue comes from its ability to potentially invert the existential forces at work in the story that these prefixes suggest. As Dostoevsky states in the introduction; "Little by little [the narrator] really does *make it clear* and 'gather his thoughts into a point.' The series of memories the narrator has evoked irresistibly leads him at last to truth; and truth irresistibly elevates his mind and his spirit. By the end, even the tone of the story changes as compared with its confused beginning. The truth is revealed quite clearly and distinctly to the unhappy man—at least as far as he is concerned."⁴⁹

Dostoevsky's "at least as far as he is concerned" draws a line between the truth the narrator has "revealed quite clearly and distinctly" to himself, and another truth toward which we, with Dostoevsky as guide, incline. The "at least" contains a loophole through which any affinities between Dostoevsky's preparatory discourse (with its function of training readers how to decode the monologue) and the narrator's text disappear as into a black hole. Dostoevsky, it would seem, knows another truth that the story serves. The narrator, readers in tow, attempts to recreate it. Clearly, the narrator fails while believing the contrary. Readers beware.

The fourth and final paragraph of the introduction to "A Gentle Creature" turns our attention again to the fantastic in Dostoevsky's fiction. Having provided a lesson on how to defamiliarize language in

---

⁴⁷ He does use the prefix *vy-* with other verbs, just not with verbs of motion or verbs that imply motion. In his revised usage of *vy-*, he attempts to move his defense in a more positive direction. Incredibly, there is a symbolic battle taking place over the meaning of *vy-*, a battle mirroring the larger one.
⁴⁸ Dostoevsky, *A Writer's Diary*, 695; 18.
⁴⁹ Dostoevsky, *A Writer's Diary*, 677–678; 5.

order to decode the text, Dostoevsky now addresses the "how" of his story. He seeks to make a second justification for the element in it he labels fantastic. He begins by saying that ". . . the process of the narrative goes on for a few hours, with breaks and interludes and in a confused and inconsistent form: at one point he talks to himself; then he seems to be addressing an invisible listener, a judge of some sort."[50] Then, in a move typical of his approach to art, he turns to the problem of verisimilitude in the narrator's monologue-for-no-one:

> But so it always happens in real life. If a stenographer had been able to eavesdrop and write down everything he said, it would be somewhat rougher and less finished than I have it here; still, it seems to me that the psychological structure would perhaps be just the same. And so it is this assumption of the stenographer recording everything (and whose account I simply polished) that I call the fantastic element in my story. Yet something quiet similar to this has already been employed more than once in art: Victor Hugo, for example, in his masterpiece *The Last Day of a Man Condemned to Death*, employed virtually this same device, and even though he did not depict any stenographer, he allowed an even greater breach of verisimilitude when he presumed that a man condemned to execution could (and would have time to) keep a diary, not only on his last day, but even in his last hour and literally in his last moment of life. But had he not allowed this fantastical element, the work itself—among the most real and most truthful of all his writing—would not have existed.[51]

Appealing to Hugo's precedent, Dostoevsky in effect asks his readers to willingly suspend disbelief. As in the case of Hugo's work, it is clearly something readers are wont to do when the work's aesthetics are of the quality we encounter in these two monologue-stories.[52] But what is important to note is that Dostoevsky's integration of the fantastic in

---

[50] Dostoevsky, *A Writer's Diary*, 678; 6.
[51] Dostoevsky, *A Writer's Diary*, 678; 6. The preface to "A Gentle Creature" might work retroactively to instruct us on how to read the complex narrative that is *Demons*. I thank Gene Fitzgerald for this insight.
[52] Interestingly, Hugo's *The Last Day of a Man Condemned to Death* has two prefaces, the first one a fictional preface written in dialogue form when the text was first published in 1827, and the second a direct authorial address in the 1832 edition. See Victor Hugo, *The Last Day of a Condemned Man and Other Prison Writings*, trans. Geoff Woollen (Oxford: Oxford University Press, 1992), 1–33.

realist art ("in a higher sense") has more to do with literary technique than with the content of the story.

Dostoevsky works diligently in his preface to secure his readers' willingness to set aside any discomfort they might feel in regard to the story's technical implausibility. As we have seen, the third paragraph draws implied author, narrator, and readers into a web of mutual implication in the tasks of encoding and deciphering the text. Dostoevsky, in a letter to a correspondent, addressed the demands placed on the writer to win reader loyalty: ". . . the fantastic in art has limits and rules. The fantastic must be contiguous with the real to such a degree that you must *almost* believe it."[53] This "almost" is a bow to readers' rational minds. But before the pawnbroker's monologue begins, we are well prepared by Dostoevsky to suspend the "almost" he projects upon us.

Dostoevsky's extended description of how the pawnbroker goes about his self-inquiry instructs readers how to proceed with the text. But more than a willing suspension of disbelief is required. The reader must also be willing to apprehend Dostoevsky's language as a self-referential coding system that brings the introduction and the monologue into one overarching design. This means that readers will see language both as a medium and as an object. Ever mindful of language's suggestive power, Dostoevsky in effect advises his readers to be wary of the surface claims of utterance and to look deeper into its capacity to both create and resolve paradoxes. In effect, "A Gentle Creature" makes the same point we have already encountered in *Notes from the House of the Dead*. When we read Dostoevsky's prefaces, we need to be prepared to take his language for more than what it appears to be at first glance.

The language of his introductions demands the same kind of attention that Bakhtin gives to Dostoevsky's fictional texts. In effect, we are asked to view his prefaces as a subgenre, if only a minor one. The imminent rules of the subgenre prescribe a reader capable of apprehending the text both as language and as commentary on language. In order to implicate the reader in this hermeneutic, Dostoevsky, in his introduction to "A Gentle Creature," insinuates to the reader how to read the

---

[53] Cited in Jackson, *Dostoevsky's Quest for Form: A Study in His Philosophy of Art* (New Haven: Yale University Press, 1966), 88. Jackson continues, in regard to the fantastic in Dostoevsky's art, "The role of the artist, then, is ultimately that of [a] seer" who seeks to reconcile the real and the ideal in the depiction of human beings, in whom "the real and the ideal merge" (91).

entire text. Readers then view the introduction as more than a mute convention, as more than a mere technical exercise, but as an essential component of the creative process in which Dostoevsky seeks to engage them. In fact, in aiding readers to shift their focus from the text to the pre-text, and then to the con-text, Dostoevsky makes the creative process a theme of his discourse. And, as we have seen previously, the aim of that discourse is to struggle with fragmentation, with the forces of disunity expressed by *vy-*, in order to confront it with the power of *so-*. The narrator may fail here, but it is essential that we readers do not. In the final analysis, this deeply humanistic purpose alters relationships between author, reader, and narrator, and thereby realizes the potential of the aesthetic word to gather people into that point which exists on the boundary of literature and reality. In the 1870s, a period of fragmentation and social chaos, Dostoevsky found the unifying power of aesthetic language in "A Gentle Creature" in the text's very first words.

To return to the early remarks about *The Diary of a Writer* and its genre *mélange*—wherein many an entry leads to yet another, followed by a veer in thematic course to yet another entry that introduces yet another—the question of just what constitutes an introduction and what does not remains in the margins. A synchronic approach to the tale's first words delivers rather discrete readings of individual texts. On only one occasion, "The Boy at Christ's Christmas Party," does the grouping of pre-text, text, and post-text seem to matter. "Bobok" and "A Gentle Creature," however, appear very much to stand alone as thought experiments with self-contained authorial introductions and follow-on tales.

The preface to "Bobok" lays out a plan for reading just about all of Dostoevsky's fiction. The issue, in John Jones' words, is that ". . . one feels an urge to smoke Dostoevsky out with the question, 'Who's talking?'"[54] The question applies to all Dostoevsky' prose fiction. The introduction points, therefore, in two directions—toward Dostoevsky's oeuvre, on the one hand, and toward the *The Diary*, on the other. In "Bobok," Dostoevsky clarifies, at least, that it is not his voice we encounter, neither in this fiction nor in his fictional prefaces. Ironically (and this catches some of the fun Dostoevsky has with encoding texts), Dostoevsky tells us this in an authentic authorial introduction.

---

[54] John Jones, *Dostoevsky* (Oxford: Clarendon Press, 1983), 250.

One presumes, therefore, that we can believe him (and this suggests some of the seriousness of Dostoevsky's engagement with texts, a seriousness that has to do with the contract he holds with his disparate readership). I am not certain, therefore, that we need relate the introduction to "Bobok" to any meta-textual theme. Drawing on Sidorov's notion that *The Diary* is first and foremost an aesthetic phenomenon, we may conclude that the foreword to "Bobok" only qualifies as art object on the margins, say as extra-textual commentary to which we appeal in a pinch, as when citing Dostoevsky's letters, notes, or journalism.

"The Boy at Christ's Christmas Party" certainly articulates *The Diary*'s binary opposition between dystopia and utopia, and constitutes an aesthetic artifact (story). But its introduction is scattershot. First the story creeps up on Dostoevsky in "A Boy with His Arm Outstretched for Alms." Then it emerges as a theme for a fictional work that Dostoevsky, in his introduction, directly claims is hardly a fiction, but, given the existence of children beggars, a verifiable social reality. The introduction, again, comes from Dostoevsky's own voice. There is no fictionalizing here—he presents an argument about the validity of the story that follows. Our hearts are meant to be rent by the boy's lot. Dostoevsky leaves his projected readers little choice.

It would seem that when Dostoevsky introduces fiction himself, he asks his readers to follow his direct advice and to fall in line. This hardly suggests open-endedness, resistance to any final word, or dialogism. No wonder Dostoevsky altered this authorial impulse, for it hardly served his profound inclination to allow readers some room for independent interpretation. Consequently, in "The Gentle Creature," the final work of fiction containing a preface in the *Diary*, and consistent with all of the diary entries, we again hear directly from the authorial persona. The preface performs all the functions we have encountered previously in his works (with the exception of "Bobok" and "The Boy"). Within the implied author's prefatorial voice, an embedded foreword takes shape, one that propels us into the pawnbroker's monologue.

Dostoevsky may have learned in *The Diary* to be wary of his own voice position when developing a story. His return to prior prefatorial practice in "A Gentle Creature" suggests as much, as does his avoidance of an introduction altogether in "Dream of a Ridiculous Man" (1877). Why, then, would he insist on writing "From the Author" yet again in the preface to his final work of fiction, *The Brothers Karamazov*?

Anxious to the End

CHAPTER 6

I

THE BROTHERS KARAMAZOV

The foreword to *The Brothers Karamazov*, titled "From the Author" ("Ot avtora") is sometimes mentioned by critics of the novel, but most often only as an aside. For example, we have Avrahm Yarmolinsky's striking judgment: "It appears from the brief and lame foreword to *The Brothers Karamazov* that Dostoevsky intended to follow it up with a sequel."[1] There are others who consider the introduction more misleading than merely ineffective or blessedly short: ". . . Although Dostoevsky himself in the introduction 'From the Author' underscores that, by his design, the most important thing is the hagiography of Alexei Fyodorovich and that specifically Alyosha is the most 'noteworthy' hero of the novel, still it is not he, but—objectively speaking, that is, in aesthetic terms— Ivan who turns out to be the more convincing hero."[2]

In these and similar instances, the only information to be gleaned from the foreword is apparently the "author's" three announcements

---

[1] Avrahm Yarmolinsky, *Dostoevsky: His Life and Art* (New York: Grove Press, 1957), 391.

[2] A. A. Belkin, "*Brat'iia Karamazovy* (sotsial'no-filosofskaia problematika)," in *Tvorchestvo F. M. Dostoevskogo*, ed. N. L. Stepanov, D. D. Blagoi, U. A. Gural'nik, B. S. Riurikov (Moscow: AN SSSR, 1959), 274. The translation is mine. In the remainder of this chapter, translations come, with an occasional modification, from Fyodor Dostoevsky, *The Brothers Karamazov*, trans. Richard Pevear and Larissa Volokhonsky (San Francisco: North Point Press, 1990). For the original, see Dostoevskii, *PSS*, XIV–XV.

that: (1) Alyosha is the hero of the novel, (2) the projected two novels represent Alyosha's biography or hagiography (*zhizneopisanie*), and (3) *The Brothers Karamazov* is merely preparatory to this second novel where Alyosha was to have figured as the unequivocal hero.³ The relative value of the introduction ceases for the critic at this point, its remaining portions considered mere flotsam and jetsam on a sea of superfluous verbiage. But it is just such material that makes the foreword what it is.⁴ Remove the details of event and character from a narrative text and what is left: abstractions, outlines, and little else. Something similar can be said of the introduction to *The Brothers Karamazov*. Attend only to the major announcements and it appears lame and hardly brief enough.⁵

The discourse of the foreword, however, has not been subjected to critical analysis. An exception comes from Maximilian Braun who has studied it in relation to the novel's type. Because the text is "preparatory" (the narrator-chronicler's word is *vstupitel'nyi*) and presents "just one moment from my hero's early youth," Braun labels *The Brothers Karamazov* an expository novel.⁶ Importantly, Braun's evidence for the claim does not come alone "from the author" in the introduction, but also from Part 1, Book 1, Chapter 2, where the quasi-personalized narrator-chronicler of the fiction announces a second novel: "This very circumstance [Dmitry's ill treatment by his father] led to the catastrophe, *an account of which forms the subject of my first introductory novel, or, better, the external side of it*."⁷

Although Braun's focus is on genre rather than on the rhetoric of the foreword, his analysis is quite helpful. But by glossing over the coincidence of the "author's" claims about the novel in the introduction and the narrator-chronicler's similar claims in the body of the

---

3   Dostoevsky, *Brothers Karamazov*, 3–4; 5–6.
4   Dostoevsky twice calls it a foreword (*predislovie*).
5   Genette would label Dostoevsky's approach to this preface a "dodge" (*esquive*) in the form of an apology for the preface's length, dullness, irrelevance, uselessness, or presumptuousness (*Paratexts*, 230–231).
6   Maximilian Braun, "*The Brothers Karamazov* as Expository Novel," *Canadian-American Slavic Studies* 6, no. 2 (1972): 199.
7   Dostoevsky, *Brothers Karamazov*, 12; 12 (my emphasis). Note that the narrator identifies the novel as his—i.e., he is its author—which suggests he may have authored the text's introduction as well, thus making what appears to be an authentic authorial preface into a fictional authorial one.

text, it misses an opportunity to penetrate the introduction's narrative technique. It is precisely in the coincidence of foreword and text that Dostoevsky suggests how we might read the preface—or re-read it.[8] There are additional hints. Given that the voice speaking to us "from the author" is self-conscious, even defensive—he worries that the first volume may not provide adequate evidence to support his assertion that Alyosha is its hero—it calls attention to itself as a marked form of discourse. That Dostoevsky would engage in tortured arguments on behalf of his narrative, especially at this stage in a now illustrious career (1879), should strike us as sufficiently odd as to draw our attention. Furthermore, since Alyosha cannot be verified as the hero of the novel without evidence provided by a sequel (Dostoevsky died before he could write it), the design of *The Brothers Karamazov*, from the claims of the foreword in any case, is left in an unfinished state. The announcement of the novel's sequel has led to speculation about what Dostoevsky had in mind for its continuation.[9] Interesting as these clues may be, in no instance of which I am aware has the introduction been analyzed as a discrete form of discourse that stands at rhetorical levels quite distinct from those that follow in the novel proper.

Stating that the foreword stands at a different discursive level from the fictional text's is not to imply that it holds fast to the author's position either. It may well be that its rhetorical situation does not coincide with that of its implied author, whose voice, by virtue of the "Ot avtora" title affixed to the introduction, we are enticed to assume is that of Dostoevsky's literary or authorial persona. It may well be the case that it is not a conventional authorial preface of the type we have seen in Lermontov's *A Hero of Our Time*, but one in which an implied author

---

[8] V. E. Vetlovskaia has posited the value of retrospection in regard to any interpretation of the novel in her "Razviazka v *Brat'iakh Karamazovykh*," in *Poetika i stilistika russkoi literatury* (Leningrad: Nauka, 1971), 195–203; retrospection belongs to memory, which is Diane Thompson's approach in her *The Poetics of Memory in "The Brothers Karamazov"* (Cambridge: Cambridge University Press, 1991).

[9] See, in particular, the treatment of such speculation in Grossman, *Dostoevsky*, 586–588; Thompson, *Poetics of Memory*, 338 n. 20; Joseph Frank, *The Mantle of the Prophet, 1871–1881* (Princeton: Princeton University Press, 2002), 484; and Igor Volgin, "Alyosha's Destiny," in *The New Russian Dostoevsky: Readings for the Twenty-First Century*, ed. Carol Apollonio (Bloomington: Slavica Publishers, 2010), 271–286.

addresses implied readers directly. On the other hand, it may well be the case that it cannot be taken as a conventional figural form of speech (where a character as narrator delivers up an introduction in his or her own voice), that is, as a feature of the author's imagined world rather than as his direct address. We again recall as examples of figural prefaces the fictional editor's introduction to Pushkin's *Tales of the Late Ivan Petrovich Belkin* and Gogol's Rudy Panko in *Evenings on a Farm Near Dikanka*. Between these distinct modes of provenance there is yet another option for identifying the voice which speaks to us "Ot avtora" in *The Brothers Karamazov*, one familiar to us thanks to Bakhtin's study of Dostoevsky's poetics—double voicing. It is to such speech, I believe, that Dostoevsky directs our attention through the odd discourse of the introduction.

II

FREE INDIRECT SPEECH

Before attending to the occurrence of double voicing (or a variant of it), let us first refresh our memory of the foreword itself. Dostoevsky published his novel in serial form from January 1879 to November 1880. Significantly, when the first entry appeared, very little of the novel had been composed—only Book 1, Chapters 1 and 2 of Part I.[10] It is unusual for authors to write an introduction before the novel is thoroughly fleshed out or even completed, and this is because a preface would then require authors to possess great foresight and a strong willingness to take risks. If daring authors require foresight, readers of those risky prefaces are in need of a strong memory. When the novel's epilogue would finally be published (as *The Brothers Karamazov* was at the end of 1880), who of the original reading public would have

---

[10] As William Mills Todd III has put it, *The Brothers Karamazov* was "the novel that [Dostoevsky] had least drafted as he began serialization"; Dostoevsky "had only written several books of the novel" at the time he began to publish it ("*The Brothers Karamazov* and the Poetics of Serialization," *Dostoevsky Studies* 7 [1986]: 87–88). It is clear, however, that he had long planned the novel and had thought out a great deal of it, at least in general outline (Frank, *The Mantle*, 390–391).

remembered the foreword of two years earlier? A readily predictable failure in any real reader's memory did not deter Dostoevsky in the least from including an introduction to the first published entry, one that envisioned not only the whole arc of *The Brothers Karamazov*, but a sequel as well. Here are the kernels from the foreword commented upon most often in the critical literature:

From the Author

> Starting out on the biography of my hero, Alexei Fyodorovich Karamazov, I find myself in some perplexity. Namely, that while I do call Alexei Fyodorovich my hero, still, I myself know that he is by no means a great man, so that I can foresee the inevitable questions, such as: What is notable about your Alexei Fyodorovich that you should choose him for your hero? What has he really done? To whom is he known, and for what? Why should I, the reader, spend my time studying the facts of his life? . . . .
>
> . . . . the trouble is that while I have one biography, I have two novels. The main novel is the second one—about the activities of my hero in our time, that is, in our present, current moment. As for the first novel, it already took place thirteen years ago and is even almost not a novel at all but just one moment from my hero's early youth. . . .[11]

This citation consists of less than a quarter of the entire foreword. But key temporal elements, in terms of the overall design, are made clear here. It contains crucial information for interpreting the narrative, not the least of which is the setting of Alyosha's "hagiography" in historical terms. The introduction appears in 1879—"the present, current moment" (most likely this moment coincides with the date of the publication of the first installment)—by which we calibrate the action of the novel "thirteen years ago" as 1866. We learn, thus, that *The Brothers Karamazov* is set in the decade in which *Crime and Punishment* and *Notes from the Underground* were published. Their actions nearly overlap. Gérard Genette states that "it is indisputable that historical awareness of the period in which a work was written is rarely immaterial to one's reading of that work."[12] Thus, if not for the foreword, we might not have been able to deduce readily the novel's temporal frame

---

[11] Dostoevsky, *Brothers Karamazov*, 3–4; 5–6 (ellipses added).
[12] Genette, *Paratexts*, 7.

with any accuracy, so crucial as it is to the novel's interpretation within Dostoevsky's oeuvre.

Furthermore, were we *not* to have the "author's" testimony that Alyosha is the hero of a two-volume biography, for which *The Brothers Karamazov* is just "one moment" in his life, we might perhaps be inclined to conclude, as many have, that Ivan and Dmitry are in fact the central dramatis personae of this first volume. Knowing the trajectory of the novel in advance (if not in detail, then in overall design),[13] the "author" asserts Alyosha's centrality but feels this notion will encounter reader resistance as the novel unfolds serially. The foreword, therefore, steers us in a direction that we as readers might not otherwise take. This is odd, for it pits "the author's" claims about Alyosha against his own narrative's dramatic focus on the other brothers. Furthermore, if the "author" of the introduction's title does not represent either the implied author "Dostoevsky" or the historical Dostoevsky himself, but the narrator-chronicler instead, then the matter becomes even more vexed.[14]

The largest portion of the foreword runs an altered vocal course. The "authorial" remarks elsewhere in the introduction sound a strained note when compared with the declarative sentences and rhetorical questions of the entries already cited. This suggests that their provenance changes as well. Yet the shift from direct address to something more figural is not abrupt. The questions "the author" puts into the reader's mouth in the first paragraph of the introduction signal a modulation

---

[13] After Dostoevsky published an installment, he conducted a good deal of research prior to composing the next. The details pertaining to the multitude of characters and their settings (e.g., Zosima and the monastery) were worked out progressively. His research slowed the novel's composition, which took roughly two years to complete rather than the one year he had anticipated. This delay caused problems for Dostoevsky and the publisher; the December 1879 entry contained an apology "Ot avtora" ("From the Author") for extending the novel into another subscription year, something that would normally have been considered a breach of contract. It is clear that this apology comes from the historical Dostoevsky and not from either his authorial persona or from the text's narrator.

[14] Genette cites many examples where the preface attempts to justify or explain the title of the work (*Paratexts*, 156–170). Perhaps, since he could foresee that Dmitry and Ivan, among others, were to be central to this novel's argument, Dostoevsky felt the need at the earliest moment to explain the novel's title— Volume One is about Ivan and Dmitry (and Smerdyakov?); Volume Two is about Alyosha. Cf. Ia. Golosovker's argument that Ivan and Zosima are the central characters (*Dostoevskii i Kant* [Moscow: Akademiia nauk, 1963], 35–45).

in tone ("What is notable about your Alexei Fyodorovich . . . ? What has he really done?" etc.). For the simple reason that these questions may be superfluous—they can be raised by most any reader in regard to most any standard narrative—we are cued to read with a wary eye. Under normal conditions, we readers give the benefit of the doubt to the implied author, whose creator knows that such questions will be answered in due course. For reasons of convention having to do with an unstated or assumed author-reader contract, these questions, in fact, need not have been raised by Dostoevsky at all. This being the case, why would Dostoevsky have his authorial persona advance so clumsily? Never in his post-exile years did he feel compelled to do so. Why now?

As Dorrit Cohn explains, the direct and indirect speech of a character in the guise of the narrator's discourse, i.e., without punctuation marks or inquit verbs ("s/he said" verbs used in reported speech), requires the provision of clues in order for it to be apprehended by readers.[15] Such hints put the reader on the lookout for a special form of speech that has been variously labeled, usually in reference to the literature of a specific language group and/or author, as free indirect style (*style indirect libre*), *erlebte Rede*, quasi-indirect discourse, double-voicing, and, in Cohn's terminology, narrated monologue.[16] The rhetorical questions in the foreword's first paragraph give us a sense that another voice is intruding almost immediately into "the author's" direct address. Alerted by those questions to a shift in voice, we turn with a more keen attentiveness to the odd utterances that immediately follow them:

> The last question [i.e., Why should *I*, the reader, spend my time studying the facts of his life?] is the most fateful one, for I can only reply: "Perhaps *you* will see [*uvidite sami*] from the novel." But suppose *they* read [*prochtut*] the novel and do not see [*ne uvidiat*], do not agree [*ne soglasiatsia*] with the noteworthiness of my Alexei Fyodorovich? I say this because, to my sorrow, I foresee it. To me he is noteworthy,

---

[15] Dorrit Cohn, *Transparent Minds: Narrative Modes for Presenting Consciousness in Fiction* (Princeton: Princeton University Press, 1978), 106.
[16] Cohn, *Transparent Minds*, 99–140. For *erlebte Rede*, quasi-indirect discourse, double-voicing, see respectively, Roy Pascal, *The Dual Voice*, 8–12; N. Voloshinov, *Marxism and the Philosophy of Langauge*, trans. L. Matejka and Irwin Titunik (Cambridge, MA: Harvard University Press, 1986), 109–160; and Bakhtin, *Problems*, 181–269.

but I decidedly doubt that I shall succeed in proving it to the reader. The thing is that he does, perhaps, make a figure, but a figure of an indefinite, indeterminate sort. Though it would be strange to demand clarity from people in a time like *ours*. One thing, perhaps, is rather doubtless: he is a strange man, even an odd one. But strangeness and oddity will sooner harm than justify any claim to attention, especially when everyone is striving to unite particulars and find at least some general sense in the general senselessness. Whereas an odd man is most often a particular and isolated case. Is that not so?[17]

This is a complex discourse hardly in keeping with the first declarative sentence "from the author" that initiates the foreword. The self-consciousness here is one thing, the opaque logic another. More remarkable still are its temporal jumps, the marked alternation of nominal and possessive pronouns in reference to the same imagined readers/persons, impersonal second- and third-person verbal forms, and an apparently unmotivated mixture of direct and reported speech. Given these clues, the near-audibility of inexplicit queries and responses ring in the background of this passage and seem to impel each successive non-sequitur-like response. The density of these marked features constitutes a set of authorial signals that guide us to double-voiced speech.

As Pascal claims in his study of dual discourse, ". . . free indirect speech is never purely and simply the evocation of a character's thought and perception, but always bears, in its vocabulary, its intonation, its syntactical composition and other stylistic features, in its content, or its context, or in some combination of these, the mark of the narrator."[18] But it is a voice through which we hear another, grounding voice in the wings, the one that delivers judgment or perspective or moral suasion. The two voices merge, interact, play with and against each other, supplant the partner here, conjoin there, alternate with each other, then fuse again. Pascal notes that free indirect speech occurs in Dostoevsky at dramatic moments in the lives of his characters: "Dostoyevsky . . . uses very fully the older methods of reproducing the inner motions of the mind—narratorial report, direct speech, and the soliloquy in inverted commas—as well as free indirect speech. The latter usually occurs at times of great inward tension, struggle, and anxiety—in

---

[17] Dostoevsky, *Brothers Karamazov*, 3; 5 (my emphases).
[18] Pascal, *The Dual Voice*, 43.

Crime and Punishment, for instance, when Raskolnikov arrives outside the old usurer's, just before he commits the murder, or when in part VI he is on his way to Svidrigailov's."[19] Raskolnikov stands at a threshold. So, too, our narrator/author. In the foreword to *The Brothers Karamazov*, the "author" seems to be under stress in that he foresees his novel will not be appreciated and his hero consigned to secondary status. Yet, it would seem unlikely that Dostoevsky himself would suffer such anxieties about his text. As an experienced writer he would hardly have been so overcome as to have committed such a strange piece of discourse to the public without some purpose.[20]

It is plausible, however, that it is not the implied author who speaks here (or who speaks solely). Apropos, the worries about the work and its reception seem more likely to belong to a novice. In fact, the narrator-chronicler of the text claims to be the one who distills the information for the presentation of his work about the Karamazov brothers during a brief if tragic period in their lives in 1866. He works from memory and other unidentified means to present his tale. In the first installment of January 1879, it is he who claims, as Braun indicates, that the work is preparatory to a second novel. Thus, it appears, we have two authors claiming provenance over *The Brothers Karamazov*—the implied author and his narrator-chronicler (unnamed and without biography, but apparently a coeval of Alyosha's). Although at different discursive levels, together they produce the discourse that follows the foreword. "From the Author," therefore, rings with a triple referent. First, it is in truth of fact the real author, Dostoevsky, who pens it. Second, it is presented through the mediacy of his author-persona, who shares the verbal field with, third, the narrator-chronicler, Alyosha's "biographer." The first is the historical person; the second an artifact of the narrative situation; and the third the intentional creation of the first. Authorial persona and narrator appear together in the foreword with their own distinct voices and experiential positions.[21]

---

[19] Pascal, *The Dual Voice*, 124.
[20] In his letters, Dostoevsky occasionally expresses concerns over individual parts of the novel. See in particular his letters to Pobedonostsev (Dostoevskii, *PSS*, XXX/1: 66–156).
[21] For a description of narrator/author layers, see Jan M. Meijer, "The Author of *Bratija Karamazovy*," in *Dutch Studies in Russian Literature* 2, no. 2 (1971): 7–15.

This triple effect is not meant to nullify the independence of character voice for which Dostoevsky is hailed (albeit not without contention among critics). Rather, we find in the introduction an elegant distribution of responsibilities that represent distinct rhetorical levels of the text and its paratext. First, the historical Dostoevsky's position can be ascertained—or rather, argued over—from materials both paratextual (title, epigraph, preface, intertitles, etc.) and epitextual (Dostoevsky's letters, comments to others, speeches, readings, apologies, published articles).[22] Second, the implied author remains wholly a byproduct of the narratological situation. We infer his position, beliefs, moral values, and attitudes toward specific characters, through the agency of the novel's discourse, its architectonics, its characters' voices, perhaps even the epigraph (although this is debatable), as well as the privileged position belonging to the epilogue. Third, the semi-personalized narrator-chronicler's image remains opaque throughout the text. But, given the conventions of the realist third-person personalized narrator, he is to be viewed as the first and primary filter of all elements of the work—he is the teller of the tale. We listen to him, even when his voice disappears into the background and the narrative takes on the effect of omniscience. Technically, it is still his voice, even though we sense the intrusion of the implied author's superior perspective (relative to the narrator's). Most critical to us in the foreword is the interaction of the two—the implied author's and the narrator-chronicler's.

   The implied author initiates the preface. His tone is neutral, matter-of-fact, learned, and worldly. His utterances lay claim to some level of order, logic, reason, and are rooted in his (inferred) literary professional experience. In the foreword, the kernel of his message can also be sensed or intuited behind the utterances of the perturbed narrator-chronicler. This latter is very little known to us—no sooner does he present himself in the first installment of the serialized novel then he disappears from the reader's view. As Pascal notes: "Authors often try to profit from the authenticity that the invention of a personalized narrator gives, without observing the limitations it imposes. *Madame Bovary* and *The Brothers Karamazov*, for instance, both begin as narratives of a specific narrator-person, who is soon utterly discarded by Flaubert and only occasionally resuscitated by Dostoyevsky, for

---

[22] See Genette for a discussion of the epitext: *Paratexts*, 344–403.

essential aspects of both novels contradict the character of a personal narrative."[23] But we learn something about Dostoevsky's narrator in the foreword through the agency of that narrator's own discourse.[24] He engages in free association, expresses a panicked illogic, produces red herrings, delivers a confused description of his readers' abilities and his critics' potential responses, and waxes and wanes in his willingness to stand his ground about the merits of his narrative. He gains confidence only by means of the support of his worldly mentor, who is active in the role of implied author. As Pascal points out, ". . . sentences and epithets which, if narratorial, would seem vague or clumsy are precise and subtle when we understand them as the thought of the character [i.e., the narrator-chronicler]; precise and subtle, that is, in delineating his thought and interpretation of experience."[25] Pascal's analysis describes effectively the relationship of the two vocal acts in the novel's foreword and prescribes how we might differentiate them.

The text comes to us through the intermediacy of the narrator-chronicler; yet we are not given an account of his person (as we might, strictly speaking, in an editor's or fictional editor's preface).[26] Were it not for the introduction, we would have been left in doubt about the narrator's qualities. It is my contention that the foreword introduces the narrator to us, not directly by any means, but by laying out the flow of his (or some of his) thoughts and emotions, his consciousness, and particularly his anxieties. In other words, free indirect speech in the foreword encapsulates some portion of the narrator's character. That portion is important to our reading of the novel. If this is the case, then the opacity of the foreword can provide greater clarity for the reader, if not completely, at least to a significant degree. Here we encounter the historical Dostoevsky's intent (intentional fallacy aside) and discover an answer to the self-doubting, perhaps even comic, questions posed in the foreword about this "preparatory" novel's utility.

---

[23] Pascal, *The Dual Voice*, 68.
[24] For an examination of the narrator-chronicler's speech characteristics, see V. E. Vetlovskaia, *Poetika romana "Brat'ia Karamazovy"* (Moscow: Nauka, 1977), 13–51.
[25] Pascal, *The Dual Voice*, 129.
[26] As we have seen, Pushkin and Gogol parody this convention.

III

AUTHORS IN DIALOGUE

A re-presentation of the foreword's opening two paragraphs allows us to see how both figural and direct ("authorial") speech interact, that is, the speech of the narrator-chronicler and that of the implied author, respectively. Odd as this may sound, it is as though the two voices are engaged in a dialogue about the text they are about to produce together.[27] The nominal pronouns that appear at the outset of the introduction provide a key to this re-presentation. They are divided between "author" and narrator in a way that suggests the two are interlocutors, the addressees of each other's alternating utterances. We can imagine a division of vocal labor along the following lines (with some modifications as well as stage directions added to the original text for purposes of clarification):

> **Narrator-chronicler to the implied author (construed as his mentor):** Starting out on the biography of my hero, Alexei Fyodorovich Karamazov, I find myself in some perplexity. Namely, that while I do call Alexei Fyodorovich my hero, still, I myself know that he is by no means a great man, so that I can foresee the inevitable questions, such as: What is notable about your Alexei Fyodorovich that you should choose him for your hero? What has he really done? To whom is he known, and for what? Why should I, the reader, spend my time studying the facts of his life?
>
> **Implied author to the narrator-novice:** The last question is the most fateful one [for you]; I can only reply [to your readers and on your behalf]: "Perhaps you will see from the novel."
>
> **Narrator-chronicler (anxiously):** But suppose they read the novel and do not see, do not agree with the noteworthiness of my Alexei Fyodorovich? I say this because, to my sorrow, I foresee it. To me he is noteworthy, but I decidedly doubt that I shall succeed in proving it to the reader. One thing, perhaps, is rather doubtless: he is a strange man, even an odd one.

---

[27] Dramatized introductions are attested in Dostoevsky's time and some of his most cherished texts used them, e.g., Victor Hugo's *The Last Day of a Condemned Man*.

Implied author: But strangeness and oddity will sooner harm than justify any claim to attention, especially when everyone is striving to unite particulars and find at least some general sense in the general senselessness.

Narrator-chronicler: [Yes, but] an odd man is most often a particular and isolated case. Is that not so?

Implied author: [I] do not agree with this last point and reply: "Not so" or "Not always so."

Narrator-chronicler (temporarily relieved): Then perhaps I shall take heart concerning the significance of my hero, Alexei Fyodorovich.

Implied author: For not only is an odd man "not always" a particular and isolated case, but, on the contrary, it sometimes happens that it is precisely he, perhaps, who bears within himself the heart of the whole.

Narrator-chronicler: [Yes, true,] while the other people of his epoch have all for some reason been torn away from it . . .

Implied author (interrupting): [. . . indeed,] by "some kind of flooding wind."

By the conclusion of the first three paragraphs of the foreword, we readers are, or might now be, sufficiently prepared to identify the narrator-chronicler's voice and to follow it through its most twisted and anxious logic, which suffuses the fourth paragraph. It presents his free indirect speech in a series of steps by which interference from, or interaction with, the implied author's voice flickers on and off. We cement our understanding of the narrator here more thoroughly than elsewhere in the text.

The transition from double-voiced speech to the narrator-chronicler's momentary solo act occurs gradually. It begins with a continuation of the implied author's and narrator-chronicler's monophonic harmony: "I would not, in fact, venture into these rather vague and uninteresting explanations but would simply begin without any foreword—if they like it, they'll read it as it is—but the trouble is that while I have just one biography [*zhizneopisanie*], I have two novels." Remembering that *The Brothers Karamazov* comes hot on the heels of Dostoevsky's tour de force performance of direct (implied) authorial address in *The Diary of a Writer*, and that he ceased writing *The Diary* in order to begin writing what was to prove to be his final work of fiction, perhaps it is not an implausible conjecture to hold that, at this moment in the foreword "From the Author," Dostoevsky himself stands before his readers, at least as much as he does in *The Diary*. For it is not the implied author who plans two novels. It is Dostoevsky himself. Nor is it the narrator who has two novels, for he is contained wholly within the first novel as a product of Dostoevsky's imagination. It appears, rather suddenly, that a third voice emerges in the introduction, one that emanates directly "From the Implied Author, Fyodor Dostoevsky" (to rewrite the preface's title).

Next we are informed that "the main novel is the second one—about the activities of my hero in our time, that is, in our present, current moment. As for the first novel, it already took place thirteen years ago and is even almost not a novel at all but just one moment from my hero's early youth."[28] Dostoevsky's biography appears to spill into this description as well. 1879 was a period of great instability, of social disorientation, of political violence—a godless time, Dostoevsky would call it. He believes he understands just how things have reached such a calamitous state and he wishes to explicate the reasons for it in his novel. (We are only two years from Dostoevsky's death and the assassination of Tsar Alexander II.) The "our time" is indeed 1879. The second novel—whether the chronicler-narrator's or Dostoevsky's—is to be entirely topical, which is not unusual for Dostoevsky. Much of his fiction is cast in the present or works quickly from the past into the present. What this means, as a consequence, is that *The Brothers Karamazov* is something of an anomaly, for it depicts, from the text's beginning to its end, the past.[29]

The dislocation of time, the "then" of *The Brothers Karamazov* and the "now" of the never-written second novel, may lie at the heart of the double-voicing of the novel's foreword. The destabilization of voices in the novel's first words replicates the dislocation of temporal schemes in the two novels planned. Together they point directly

---

[28] Dostoevsky, *Brothers Karamazov*, 3–4; 6.
[29] Dostoevsky's fiction is often retrospective, but not historical in a conventional sense. In the texts we have examined up to *The Brothers Karamazov*, the time of narration occurs almost immediately following the action. The same holds true for *Crime and Punishment*, *The Idiot*, and *The Adolescent*—texts that lack properly labeled forewords. But in *The Brothers*, more than a decade separates narrative from narrated time.

toward the chaotic forces at work from the 1860s to the late 1870s in social, political, spiritual, and economic spheres. The aesthetic unity that can be derived from all manner of chaos is clear to our narrators: "It is impossible for me to do without this first novel, or much in the second novel will be incomprehensible."[30] The two texts bear a cause and effect relationship. If the narrator-chronicler's hagiography succeeds in delivering up the tale adequately, then Dostoevsky's novel does, too. The insecurities that the narrator-chronicler confesses in the first paragraphs, and the aggressive response to foreseen negativity in response to *The Brothers Karamazov*, reveal the author's anxieties to us as well. Ecce homo.

At this point, however, the author, momentarily unmasked, slips out of sight, disguised again by the discourse with which the foreword began: "Thus my original difficulty becomes even more complicated, for if I, that is, the biographer [*biograf*] himself, think that even one novel may, perhaps, be unwarranted for such a humble and indefinite hero, then how will it look if I appear with two; and what can explain such presumption on my part?"[31] Here we return to the insecurity-based quandary of the narrator-chronicler whom the implied author alone seems able to embolden. We note that the utterance identifies the vocalist as "biographer." The implied author is just that—a fragment of an authentic personage represented in dramatic, fictional form in the foreword as the narrator's interlocutor and mentor. Dostoevsky himself is a novelist, something more than a biographer. The worry expressed at this moment in the text belongs to the narrator-chronicler.

In the fifth paragraph the implied author's voice begins to intrude again, moving our focus in stages from the consciousness of the narrator-chronicler (and of the sudden presence of Fyodor Dostoevsky) to his own perspective. It is worthwhile examining the process by which we are led back to the dual voices of the introduction's first three paragraphs. The first step in the process occurs with the first sentence: "Being at a loss to resolve these questions [about the sequel and reader response to the first volume], I am resolved to leave them

---

[30] Dostoevsky, *Brothers Karamazov*, 4; 6.
[31] Dostoevsky, *Brothers Karamazov*, 4; 6.

without any resolution."[32] Who delivers this utterance? It might be the implied author speaking on his own behalf. But it represents the voice of the narrator-chronicler equally well. Such binary thinking, however, is not apropos. It is more likely that the grammatical first person singular pronoun represents both voices. It is as though they are singing in unison—two vocalists, the same notes, and the same lyrics (thus, both appropriately use the pronoun "I"). Were the moment to be staged, we would have the narrator-chronicler and the implied author speaking this line together in unison.

But, we must not confuse this unity of one script and two voices with a merger of their functions. In this sense their intonations differ even as their lyrics are word-for-word alike. On the one hand, the narrator-chronicler (whose voice dominates in that it was the most recently heard in solo performance) continues his confused discourse, becoming more emotional, defensive, even belligerent. On the other hand, the implied author steps in again to lend the novice a hand. In a matter-of-fact way the implied author begins to wrest his portion of the discourse from his partner. We can imagine the background message just audible behind the surface utterance: "I have let my callow friend wander [in paragraph four]; there's no making sense of his formulations, so let us simply forget about it and move on."

In the second step of the process of voice merger—which functions as an act of clarification that is not available to the narrator-chronicler—the ruse of the introduction is laid bare. The exchange continues in a tag-team manner with the narrator picking up the implied author's cue:

> **In unison:** To be sure, the insightful reader will already have guessed long ago that that is what I've been getting at from the very beginning . . .
>
> **Narrator-chronicler (self-consciously quoting a dissatisfied reader):** . . . and will only be annoyed with me for "wasting fruitless words and precious time."
>
> **Implied author (quoting his interlocutor's hypothetical quote):** To this I have a ready answer: I have been "wasting fruitless words and

---

[32] Dostoevsky, *Brothers Karamazov*, 4; 6.

precious time," first, out of politeness, and, second, out of cunning. At least I have given some warning beforehand.

Narrator-chronicler (quoting his interlocutor's earlier formulation): In fact, I am even glad that my novel broke itself into two stories "while preserving the essential unity of the whole . . ."

Implied narrator: . . . [Yes,] having acquainted himself with the first story, the reader can decide for himself whether it is worth his while to begin the second.

Narrator-chronicler (magnanimously): Of course, no one is bound by anything: he can also drop the book after two pages of the first story and never pick it up again.

Implied narrator (sardonically): But still there are readers of such delicacy that they will certainly want to read to the very end so as to make no mistake in their impartial judgment. Such, for instance, are all Russian critics.

Narrator-chronicler (picking up the same intonation): Faced with these people, I feel easier in my heart: for, in spite of their care and conscientiousness, I am nonetheless providing them with the most valid pretext for dropping the story at the first episode of the novel.

In unison: Well, that is the end of my foreword [*predislovie*]. I quite agree that it is superfluous, but since it is already written, let it stand. And now to business.[33]

One might divide the discourse differently than I have here. For example, it might be more appropriate to join the two where I have made them appear distinct, or to crisscross voices and content at different moments, or to dispense with the hierarchical relationship in which I have cast their parts. The point, however, is that at least two voices operate at the surface level in the foreword. And a second is that it serves the real author's purposes (disavowals aside) to embed these voices into the discourse at the outset of a sustained effort of serial publication on his part. But this begs important questions. What is the utility of the introduction? Does it serve the text in any useful manner, or does it remain merely superfluous—even with its vocal identities fleshed out? It is difficult, if not impossible (thank God), to answer

---

[33] Dostoevsky, *Brothers Karamazov*, 4; 6 (my ellipses).

these queries definitively, but some useful concluding remarks can be made.

Paraphrasing Genette, reading a text with an introduction (epigraph, dedication or other paratextual material) and reading the same text without one must necessarily represent quite different experiences.[34] Paratexts influence how we apprehend texts, and texts cast a large backshadow over their paratexts. Each in some measure influences the other, if disproportionately. In our example, the foreword serves to influence our first reading of the text in one direction, and on the occasion of subsequent readings, in quite another. A January 1879 reading is influenced by the claims initially discussed—Alyosha, hero, sequel. The introduction serves to highlight the design of the imminent text by clarifying the work's title—it is about the Karamazov brothers, true, but it anticipates an expansive treatment of only one of them, Alyosha, in the future. *The Brothers Karamazov* focuses most on the other brothers, Dmitry, Ivan, and in important thematic ways, Smerdyakov (if, indeed, he is a half brother) and, of course, Alyosha's spiritual father, Zosima. The foreword, on first reading, attempts to make this much clear. Or does it? Under the impress of dual speech (or the dramatized dialogue I've laid out), alternative renderings are also made possible.

The preface provides us with a fine example of double voicing in Dostoevsky as it replicates the key features of free indirect speech—third person narrative providing an impressionistic sample of the voice of a first person who has been stripped of both indirect and direct speech signs, i.e., inquit verbs or quotation marks. It may very well be that both perspectives and speech types given to us by the implied author and the narrator-chronicler represent the real Dostoevsky's deep-seated anxieties about the novel and represent simultaneously his enthusiasm for the massive themes he plans on developing in the course of the novel's serialization. The epitext certainly suggests these contrary emotions, especially Dostoevsky's letters written over the course of the novel's composition and publication month by month—with occasional lapses.[35] Free indirect speech gains Dostoevsky some distance from the

---

[34] Genette, *Paratexts*, 10–12.
[35] Todd, "Poetics of Serialization," 97.

responsibility that direct authorial address assumes in the author-reader contract that we have witnessed already in *The Diary of a Writer*.[36]

The quirks that arise from the narrator-chronicler's utterances must give us pause when considering the manner of mind that produces both *The Brothers Karamazov* and its foreword, wherein claims of a sequel can be questioned. The novel is justifiably famous, its depths unfathomable, its questions eternal, its problems intractable, and its impact unforgettable. Miracle it is, then, that the novice narrator is capable of transmitting "his" Volume One to us in the final form we have in hand. It goes without saying that the narrator's success has everything to do with the author himself. He frames his novel within the limitations of his narrator-chronicler, then explodes those limitations with his own virtuosity. Dostoevsky achieves this aesthetic effect, as many critics have noted, by dispensing with the pretense of a semi-personalized narrator after the first pages of the novel have been composed; I say "semi-" because most of what we have of the narrator-chronicler, his mind and emotions, is what we are presented in the introduction.[37] The narrator's occasional remarks within the text, either foreshadowing Volume Two (e.g., statements of the type "Alyosha would remember this for the rest of his life") or reflecting upon his inability to remember scenes and events exactly as they occurred, destabilize our reading. In Gogolian fashion, they both give to us and take away from us any confidence we might wish to have in him as mediator of first note. At a minimum, the introduction supplies a hint about the quality of his character. And with that small crust proffered, we consume the whole loaf.

But can this crust really nourish us? Are we left merely with the caution that we must be wary of narrators and their claims, especially Dostoevsky's? Or the truism that texts are always mediated? Are we forced to agree with the implied author's and narrator's joint summary judgment: "I quite agree that [the foreword] is superfluous . . ."? Enter the author. His irony drips.

---

[36] Free indirect speech may also mask Dostoevsky's desires, one of which may have been to replicate Balzac, Hugo, and Zola in their multivolume projects. Genette argues that either modesty or its opposite can motivate complex fictional prefaces of the type encountered in *The Brothers Karamazov* (*Paratexts*, 207). In Dostoevsky's case, we find both anxiety and bravado.

[37] Vetlovskaia deduces some of the narrator's character from his speech genres (*Poetika romana "Brat'ia Karamazovy"* [Leningrad: Nauka, 1977], 13–51).

To appreciate just how unusual Dostoevsky's introduction is—not only for his own body of work, but for literature in general—we appeal again to Genette, who provides perspective on the matter. He produces an informal two-fold typology of prefaces in his *Paratexts*. We reviewed them at the outset of this study: authorial, allographic, and actorial; plus authentic, fictional, and apocryphal forms of these three types.[38] Dostoevsky almost exclusively uses the fictional varieties of authorial introduction. Once, in *Dead House*, we find an allographic foreword in his work, and the actorial form is activated surreptitiously in many of his works where the narrator also plays some indeterminate role in the plot. Despite Genette's scouring the literature, in no instance does he locate a preface that engages in a combination of these types simultaneously. Remarkably, Dostoevsky's does. His is a foreword that delivers readers a combination of a disavowing authorial prologue, a fictive allographic preface, and even a fictive actorial introduction. As Genette notes, all the subtypes normally represent distinct prefatorial subgenres that do not overlap.[39] Dostoevsky developed an introduction to *The Brothers Karamazov* by inviting his literary persona and fictional narrator-chronicler to perform the speech acts together in dialogic form, that is, as dramatized free indirect speech. As prefaces go, it is unique in the dramatic way it presents dual, even triple voicing.

It is not sufficient, however, to leave Dostoevsky's foreword to *The Brothers Karamazov* on a mere formal note. There is more to it than the virtuoso performance of several voices. The substance of the preface "From the Author" calls for something more than a depiction of its covert dialogue between authorial types—the master and the novice. It is of great import that the implied author's (the master's) mask slips in the introduction. We get a sneaking suspicion that the poor novice's insecurities are no more and no less than Dostoevsky's own. Authors run great risks when they subject their work to the judgment of diverse and independent audiences. It appears that great authors, too, can suffer such anxiety even in their very final "first words."

---

[38] "Fictional actorial," Genette claims, is a redundancy (*Paratexts*, 178–179). Rather than using "fictional authorial," however, I think that "fictional actorial" is also apropos in describing the narrator-chronicler of *The Brothers Karamazov*. In this he is similar to Anton Lavrentievich in *Demons*.

[39] Genette, *Paratexts*, 184–188.

Conclusion

We began this study with a discussion of the variety of names Dostoevsky utilized to label his introductions. We conclude both with a discussion of the variety of forms they take and with speculations on the reason for this variety. The array of prefatorial types is remarkable. They can appear in a footnote. They sometimes dissolve into a first chapter. They can be walled off from the following narrative, being complete narratives unto themselves. They might first appear to follow convention, but then suddenly break with it. Voices multiply within the discourse. Readers are led (by a preface label or a signature) to think the authorial persona is speaking, only to find clues that lead to yet other voices. In Dostoevsky's oeuvre, what is foreword can sometimes work backward.

Three of Dostoevsky's first-person narratives do not contain introductions: *The Humiliated and Insulted*, "The Gambler," and *The Adolescent*.[1] Three of the first-person novels present conventional introductions, conventional in the sense that upon a first encounter with them the reader can glean information useful to apprehending some basic elements of the upcoming text: *The Village of Stepanchikovo*, *Notes from the House of the Dead*, and *Demons*. And three novels are prefaced in three unconventional ways: *Notes from the House of the Dead*, *Notes from the Underground*, and *The Brothers Karamazov*.[2]

---

[1] The narrator-protagonist, Arkady Markarovich Dolgoruky, refers to his first remarks as his "foreword" (*predislovie*); Dostoevsky refrains from using any label for the novel's first words.

[2] *House of the Dead* is included twice because of its dual nature. The editor's allographic introduction is conventional; Dostoevsky's embedded preface is unique.

Each experiments with the subgenre and provides a unique experience relative to the others.

As a consequence of his experimentation with first words, it is difficult to hold Dostoevsky's prefaces to a rigid set of expectations or to corral them together into a unified theory that can adequately contain their diversity. Nevertheless, the introductions share several invariant features. First, in *The Diary of a Writer* Dostoevsky speaks in the voice of his authorial persona on the four occasions when he provides an introduction (or layers of introduction) to a piece of fiction; in all other prefaces he does not speak for himself. Second, Dostoevsky's forewords are built out of a destabilizing discourse. Who is speaking and why they speak is puzzling, and not only on a first reading. Third, the introductions all play with reader expectations about what prefaces in realist practice are or should be. Fourth, whenever Dostoevsky published an originally serialized work in a subsequent full edition of the text, he always retained the original preface. And he never added a foreword to a work that lacked one in the first place. When he put them to use, Dostoevsky intended them to remain there permanently. Beyond these constants, Dostoevsky's use of introductions inclines toward diversity.

Dostoevsky utilized forewords for first-person narratives only. To escape uniformity, and thus to challenge himself and his readers, he changed their shape at every turn. For example, the apparent similarity between the "Introductory"/Chapter One of *The Village of Stepanchikovo* and the "Instead of an Introduction"/Chapter One of *Demons* is merely cosmetic. In *Demons* Dostoevsky changed the function of *Stepanchikovo*'s dual-purpose preface. He linked the introduction to the final chapters of *Demons* and thereby reshaped its contours to lead us to a possible third story (the narrator's complicity in the intrigue). The potential for a third story in *Stepanchikovo* was not realized, but Dostoevsky built on it subsequently. In another instance, Dostoevsky recycled the label "From the Author" of "A Gentle Creature" and reused it in *The Brothers Karamazov*. But the referent for the noun "author" differs from one work to the other; the implied author addresses his readers in the former, and a divided authorial persona performs in the latter. Another loosening of the signifier-signified relationship occurs in *Demons* where Dostoevsky labeled the preface "Instead of an Introduction," which points toward the fact that it functions as something other than what might normally be expected. It became a Chapter One. And in yet another instance, the footnoted introduction to *Notes from the Underground* draws its inspiration from the many footnotes Dostoevsky attached to stories and articles not of his making in *Time* and *Epoch*. By affixing his name to the footnote, he created the illusion that he was speaking for himself in *Underground*. But he wasn't. In sum, Dostoevsky multiplied the forms of first-person narrative in his introductions so that even those that appear to be alike differ in important ways.

All the texts we have examined present first-person narratives, from *The Village of Stepanchikovo* to *The Brothers Karamazov*. But there is no hard and fast rule to be gleaned from this fact. *Humiliated and Insulted* (1861), "The Gambler" (1866), and *The Adolescent* (1875), all first person narratives, do not contain forewords. Thus, introductions appear in the fiction under one narratological condition: first-person discourse. But this condition does not dictate the use of an introduction. *Humiliated and Insulted* and *The Adolescent* are generally considered inferior works in Dostoevsky's oeuvre, but this is not because they lack prefaces. If this were the case, then *The Village of Stepanchikovo* would have gone without and "The Gambler" would certainly have acquired one. No, there is something different going on in the prefaced first-person narratives. Another narrative strategy affects the use of prefaces in Dostoevsky's art. That strategy pertains to three interrelated devices: the verbal equivalent of a picture frame, rhetorical framing, and frame narratives.

One of the key consequences of Dostoevsky's choice of a type of fictional introduction has to do with its framing capacity. Or, conversely, Dostoevsky's choice of a frame for any given work determined the preface he developed for it. Different works called for different approaches. Furthermore, the interaction of foreword and frame was dynamic. Dostoevsky learned from each attempt. As we have just seen, he capitalized on the potential of any given form and reshaped it for new purposes, most often in the direction of multiple voicing, greater rhetorical complexity, and narratological depth.

For instance, and as we have seen already, the opportunity for exploiting the frame narrative to produce a third story that was missed in *The Village of Stepanchikovo* was seized in *Demons*. These two novels represent the only two instances where there is a complete structure surrounding the story. Front and back portions of the text meet to create a frame narrative. In all the other works with introductions, Dostoevsky appealed to alternative models of the device.

In *Notes from the Underground* Dostoevsky wished to provide a preparatory set of remarks that would frame his narrative. In it he provides a context—argumentative and historical—for the subsequent presentation. The result is a prologue, something rarely used by Dostoevsky except in his journalism. In *Underground* the vocal performance shares rhetorical features with the theater. A figure introduces facets of the drama that is about to commence, and does so from the very stage on which the monologue unfolds. In some of his remarks, he also adopts the voice of the protagonist, thus foreshadowing the Underground Man's vocal strategies. This rhetorical framing suited Dostoevsky's purposes in setting the scene, and a footnoted introduction fit that framing purpose.

Notes from the House of the Dead presents a self-contained frame, akin, let us say, to those we find around pictures. The figure of the fictional editor who introduces Goryanchikov's *House of the Dead* memoir is developed in near complete conformity with convention. The introduction is entirely closed off narratologically and chronotopically from Goryanchikov's text. But the walled-off frame of the editor's discourse (in his misguided attempt to contextualize Goryanchikov's memoir) is broken apart by the implied author who subverts the editor's position in the text's very first utterances. Here Dostoevsky set two points of view in opposition to each other: bourgeois self-content versus the quest for self knowledge and spiritual growth. He chose a frame, set off from the text, that ends up depicting the editor more than Goryanchikov. The introduction therefore comes off more like the shortest of short stories, framed and contained unto itself, about the editor's perspective on life. The fictional allographic preface, similar to the one in Pushkin's *Belkin Tales*, suited Dostoevsky's purposes precisely.

Dostoevsky opted for these three types when developing a first-person narrative for which he felt the need of a frame: frame narrative with its third-tale potential, framing preface with its rhetorical positioning, and the picture-framed introduction whole unto itself as a separable text. Dostoevsky chose from these frame types as he contemplated how to set his readers loose into his tale. But he was not content with any given form. Because they were odd, they challenged readers to deal with them as discrete elements of the narrative. Dostoevsky seems never to have been satisfied with the results, so he continued to tinker. As a result, his prefatorial practice evolved at each step. In keeping with his inclination to mystify readers at the outset of a new tale, Dostoevsky developed the form for the last time in his final work of fiction.

In yet another challenge to his readers, the preface-frame connection that governed his practice throughout the exile years dissolves in *The Brothers Karamazov*. Dostoevsky asks us one more time to abandon any automatic reading habits we have acquired and to deal with the foreword to *The Brothers Karamazov* on its own new terms. In developing his foreword, Dostoevsky again appealed to prior practice. This preface "From the Author" possesses affinities with "A Gentle Creature" in terms of its label, with *Underground* in terms of double-voicing, and with *House of the Dead* in the way the text of the introduction is walled off from the narrative itself. But again Dostoevsky reworks these earlier forms to achieve something unique. In *The Brothers Karamazov* "From the Author" becomes "From Two Authors." Free indirect speech of *Underground*'s footnoted introduction becomes a dramatic dialogue between two distinct figures. In *The Brothers Karamazov* the possibility of a covert message, in the style of the introduction to *House of the Dead*, was jettisoned.

The rich and suggestive play in which Dostoevsky engaged in his many introductions prior to *The Brothers Karamazov* is almost completely abandoned in his last novel. There is nothing embedded linguistically or structurally that might assist us in encountering the text, no ideological claims limned, no telling identification of the work's genre (other than the novel's sequel), and precious little presaging of the work's themes. We are left, in the first words of Dostoevsky's final work, with an author in meta-dialogue with another author, a practiced writer speaking with a novice, an accomplished Dostoevsky persona imagining a new work together with a projected self that suffers the many anxieties that the creative act provokes. Rather than being "brief and lame," this introduction seems frighteningly honest and revealing.

To summarize, Dostoevsky used different labels for his introductions to call our attention to them, so that we might attend to them.

He created different forms of preface to underscore the importance of de-automatized perception. He challenged, and continues to challenge, us to extend our awareness beyond the text to the process of creation itself. Not to belabor the obvious, we are asked to realize that a preface comes at us first in our reading because Dostoevsky chose these specific utterances to initiate the work. In his choices we encounter the creative artist himself.

To appreciate just what this means for the limited and focused device introductions represent for prose fiction, we can now summarize the choices Dostoevsky had before him each time he published a new work or began to publish a new work serially. For omniscient narrative and for *The Diary of a Writer*, Dostoevsky had a clear, perhaps restrictive, sense of what he wished to do for his text's first words: no foreword for omniscient narrations; authentic (implied) authorial address for *The Diary*. But for the vast majority of his post-exile fiction, he opted for first-person narratives in which the word is destabilized, for Dostoevsky's narrators suffer a limited perspective, and they are prone to error and riven by subjectivity, often to the extent of thorough unreliability.

When we consider Dostoevsky's choice to include a preface in any given work (or a zero preface, as the case may be), it is useful to recall the open moment he occupied when creating it. He could opt, for example, to use one of the normative forewords taken from the canon (Pushkin, Gogol, Lermontov), which he did with *Stepanchikovo* and *House of the Dead*; or he could innovate, which he did most everywhere else either by using hybrid forms of the typologies that Genette describes or by fusing or separating the vocal performance of the preface from the story's discourse.

Except for *The Diary*, where it was called for by the work's threshold nature, Dostoevsky shied away from an authentic authorial introduction, the most commonly attested type in literature. Dostoevsky did not wish to be overtly directive in his fiction. Nor did he wish to "poke his nose out of his hole into the great world" in the manner of Gogol's Rudy Panko. Like his beloved Pushkin, he chose to remain in the background and to allow other voices to speak, not for him, but for themselves. We might call it cover. But I think this too reductive a position to take. Better to call it Dostoevskian dialogism, a dialogism that begins with the text's first words.

Conclusion

What we understand as Dostoevsky's antipathy to any final word, any absolute judgment, allows us to apprehend authorial freedom and therefore to reconnect with the open and free moment that the creative artist provides our experience. In his fiction's introductions, in their initial utterances, Dostoevsky inscribed his first, finalized aesthetic choices onto the page. And he insisted on them remaining there into the ages. They mattered to him.

Bibliography

Prose Fiction

Bestuzhev-Marlinskii, A. A. *Vtoroe polnoe sobranie sochinenii*. 4 vols. St. Petersburg: n.p., 1847.

Bulgarin, Faddei. *Sochineniia*. Moscow: Sovremennik, 1990.

Chernyshevsky, Nikolai. *What is to be Done?* Translated by Michael R. Katz. Cornell: Cornell University Press, 1989.

Dostoevskii, F. M. *Polnoe sobranie sochinenii v 30-i tomakh*. Leningrad: Nauka, 1972–1990.

———. "Zapiski iz podpol'ia." *Epokha*, no. 1 (1864): 497–519; no. 2 (1864): 293–367.

Dostoevsky, F. M. *The Brothers Karamazov*. Translated by Richard Pevear and Larissa Volokhonsky. San Francisco: North Point Press, 1990.

———. *Demons*. Translated by Richard Pevear and Larissa Volokhonsky. New York: Vintage Books, 1994.

———. *A Gentle Creature and Other Stories*. Translated by Alan Myers. New York: Oxford University Press, 1995.

———. *Memoirs from the House of the Dead*. Edited by Ronald Hingley. Translated by Jessie Coulson. New York: Oxford University Press, 1983.

———. *Notes from Underground*. Translated by Richard Pevear and Larissa Volokhonsky. New York: Vintage Books, 1994.

———. *Pis'ma v chetyrekh tomakh*. Edited by A. Dolinin. Moscow: Akademiia and Golitizdat, 1928–1959.

———. *The Unpublished Dostoevsky*. Edited by Carl Proffer. Ann Arbor: Ardis, 1973.

———. *The Village of Stepanchikovo and its Inhabitants*. Translated by Ignat Avsey. Ithaca: Cornell University Press, 1987.

———. *Winter Notes on Summer Impressions*. Translated by David Patterson. Evanston: Northwestern University Press, 1988.

———. *Writer's Diary*, 2 vols. Translated by Kenneth Lantz. Evanston: Northwestern University Press, 1994.
Dostoevskii, Mikhail and Fedor, eds. *Epokha*. St. Petersburg: n.p., 1864–1865.
———. *Vremia*. St. Petersburg: n.p., 1861–1863.
Eliot, Charles W. *Prefaces and Prologues to Famous Books*. In *The Five Foot Shelf of Books*, vol. 37. New York: Collier and Son, 1910.
Gertsen, A. I. *Byloe i dumy*. 2 vols. Moscow: Khudlit, 1987.
Gogol, Nikolai. *The Complete Tales of Nikolai Gogol*, 2 vols. Edited by Leonard J. Kent. Chicago: The University of Chicago Press, 1985.
———. *Dead Souls*. Translated by D. J. Hogarth. London: J. M. Dent and Sons, 1931.
———. *Sobranie khudozhestvennykh proizvedenii v piati tomakh*. Moscow: Akademiia nauk SSSR, 1960.
Goncharov, Ivan. *Oblomov*. Translated by Stephen Pearl. New York: Bunim & Bannigan, 2006.
Greshman, Herbert S. and Kernan B. Whitworth, Jr., eds. *Anthology of Critical Prefaces to the Nineteenth Century French Novel*. Columbia: University of Missouri Press, 1962.
Grigorovich, D. V. *Izbrannye sochinenii*. Moscow: Khudlit, 1955.
Herzen, A. I. *Who is to Blame?* Translated by Michael R. Katz. Cornell: Cornell University Press, 1984.
Hugo, Victor. *The Last Day of a Condemned Man and Other Prison Writings*. Translated by Geoff Woollen. Oxford: Oxford University Press, 1992.
James, Henry. *The Art of the Novel: Critical Prefaces by Henry James*. Edited by Richard P. Blackmur. New York: C. Scribner's Sons, 1934.
Karamzin, N. N. *Letters of a Russian Traveler: 1789–1790*. Translated by Florence Jonas. New York: Columbia University Press, 1957.
———. *Pis'ma russkogo puteshestvennika*. Leningrad: Nauka, 1984.
Lazhechnikov, I. I. *Sochineniia v dvukh tomakh*. Moscow: Khudlit, 1986.
Lermontov, Mikhail. *A Hero of Our Time*. Translated by Vladimir Nabokov. Ann Arbor, MI: Ardis Press, 1988.
———. *Polnoe sobranie sochinenii v piati tomakh*. Moscow: Akademiia, 1936–1952.
Lesage, Alain-René. *The Adventures of Gil Blas de Santillana*. Translated by Tobias Smollett. 2 vols. London: Oxford University Press, 1928.
Marvels of the East (British Library, Cotton MS Vitellius A XV) https:imagesonline.bl.uk/?service=search&action=do_quick_search&language=en&q=Marvels+of+the+East.
Narezhnyi, V. V. *Izbrannye sochineniia v dvukh tomakh*. Moscow: Khudlit, 1956.
Odoevskii, V. F. *Sochineniia v dvukh tomakh*. Moscow: Khudlit, 1981.
Odoevsky, Vladimir F. *Russian Nights*. Translated by Olga Olienikov and Ralph E. Matlaw. New York: E. P. Dutton & Co., 1965.

Pushkin, Alexander. *Complete Prose Fiction*. Translated by Paul Debrezeny. Stanford: Stanford University Press, 1983.
———. *Sobranie sochinenii v desiati tomakh*. Moscow: Khudlit, 1960.
Scott, Sir Walter. *Ivanhoe*. Norwalk, CT: The Heritage Press, 1950.
———. *The Prefaces to the Waverley Novels by Sir Walter Scott*. Edited by Mark A. Weinstein. Lincoln: University of Nebraska Press, 1978.
Senkovsky, Osip. *The Fantastic Journeys of Baron Brambeus*. Translated by Louis Pedrotti. New York: P. Lang, 1993.
Vel'tman, Aleksandr. *Osip Senkovsky's "The Fantastic Journeys of Baron Brambeus."* Translated by Louis Pedrotti. New York: Peter Lang, 1993.
Zagoskin, M. N. *Sochineniia v dvukh tomakh*. Moscow: Khudlit, 1987.

Scholarly Works Consulted

Abbott, H. Porter. *The Cambridge Introduction to Narrative*. Cambridge: Cambridge University Press, 2002.
Aitken, Gillon and David Budgen. *Alexander Pushkin: The Tales of Belkin*. London: Angel Classics, 1983.
Alexandrov, V. E. "The Narrator as Author in Dostoevskij's *Besy*." *Russian Literature* 15 (1984): 243–254.
Alkire, Gilman H. "Gogol' and Bulgarin's *Ivan Vyzhigin*." *Slavic Review* 28, no. 2 (1969): 289–296.
Allain, Louis. "'Krotkaia' i samoubiitsy v tvorchestve F. M. Dostoevskogo." *Dostoevsky Studies* 4 (2000): 43–52.
Altman, Jane G. *Epistolarity: Approaches to a Form*. Columbus: Ohio State University Press, 1982.
Al'tman, M. S. "Gogolevskie traditsii v tvorchestve Dostoevskogo." *Slavia* 30, no. 3 (1961): 443–461.
Altshuller, Mark. "The Walter Scott Motifs in Nikolay Gogol's Story *The Lost Letter*." *Oxford Slavonic Papers* 22 (1989): 81–88.
Andersen, Zsuzsanna Bjørn. "The Concepts of Domination and Powerlessness in F. M. Dostoevsky's 'A Gentle Spirit.'" *Dostoevsky Studies* 4 (2000): 53–60.
Anderson, Nancy K. *The Perverted Ideal in Dostoevsky's "The Devils."* New York: Peter Lang, Middlebury Studies in Russian Language and Literature, 1997.
Andreeva, A. N., ed. *Poetika zaglaviia*. Moscow-Tver': Liliia, 2005.
Annenkov, P. V. *Literaturnye vospominaniia*. Moscow: Khudlit, 1960.
Apollonio, Carol, ed. *The New Russian Dostoevsky: Readings for the Twenty-First Century*. Bloomington: Slavica, 2010.
———. "Prophecy in 'The Peasant Marei.'" *Dostoevsky Studies* 18 (2014): 45–58.
Bagby, Lewis. *Alexander Bestuzhev-Marlinsky and Russian Byronism*. University Park: Pennsylvania University Press, 1995.

———. "'Brief and Lame': The Introduction to Dostoevsky's *The Brothers Karamazov.*" *Slavic and East European Journal* 55, no. 2 (2011): 229–244.

———. "Chronotopoi of Pre-Conversion: *Notes from a Dead House.*" *California Slavic Studies* 18, no. 3 (1995): 39–53.

———. "Dostoyevsky's *Notes from a Dead House.*" *The Modern Language Review* 81, no. 1 (1986): 139–152.

———, ed. *Lermontov's "A Hero of Our Time: A Critical Companion."* Evanston: Northwestern University Press and The American Association of Teachers of Slavic and East European Languages, 2002.

———. "Vvedenie v 'Krotkuiu': Pisatel'/Chitatel'/Ob"ekt." *Dostoevsky Studies* 9 (1988): 127–135.

Bakhtin, Mikhail M. *The Dialogic Imagination.* Edited by Michael Holquist. Translated by Caryl Emerson and Michael Holquist. Minneapolis: University of Minnesota, 1984.

———. *Problems of Dostoevsky's Poetics.* Edited and translated by Caryl Emerson. Minneapolis: University of Minnesota Press, 1984.

———. *Problemy poetiki Dostoevskogo.* Moscow: Khudlit, 1972.

———. *Sobranie sochinenii.* Moscow: Russkie slovari: iazyki slavianskoi kul'tury, 2002.

———. *Voprosy literatury i estetiki.* Moscow: Khudlit, 1975.

Belkin, A. A. "*Brat'iia Karamazovy* (sotsial'no-filosofskaia problematika)." In *Tvorchestvo F. M. Dostoevskogo*, edited by N. L. Stepanov, D. D. Blagoi, U. A. Gural'nik, and B. S. Riurikov, 265–292. Moscow: Akademiia nauk SSSR, 1959.

Belknap, Robert L. "'The Gentle Creature' as the Climax of a Work of Art that Almost Exists." *Dostoevsky Studies* 4 (2000): 35–42.

———. "Memory in *The Brothers Karamazov.*" In *Dostoevsky. New Perspectives*, edited by Robert Louis Jackson, 227–242. Englewood Cliffs, NJ: Prentice-Hall, 1984.

———. "The *Siuzhet* of Part One of *Crime and Punishment.*" In *Dostoevsky on the Threshold of Other Worlds (Essays in Honour of Malcolm V. Jones)*, edited by Sarah Young and Lesley Milne, 153–156. Ilkeston: Bramcote Press, 2006.

———. *The Structure of The Brothers Karamazov.* The Hague: Mouton, 1968.

———. "The Unrepentant Confession." In *Russianness: Studies on a Nation's Identity (In Honor of Rufus Mathewson)*, 113–123. Ann Arbor: Ardis, 1990.

Berdiaev, Nikolai. *Dostoevsky.* New York: Meridian Books, 1966.

Bernstein, Michael Andre. *Bitter Carnival: Ressentiment and The Abject Hero.* Princeton, NJ: Princeton University Press, 1992.

Bethea, David M. *Realizing Metaphors: Alexander Pushkin and the Life of the Poet.* Madison: Wisconsin University Press, 1998.

Bethea, David M. and Sergei Davydov. "Pushkin's Saturnine Cupid: The Poetics of Parody in *The Tales of Belkin*." *PMLA* 96, no. 1 (Jan. 1981): 8–21.

Bitsilli, P. M. "K voprosu o vnutrennei forme romana Dostoevskogo." In *O Dostoevskom: Stat'i*, edited by Donald Fanger, 3–71. Providence: Brown University Press, 1966.

Blackmur, R. P., ed. *The Art of the Novel: Critical Prefaces by Henry James*. New York: Charles Scribner's Sons, 1937.

———. "*The Brothers Karamazov*." In *Eleven Essays in the European Novel*, 185–243. New York and Burlingame: Harcourt, Brace & World, 1964.

Bocharov, S. G. "Bezdna prostranstva." In *Povesti Belkina: K 200-letiiu so dnia rozhdeniia A. S. Pushkina*, edited by N. K. Gei and I. L. Popova, 461–479. Moscow: Nasledie, 1999.

———. *Poetika Pushkina: Ocherki*. Moscow: Nauka, 1974.

Bojanowska, Edyta M. *Nikolai Gogol: Between Ukrainian and Russian Nationalism*. Cambridge: Harvard University Press, 2007.

Booth, Wayne C. *The Rhetoric of Fiction*. Chicago: University of Chicago Press, 1961.

Børtnes, Jostein. "Polyphony in *The Brothers Karamazov*: Variations on a Theme." *Canadian-American Slavic Studies* 17, no. 3 (1983): 402–411.

Børtnes, Jostein and Ingunn Lunde, eds. *Cultural Discontinuity and Reconstruction: the Byzanto-Slav Heritage and the Creation of a Russian National Literature in the Nineteenth Century*. Oslo: Solum Forlag, 1997.

Braun, Maximilian. "*The Brothers Karamazov* as an Expository Novel." *Canadian-American Slavic Studies* 6 (1972): 199–208.

Briggs, A. D. P. *Alexander Pushkin: A Critical Study*. Totowa, NJ: Barnes and Noble Books, 1983.

Bulanov, A. M. "Stat'ia Ivana Karamazova o tserkovno-obshchestvennom sude v ideino-khudozhestvennoi structure poslednego romana Dostoevskogo." In *F. M. Dostoevskii: materialy i issledovaniia*, edited by A. S. Dolinin, 125–136. Leningrad: Nauka, 1944.

Burnett, Leon, ed. *F. M. Dostoevsky 1821–1881: A Centenary Collection*. Oxford: Holdan Books, 1981.

Cardici, Paul F. "Dostoevsky's Underground as Allusion and Symbol." *Symposium* 28 (1974): 248–258.

Catteau, J. "De la structure de *La Maison des Morts* de F. M. Dostoevskij." *Revue des études slaves* 54 (1982): 63–72.

———. *Dostoevsky and the Process of Literary Creation*. Translated by Audrey Littlewood. Cambridge: Cambridge University Press, 1989.

———. "The Paradox of the Legend of the Grand Inquisitor in *The Brothers Karamazov*." In *Dostoyevsky. New Perspectives*, edited by Robert Louis Jackson, 243–254. Englewood Cliffs, NJ: Prentice-Hall 1984.

Chances, Ellen. "Literary Criticism and the Ideology of 'Pochvennichestvo' in Dostoevsky's Thick Journals *Vremia* and *Epokha*." *Russian Review* 34 (1975): 151–164.

———. "Počvenničestvo—Evolution of an Ideology," *Modern Fiction Studies* 20 (1975): 543–551.

———. "Pochvennichestvo: Ideology in Dostoevsky's Periodicals," *Mosaic* 7, no. 2 (1974): 71–88.

Chicherin, A. V. "Poeticheskii stroi iazyka v romanakh Dostoevskogo." In *Tvorchestvo F. M. Dostoevskogo*, edited by N. L. Stepanov, D. D. Blagoi, U. A. Gural'nik, and B. S. Riurikov, 417–444. Moscow: Akademiia nauk SSSR, 1959.

Christa, Boris. "'Money Talks': The Semiotic Anatomy of 'Krotkaia.'" *Dostoevsky Studies* 4 (2000): 143–152.

Cohn, Dorrit. *Transparent Minds: Narrative Modes for Presenting Consciousness in Fiction*. Princeton: Princeton University Press, 1978.

Connolly, Julian W. *Intimate Stranger: Meetings with the Devil in Nineteenth-Century Russian Literature*. Middlebury Studies in Russian Language and Literature. New York: Peter Lang, 2001

Consigny, Scott. "The Paradox of Textuality: Writing as Entrapment and Deliverance in *Notes from Underground*." *Canadian-American Slavic Studies* 12 (1978): 341–352.

Cox, Gary. "Geographic, Sociological, and Sexual Tensions in Gogol's Dikan'ka Stories." *Slavic and East European Journal* 24 (1980): 219–232.

Cravens, Craig. "The Strange Relationship of Stavrogin and Stepan Trofimovich as Told by Anton Lavrent'evich G-v." *Slavic Review* 59, no. 4 (2000): 782–801.

Danov, David K. *The Dialogic Sign: Essays on the Major Novels of Dostoevsky*. New York: Peter Lang, 1991.

———. "Notes on Generating a Text: *The Brothers Karamazov*." *Modern Language Studies* 11 (1980–1981): 75–95.

———. "Stavrogin's Teachings: Reported Speech in *The Possessed*." *Slavic and East European Journal* 32 (1988): 213–224.

Davison, Roy M. "Aspects of Novelistic Technique in Dostoevskii's *Besy*." In *From Pushkin to Palisandriia: Essays on the Russian Novel in Honor of Richard Freeborn*, edited by Arnold McMillin, 83–95. New York: St. Martin's Press, 1990.

———. "*The Devils*: The Role of Stavrogin." In *New Essays on Dostoyevsky*, edited by Malcolm V. Jones and Garth M. Terry, 95–114. Cambridge: Cambridge University Press, 1983.

Davydov, Sergei. "Pushkin's Merry Undertaking and 'The Coffinmaker.'" *Slavic Review* 44, no. 1 (1985): 30–48.

Debreczeny, Paul. *The Other Pushkin*. Stanford: Stanford University Press, 1983.

———. *Social Functions of Literature: Alexander Pushkin and Russian Culture.* Stanford: Stanford University Press, 1997.

Demin, A. S., A. S. Eleonskaia, L. A. Itigina, A. S. Kurilov, Iu. A. Labyntsev, L. I. Sazonova, L. A. Sofronova, and L. A. Chernaia, eds. *Tematika i stilistika predislovii i poslesłovii.* Moscow: Nauka, 1981.

Dolinin, A. S., ed. *Dostoevskii: Stat'i i materialy: sbornik statei.* Leningrad and Moscow: Mysl', 1924.

———. "K istorii sozdaniia *Brat'ia Karamazovy*." In *F. M. Dostoevskii: Materialy i issledovaniia*, edited by A. S. Dolinin, 9–80. Leningrad: AN SSSR, 1934.

———. "Krotkaia." In *F. M. Dostoevskii: Stat'i i materialy*, Vol. 2, edited by A. S. Dolinin, 423–438. Leningrad: Mysl', 1925.

Dowler, Wayne. *Dostoevsky, Grigor'ev, and Native-Soil Conservatism.* Toronto: University of Toronto Press, 1982.

Driessen, F. C. *Gogol as a Short-Story Writer.* Translated by Ian F. Finlay. The Hague: Mouton and Co., 1965.

Egorenkova, G. I. "Siuzhetnost' kompozitsii (nekotorye osobennosti khudozhestvennoi struktury romana Dostoevskogo *Brat'ia Karamazovy*)." *Filologicheskie nauki* 6 (1976): 14–24.

Erlich, Victor. *Gogol.* New Haven: Yale University Press, 1969.

———, ed. *Twentieth Century Russian Literary Criticism.* New Haven: Yale University Press, 1975.

Etov, V. I. *Dostoevskii: Ocherk tvorchestva.* Moscow: Prosveshchenie, 1968.

Evnin, F. I. "Roman *Besy*." In *Tvorchestvo F. M. Dostoevskogo*, edited by N. L. Stepanov, D. D. Blagoi, U. A. Gural'nik, and B. S. Riurikov, 215–264. Moscow: Akademiia nauk SSSR, 1959.

———. "Roman *Prestuplenie i nakazanie*." In *Tvorchestvo Dostoevskogo*, edited by N. L. Stepanov, D. D. Blagoi, U. A. Gural'nik, and B. S. Riurikov, 128–172. Moscow: Akademiia nauk SSSR, 1959.

Fanger, Donald. *The Creation of Nikolai Gogol.* Cambridge, MA: Harvard University Press, 1979.

Fitzgerald, Gene D. "Antithetic Stylistic Elements in Dostoevskij's Narrative." PhD dissertation, University of Wisconsin, 1971.

———. "Anton Lavrent'evic G-v: The Narrator as Recreator in Dostoevsky's *The Possessed*." In *New Perspectives on Nineteenth-century Russian Prose*, edited by G. J. Gutsche and L. G. Leighton, 121–134. Columbus: Slavica, 1982.

———. "The Chronology of F. M. Dostoevskij's *The Possessed*." *Slavic and East European Journal* 27 (1983): 19–46.

Forrester, James. *Why You Should: The Pragmatics of Deontic Speech.* Hanover, NH: University Press of New England for Brown University Press, 1989.

Fortunatov, N. M. "Cherty arkhitektoniki Dostoevskogo." In *Puti iskanii: O masterstve Pisatelia*, 84–104. Moscow: Sovetskii pisatel', 1974.

Frank, Joseph. *Dostoevsky*. 5 vols. Princeton: Princeton University Press, 1976–2002.

———. "Dostoevsky's Discovery of 'Fantastic Realism.'" *Russian Review* 27 (1968): 286–295.

———. "Dostoevsky: The Encounter with Europe." *Russian Review* 22 (1963): 237–252.

Franklin, Simon. "Novels without Ends: Notes on *Eugene Onegin* and *Dead Souls*." *Modern Language Review* 79 (1984): 372–383.

Frantz, Philip E. *Gogol: A Bibliography*. Ann Arbor, MI: Ardis Press, 1989.

Frazier, Melissa. *Frames of the Imagination: Gogol's* Arabesques *and the Romantic Question of Genre*. New York: Peter Lang, 2000.

———. *Romantic Encounters: Writers, Readers, and the "Library for Reading."* Stanford: Stanford University Press, 2007.

Fridlender, G. M. "Novye knigi o Dostoevskom." *Russkaia literature* 2 (1964): 179–190.

———. "Put' Dostoevskogo k romanu-epopee." In *Dostoevskii: Materialy i issledovaniia* 8, edited by G. M. Fridlender, 159–176. Leningrad: Nauka, 1988.

———. *Realizm Dostoevskogo*. Moscow and Leningrad: Nauka, 1964.

Fusso, Susanne. "Husbands and Lovers: Vaudeville Conventions in 'Another Man's Wife,' 'The Jealous Husband,' and *The Eternal Husband*." In *Before They Were Titans: Essays on the Early Works of Dostoevsky and Tolstoy*, edited by Elizabeth Cheresh Allen, 61–92. Brighton, MA: Academic Studies Press, 2015.

———. "Maidens in Childbirth: The Sistine Madonna in Dostoevskii's *Devils*." *Slavic Review* 54, no. 2 (1995): 261–275.

Fusso, Susanne and Priscilla Meyer, eds. *Essays on Gogol: Logos and the Russian Word*. Evanston: Northwestern University Press, 1992.

Gavrilova, Iu. Iu. "Nepreryvnost' povestvovaniia." In *Povesti Belkina: K 200-letiiu so dnia rozhdeniia A. S. Pushkina*, edited by N. K. Gei and I. L. Popova, 555–575. Moscow: Nasledie, 1999.

Gei, N. K. "Mir *Povestei Belkina*." In *Povesti Belkina: K 200-letiiu so dnia rozhdeniia A. S. Pushkina*, edited by N. K. Gei and I. L. Popova, 384–460. Moscow: Nasledie, 1999.

Genette, Gérard. *Paratexts: Thresholds of Interpretation*. Translated by Jane E. Lewin. Cambridge: Cambridge University Press, 1997.

Gershman, Herbert S. and Kernan B. Whitworth, Jr., eds. *Anthology of Critical Prefaces in the Nineteenth Century French Novel*. Columbia, MO: University of Missouri Press, 1962.

Gibian, George. "The Grotesque in Dostoevsky." *Modern Fiction Studies* 4 (1958): 262–270.

Gippius, V. V. *Gogol'*. Leningrad: Mysl', 1924.

———. *Ot Pushkina do Bloka*. Moscow and Leningrad: Nauka, 1966.

Gleason, Abbot. *Young Russia*. New York: The Viking Press, 1980.

Goloskover, Ia. *Dostoevskii i Kant*. Moscow: Akademiia nauk, 1963.

Grayson, Jane and Faith Wigzell, eds. *Gogol: Text and Context*. New York: St. Martin's Press, 1989.

Gregg, Richard. "The Curse of Sameness and the Gogolian Esthetic: 'The Tale of the Two Ivans' as Parable." *Slavic and East European Journal* 312 (1987): 1–9.

Grishin, D. V. *Dostoevskii-chelovek, pisatel' i mify: Dostoevskii i ego "Dnevnik pisatelia."* Melbourne: Melbourne University Press, 1971.

Grossman, L. P. *Dostoevsky: His Life and Work*. Translated by Mary Mackler. New York: The Bobbs-Merrill Co., 1975.

———. *Poetika Dostoevskogo*. Moscow: Gosudarstvennaia akademiia khudozhestvennykh nauk, 1925.

———. "The Stylistics of Stavrogin's Confession: A Study of the New Chapter of *The Possessed*." In *Critical Essays on Dostoevsky*, edited by Robin Feuer Miller, 148–158. Boston: G. K. Hall, 1986.

———. "Stilistika Stavrogina." In *Poetika Dostoevskogo*, 144–163. Moscow: Akademiia nauk, 1925.

Gutsche, George. "Dinner at Smirdin's: Forces in Russian Print Culture in the Early Reign of Nicholas I." In *The Space of the Book*, edited by Miranda Remnek, 54–81. Toronto: University of Toronto Press, 2011.

———. "Puškin and Belinskij: The Role of the Offended Provincial." In *New Perspectives on Nineteenth-Century Russian Prose*, edited by George J. Gutsche and Lauren G. Leighton, 41–59. Columbus, OH: Slavica, 1982.

Hingley, Ronald. *The Undiscovered Dostoyevsky*. London: Hamish Hamilton, 1962.

Holland, Kate. "The Fictional Filter: 'Krotkaia' and *The Diary of a Writer*." *Dostoevsky Studies* 4 (2000): 95–116.

———. *The Novel in the Age of Disintegration: Dostoevsky and the Problem of Genre in the 1870s*. Evanston: Northwestern University Press, 2013.

Holquist, James M. "Plot and Counter-plot in *Notes from the Underground*." *Canadian-American Slavic Studies* 6 (1972): 225–238.

Holquist, Michael. *Dostoevsky and the Novel*. Princeton: Princeton University Press, 1971.

Horst-Jurgen, Gerigk, ed. *"Die Bruder Karamasow," Dostojewskijs letzter Roman in heutiger Sicht*. Dresden: Dresden University Press, 1997.

Hudspith, Sarah. *Dostoevsky and the Idea of Russianness*. London: RoutledgeCurzon, 2004.

Iakubova, Rima. "Dostoevsky's Novel *Demons* and the Russian Balagan." In *The New Russian Dostoevsky*, edited by Carol Apollonio, 189–216. Bloomington: Slavica, 2010.

Iakubovich, D. P. "Predislovie k 'Povestiam Belkina' i povestvovatel'nye priemy Val'ter Skotta." In *Pushkin v mirovoi literature: sbornik statei*, 160–187. Leningrad: Gos. izdatel'stvo, 1926.

Isenberg, Charles. *Telling Silence: Russian Frame Narratives of Renunciation.* Evanston: Northwestern University Press, 1993.

Ivanchikova, Ye. A. *Sintaksis khudozhestvennoi prozy Dostoevskogo.* Moscow: n.p., 1979.

Ivask, George. "Dostoevsky's Wit." *Russian Review* 21 (1962): 154–164.

Jackson, Robert Louis. "Aristotelian Movement and Design in Part Two of *Notes from Underground*." In *Dostoevsky: New Perspectives*, edited by Robert Louis Jackson, 66–81. Englewood Cliffs, NJ: Prentice Hall, 1984.

———. *The Art of Dostoevsky: Deliriums and Nocturnes.* Princeton: Princeton University Press, 1981.

———. *Close Encounters: Essays on Russian Literature.* Boston: Academic Studies Press, 2013.

———. "Dostoevsky's Critique of the Aesthetics of Dobroliubov." *Slavic Review* 23 (1964): 258–274.

———, ed. *Dostoevsky: New Perspectives.* Englewood Cliffs, NJ: Prentice Hall, 1984.

———. *Dostoevsky's* Notes from the Underground *in Russian Literature.* Westport: Greenwood Press, 1981.

———. *Dostoevsky's Quest for Form: A Study of His Philosophy of Art.* New Haven: Yale University Press, 1966.

———, ed. *A New Word on "The Brothers Karamazov."* Evanston: Northwestern University Press, 2004.

Janda, Laura A. et al. *Why Russian Aspectual Prefixes Aren't Empty: Prefixes as Verb-Classifiers.* Bloomington, IN: Slavica, 2013.

Jones, John. *Dostoevsky.* Oxford: Clarendon Press, 1983.

Jones, Malcolm V. *Dostoevsky: The Novel of Discord.* London: Paul Elek, 1976.

———. *Dostoyevsky after Bakhtin: Readings in Dostoyevsky's Fantastic Realism.* Cambridge: Cambridge University Press, 1990.

———. "Dostoyevsky: Driving the Reader Crazy." *Essays on Poetics* 12, no. 1 (1987): 57–80.

Jones, Malcolm V. and G. M. Terry, eds. *New Essays on Dostoyevsky.* New York: Cambridge University Press, 1983.

Jovanović, Milivoje. "Tekhnika romana tain v *Bratiiakh Karamazovykh*." *Dostoevsky Studies* 8 (1987): 45–72.

Kabat, Geoffrey C. *Ideology and Imagination: The Image of Society in Dostoevsky.* New York: Columbia University Press, 1978.

Karaulov, Iu. N. and E. L. Ginzburg, eds. *Slovo Dostoevskogo.* Moscow: Azbukovnik, 2001.

Kariakin, Iu. "Zachem khroniker v *Besakh*?" In *Dostoevsky: Materialy i issledovaniia* 5, 113–131. Leningrad: Nauka, 1983.

Karlova, T. S. "O strukturnom znachenii obraza *Mertvogo doma*." In *Dostoevsky: materialy i issledovaniia*, edited by G. M. Fridlender, 135–146. Moscow: Nauka, 1974.

Kavanagh, T. M. "Dostoyevsky's *Notes from Underground*: The Form of the Fiction." *Texas Studies in Language and Literature* 14 (1972): 491–507.

Kelly, Aileen. "Dostoevskii and the Divided Conscience." *Slavic Review* 47, no. 2 (1988): 239–260.

Khagi, Sofya. "Silence and the Rest: The Inexpressible from Batiushkov to Tiutchev." *Slavic and East European Journal* 48 (2004): 41–61.

Kim, Sang Hyun. *Aleksandr Pushkin's "The Tales of Belkin."* Lanham, MD: University Press of America, 2008.

Kirai, D. "Dostoevskii i nekotorye voprosy estetiki romana." In *Dostoevskii: Materialy i issledovaniia*, 1, edited by G. M. Fridlender, 83–99. Moscow: Nauka, 1974.

Kirai, Nina. "Dostoevskii: 'Krotkaia'—teatr pamiati." *Dostoevsky Studies* 4 (2000): 61–70.

Kiraly, Gyula. "Nedeklarirovannyi avtor v romanakh Dostoevskogo." *Bulletin of the International Dostoevsky Society* 7 (1977): 100–112.

Kirpotin, V. Ia. "*Brat'ia Karamazovy* kak filosofskii roman." *Voprosy literatury* 12 (1983): 106–135.

———. *Dostoevskii-khudozhnik: Etiudy i issledovaniia*. Moscow: Sovetskii pisatel', 1972.

———. *Dostoevskii v shestidesiatye gody*. Moscow: Khudlit, 1966.

———. "U istokov romana-tragedii: Dostoevskii, Pushkin, Gogol'." In *Dostoevskii i russkie pisateli: Traditsii, novatorstvo, masterstvo: sbornik statei*, edited by V. Ia. Kirpotin, 43–120. Moscow: Sovetskii pisatel', 1972.

———. "*Zapiski iz mertvogo doma*." In *Tvorchestvo Dostoevskogo*, edited by N. L. Stepanov, D. D. Blagoi, U. A. Gural'nik, B. S. Riurikov, 101–127. Moscow: Akademiia nauk, 1959.

———. "*Zapiski iz podpol'ia* F. M. Dostoevskogo." *Russkaia literatura* 1 (1964): 27–48.

Kjetsaa, Gier. *Dostoevsky and His New Testament*. Oslo: Solum Forlag A. S., 1984.

———. *Fyodor Dostoevsky: A Writer's Life*. Translated by Siri Hustvedt and David McDuff. New York: Viking, 1987.

Kleespies, Ingred. *A Nation Astray: Nomadism and National Identity in Russian Literature*. Dekalb: Northern Illinois Press, 2012.

Kodjak, Andrej. *Pushkin's I. P. Belkin*. Columbus, OH: Slavic Publishers, Inc., 1979.

Komarovich, V. L. "'Mirovaia garmoniia' Dostoevskogo." In *O Dostoevskom*, edited by Donald Fanger, 119–149. Providence: Brown University Slavic Reprint, 1966.

Kovacs, Arpad. "Pamiat' kak printsip siuzhetnogo povestvovaniia: *Zapiski iz podpol'ia*." *Weiner slawistishcer almanach* 16 (1985): 81–97.

———. "Printsipy poeticheskoi motivatsii v romane *Besy*." *Dostoevsky Studies* 5 (1984): 49–62.

———. "Problema povestvovatelia i avtora romanov Dostoevskogo v sovremennoi sovetskoi poetike." *Canadian-American Slavic Studies* 15 (1981): 545–553.

Kovsan, M. L. "Khudozhestvennoe vremia v romane F. M. Dostoevskogo *Besy*. *Filologicheskie nauki* 5 (1982): 24–30.

Leatherbarrow, W. J. *The Brothers Karamazov*. Cambridge: Cambridge University Press, 1992.

———, ed. *The Cambridge Companion to Dostoevskii*. Cambridge: Cambridge University Press, 2002.

———, ed. *Dostoevsky's* The Devils: *A Critical Companion*. Evanston: Northwestern University Press, AATSEEL Critical Companions to Russian Literature, 1999.

———. "Pushkin and the Early Dostoevsky." *Modern Language Review* 74, no. 2 (1979): 368–385.

Levin, V. I. "Dostoevskii, 'podpol'nyi paradoksalist' i Lermontov." *Izvestiia Akademii nauk SSSR. Seriia literatury i iazyka* 31 (1972): 142–156.

Lezhnev, A. *Proza Pushkina: Opyt stilevogo issledovaniia*. Moscow: Khudlit, 1966.

———. *Pushkin's Prose*. Translated by Roberta Reeder. Ann Arbor: Ardis Press, 1983.

Likhachev, D. S. "Letopisnoe vremia u Dostoevskogo." In *Poetika drevnerusskoi Literatury*, 319–334. Leningrad: Nauka, 1971.

———. "'Nebrezhenie slovom' u Dostoevskogo." In *Dostoevskii: Materialy i issledovaniia*, vol. 2, edited by G. M. Fridlender, 30–41. Leningrad: Nauka, 1976.

———. "'Predislovnyi rasskaz' Dostoevskogo." In *Poetika i stilistika russkoi literatury: Pamiati akademiki Viktora Vladimirovicha Vinogradova*, edited by M. P. Alekseev, 189–194. Leningrad: Nauka, 1971.

Linner, S. "Dostoevskii's Moral Authority." *Canadian-American Slavic Studies* 17 (1983): 412–421.

Livermore, Gordon. "Stepan Verkhovensky and the Shaping Dialectic of Dostoevsky's *Devils*." In *Dostoevsky: New Perspectives*, edited by Robert Louis Jackson, 176–192. Englewood Cliffs, NJ: Prentice Hall, 1984.

Lounsbery, Anne. "Dostoevskii's Georgraphy: Centers, Peripheries, and Networks in *Demons*." *Slavic Review* 66, no. 2 (2007): 211–229.

———. *Thin Culture, High Art: Gogol, Hawthorne, and Authorship in Nineteenth-Century Russia and America*. Cambridge, MA: Harvard University Press, 2007.

Magarshack, David. *Dostoevsky's Occasional Writings*. Evanston: Northwestern University Press, 1963.

Mann, Iu. *Poetika Gogolia: Variatsii k teme*. Moscow: Coda, 1996.

Martinsen, Deborah A. *Surprised by Shame: Dostoevsky's Liars and Narrative Exposure*. Columbus: The Ohio State University Press, 2003.

Mashinskii, S. *Khudozhestvennyi mir Gogolia*. Moscow: Prosveshchenie, 1979.

Matlaw, Ralph. *The Brothers Karamazov: Novelistic Technique*. The Hague: Mouton, 1957.

———. "Structure and Integration in *Notes from Underground*." In *Notes from Underground*, edited by Robert G. Durgy and translated by Serge Shishkoff, 181–203. Washington, DC: University Press of America, 1969.

McCracken-Flesher, Caroline. *Possible Scotlands: Walter Scott and the Story of Tomorrow*. Oxford: Oxford University Press, 2005.

McGuire, Robert A. *Exploring Gogol*. Stanford: Stanford University Press, 1994.

———. *Gogol from the Twentieth Century*. Princeton: Princeton University Press, 1974.

McLean, Hugh. "Gogol's Retreat from Love: Towards an Interpretation of *Mirgorod*." In *American Contributions to the Fourth International Congress of Slavists*, 225–245. The Hague: Mouton, 1958.

Meerson, Olga. *Dostoevsky's Taboos*. Dresden: Dresden University Press, 1998,

Meijer, J. M. "The Author of *Bratiia Karamazovy*." *Dutch Studies in Russian Literature* 2, no. 2 (1971): 7–46.

———. "A Note on Time in *Bratija Karamazovy*." In *The Brothers Karamazov by F. M. Dostoevskij*, edited by Jan van der Eng and J. M. Meijer, 47–62. The Hague: Mouton and Co., 1971.

———. "Situation Rhyme in a Novel of Dostoevskij." In *Dutch Contributions to the Fourth International Congress of Slavists*, 115–128. The Hague: Mouton and Co., 1958.

———. "The Sixth Tale of Belkin." In *The Tales of Belkin by A. S. Puškin*, edited by Jan van der Eng, 110–134. The Hague: Mouton and Co., 1968.

———. "Some Remarks on Dostoevskij's *Besy*." In *Dutch Contributions to the Fifth International Congress of Slavists*, 125–144. The Hague: Mouton and Co., 1963.

———. "Stilistika Stavrogina." In *Poetika Dostoevskogo*, 144–163. Moscow: Akademiia nauk, 1925.

Merrill, Reed. "The Mistaken Endeavor. Dostoevsky's *Notes from Underground*." *Modern Fiction Studies* 18 (1972): 505–516.

Meyer, Priscilla. "Lermontov's Reading of Pushkin: *The Tales of Belkin* and *A Hero of Our Time*." In *The Golden Age of Russian Literature and*

Thought, edited by Derek Offord, 58–75. New York: St. Martin's Press, 1992.

Meyer, Priscilla and Stephen Rudy, eds. *Dostoevsky and Gogol: Texts and Criticism*. Ann Arbor: Ardis Press, 1979.

Miller, Robin Feuer. *"The Brothers Karamazov": Worlds of the Novel*. New Haven: Yale University Press, 2008.

———, ed. *Critical Essays on Dostoevsky*. Boston: G. K. Hall, 1987.

———. *Dostoevsky and "The Idiot": Author, Narrator and Reader*. Cambridge: Harvard University Press, 1981.

Mirsky, D. S. *Critical Essays on Dostoevsky*. Boston: G. K. Hall, 1986.

———. *A History of Russian Literature*. New York: Knopf, 1958.

Mochizuki, Tetsuo. "The Pendulum is Swinging Insensibly and Disgustingly: Time in 'Krotkaia.'" *Dostoevsky Studies* 4 (2000): 71–82.

Mochulsky, Konstantin. *Dostoevsky: His Life and Work*. Translated by Michael A. Minihan. Princeton: Princeton University Press, 1973.

Moeller-Sally, Stephen. "0000; or, The Sign of the Subject in Gogol's Petersburg." In *Russian Subjects: Empire, Nation and the Culture of the Golden Age*, edited by Monika Greenleaf and Stephen Moeller-Sally, 325–346. Evanston: Northwestern University Press, 1998.

Monas, Sidney. *The Third Section: Police and Society in Russia under Nicholas I*. Cambridge: Harvard University Press, 1961.

Monter, Barbara Heldt. "The Quality of Dostoevskij's Humor: *The Village of Stepanchikovo*." *Slavic and East European Journal* 17 (1973): 33–41.

Moore, Gene M. "The Voices of Legion: The Narrator of the Possessed." *Dostoevsky Studies* 6 (1985): 51–65.

Mørch, Audun J. "Dostoevskij's *Besy*: Revolutionaries with Speech Deficiency." *Scando-Slavica* 39 (1993): 62–73.

Morson, Gary Saul. *The Boundaries of Genre: Dostoevsky's Diary of a Writer and the Traditions of Literary Utopia*. Austin: University of Texas Press, 1981.

———. "Conclusion: Reading Dostoevskii." In *The Cambridge Companion to Dostoevskii*, edited by W. J. Leatherbarrow, 212–234. Cambridge: Cambridge University Press, 2002.

———."The Heresiarch of *Meta*." *PTL: A Journal for Descriptive Poetics and Theory of Literature* 3 (1978): 407–427.

———. *Hidden in Plain View: Narrative and Creative Potentials in "War and Peace."* Stanford: Stanford University Press, 1987.

———. "Introductory Study." In *Fyodor Dostoevsky: A Writer's Diary*, 2 vols. Translated by Kenneth Lantz, I: 1–117. Evanston: Northwestern University Press, 1994.

———. *Narrative and Freedom: The Shadows of Time*. New Haven: Yale University Press, 1994.

———. *Prosaics and Other Provocations: Empathy, Open Time, and the Novel*. Boston: Academic Studies Press, 2013

———. "Verbal Pollution in *The Brothers Karamazov*." *PTL: A Journal for Descriptive Poetics and Theory of Literature* 3 (1978): 223–233.

Moser, Charles. *Anti-Nihilism in the Russian Novel of the 1860s*. The Hague: Mouton and Co., 1964.

———. "The *Brothers Karamazov* as a Novel of the 1860s." *Dostoevsky Studies* 7 (1986): 73–80.

———. "Dostoevsky and the Aesthetics of Journalism." *Dostoevsky Studies* 3 (1982): 27–41.

———. "Stepan Trofimovič Verkhovenskij and the Esthetics of His Time." *Slavic and East European Journal* 29 (1985): 157–163.

Murav, Harriet. *Holy Foolishness: Dostoevsky's Novels and the Poetics of Cultural Critique*. Stanford: Stanford University Press, 1992.

Natov, Nadine. "The Ethical and Structural Significance of the Three Temptations in *The Brothers Karamazov*." *Dostoevsky Studies* 8 (1987): 3–44.

———. "Rol' filosofskogo podteksta v romane *Besy*." *Zapiski russkoi akademicheskoi gruppy v SShA* 14 (1981): 69–100.

Natova, Nadin. "Novella 'Krotkaia' kak sintez mnogikh predshestvuiushchikh tem i kharakterov v proizvedeniiakh Dostoevskogo." *Dostoevsky Studies* 4 (2000): 5–34.

Nechaeva, V. S. *Zhurnal M. M. i F. M. Dostoevskykh 'Epokha' 1864–1865*. Moscow: Khudlit, 1975.

———. *Zhurnal M. M. i F. M. Dostoevskykh 'Vremia' 1861–1863*. Moscow: Khudlit, 1974.

Neühauser, Rudolph. "*The Brothers Karamazov*: A Contemporary Reading of Book VI, 'The Russian Monk.'" *Dostoevsky Studies* 7 (1986): 135–151.

———. "Observations on the Structure of *Notes from Underground* with Reference to the Main Themes of Part II." *Canadian-American Slavic Studies* 6 (1972): 239–255.

———. "Romanticism in the Post-Romantic Age: A Typological Study of Antecedents of Dostoevskii's Man from Underground." *Canadian-American Slavic Studies* 8 (1974): 333–358.

———. "The Structure of *The Insulted and Injured*." *Forum International* 3 (1980): 48–60.

Nilsson, Nils Ake. "Rhyming as a Stylistic Device in *Crime and Punishment*." *Russian Literature* 4 (1973): 65–71.

Oats, Joyce Carol. "Tragic Rites in Dostoyevsky's *The Possessed*." In *Contraries: Essays*, 17–50. New York: Oxford University Press, 1981.

Orwin, Donna Tussing. *Consequences of Consciousness: Turgenev, Dostoevsky, and Tolstoy*. Stanford: Stanford University Press, 2007.

O'Toole, E. Michael. *Structure, Style and Interpretation in the Russia Short Story*. New Haven: Yale University Press, 1982.

———. "Structure and Style in the Short Story: Dostoevsky's *A Gentle Creature*." In *F. M. Dostoevsky (1821–1881): A Centenary Collection*, edited by Leon Burnett, 1–36. Essex: University of Essex Press, 1981.

Pascal, Roy. *The Dual Voice (Free Indirect Speech and its functioning in the nineteenth-century European novel)*. Manchester: Manchester University Press, 1977.

Passage, Charles E. *Character Names in Dostoevsky's Fiction*. Ann Arbor: Ardis Press, 1982.

Peace, Richard. *Dostoyevsky. An Examination of the Major Novels*. Cambridge: Cambridge University Press, 1971.

———. *The Enigma of Gogol*. Cambridge: Cambridge University Press, 1981.

Pedrotti, Louis. *Józef-Julian Sękowski: The Genesis of a Literary Alien*. Berkeley: University of California Press, 1965.

Perlina, Nina. *Varieties of Poetic Utterance: Quotation in "The Brothers Karamazov."* Lanham: University Press of America, 1985.

Pervushin, N. V. "Dostoevsky's Foma Opiskin and Gogol'." *Canadian Slavonic Papers/Revue Canadienne des Slavistes* 14, no. 1 (1972): 87–91.

Pervushin, Nikolai. "Epilogi v proizvedeniiakh Dostoevskogo." In *Zapiski russkoi akademicheskoi gruppy v SShA (Transactions of the Association of Russian-American Scholars in the USA)*, edited by A. P. Obolensky and N. Natov, 158–168. New York: New York Association of Russian-American Scholars in the USA, 1981.

Peschio, Joe. *The Poetics of Impudence and Intimacy in the Age of Pushkin*. Madison: The University of Wisconsin Press, 2012.

Peschio, Joseph and Igor' Pil'shchikov. "The Proliferation of Elite Readerships and Circle Poetics in Pushkin and Baratynskii (1820s–1830s)." In *The Space of the Book*, edited by Miranda Remnek, 82–107. Toronto: University of Toronto Press, 2011.

Petrunina, N. N. *Proza Pushkina: puti evoliutsii*. Leningrad: Nauka, 1987.

Pike, Christopher R. "Formalist and Structuralist Approaches to Dostoyevsky." In *New Essays on Dostoyevsky*, edited by Malcolm V. Jones and Garth M. Terry, 187–214. Cambridge: Cambridge University Press, 1983.

Pil'shchikov, Igor'. "On Baratynsky's 'French trifle': *The Elysian Fields* and its Context." *Essays in Poetics* 19, no. 2 (1994): 62–93.

Pomar, Mark G. "Aleša Karamazov's Epiphany: A Reading of 'Cana of Galilee.'" *Slavic and East European Journal* 27 (1983): 47–56.

Pomorska, Krystyna. "On the Problem of Parallelism in Gogol's Prose: 'A Tale of the Two Ivans.'" In *The Structural Analysis of Narrative Texts:*

Conference Papers, edited by Andrej Kodjak, Michael J. Connolly, and Krystyna Pomorska, 31–43. Columbus, OH: Slavica, 1980.

Pope, Richard. "Peter Verkhovensky and the Banality of Evil." In *Dostoevsky and the Twentieth Century: The Ljubljana Papers*, edited by Malcolm V. Jones, 39–47. Nottingham: Astra, 1993.

Popova, I. L. "Smekh i slezy v *Povestiakh Belkina*." In *Povesti Belkina: K 200-letiiu so dnia rozhdeniia A. S. Pushkina*, edited by N. K. Gei and I. L. Popova, 480–509. Moscow: Nasledie, 1999.

———. "Tvorcheskaia istoriia *Povestei Belkina*." In *Povesti Belkina: K 200-letiiu so dnia rozhdeniia A. S. Pushkina*, edited by N. K. Gei and I. L. Popova, 181–206. Moscow: Nasledie, 1999.

Proctor, Thelwall. *Dostoevskij and the Belinskij School of Literary Criticism*. The Hague: Mouton, 1969.

Pukhachev, Sergei. "Kinesic Observations on Dostoevsky's Novel *Demons*." In *The New Russian Dostoevsky*, edited by Carol Apollonio, 189–216. Bloomington: Slavica, 2010.

Remnek, Miranda. "The Expansion of Russian Reading Audiences, 1828–1848," PhD Dissertation. Berkeley: University of California, 1999.

———. "'A Larger Portion of the Public': Fiction, Journals & Female Readers in the Early Reign of Nicholas I." In *An Improper Profession: Women, Gender & Journalism in Late Imperial Russia*, edited by Barbara Norton and Jehanne Gheith, 26–52. Durham, NC: Duke University Press, 2001.

———. "Russian Literary Almanacs in the 1820s and Their Legacy." *Publishing History* 17 (1985): 65–86.

Reyfman, Irina. *Ritualized Violence Russian Style: The Duel in Russian Culture and Literature*. Stanford: Stanford University Press, 1999.

Rice, Martin. *Dostoevsky and the Healing Art: An Essay in Literary and Medical History*. Ann Arbor: Ardis Press, 1985.

———."Dostoevskii's *Notes from Underground* and Hegel's *Master and Slave*." *Canadian-American Slavic Studies* 8 (1974): 359–369.

Romberg, Bertil. *Studies in the Narrative Technique of the First-Person Novel*. Stockholm: Lund, 1962.

Rosen, Nathan. "Breaking out of the Underground: The 'Failure' of *A Raw Youth*." *Modern Fiction Studies* 4 (1958): 225–239.

———. "Chaos and Dostoevsky's Women." *Kenyon Review* 20 (1958): 257–277.

———. "Style and Structure in *Brothers Karamazov*." *Russian Literature Triquarterly* 1 (1971): 352–365.

Rosenblium, L. M. *Tvorcheskie dnevniki Dostoevskogo*. Moscow: Nauka, 1981.

Rosenshield, Gary. *Crime and Punishment: The Techniques of the Omniscient Author*. Lisse: Peter de Ridder, 1978.

———. "The Fate of Dostoevskij's Underground Man: The Case for an Open Ending." *Slavic and East European Journal* 28 (1984): 324–339.

———. "Point of View and Imagination in Dostoevskij's 'White Nights.'" *Slavic and East European Journal* 21 (1977): 191–203.

Rowe, W. W. "*Crime and Punishment* and *Brothers Karamazov*: Some Comparative Observations." *Russian Literature Triquarterly* 10 (1974): 331–342.

Ruud, Charles A. *Fighting Words: Imperial Censorship and the Russian Press, 1804–1906*. Toronto: University of Toronto Press, 1982.

Said, Edward W. *Beginnings: Intention and Method*. New York: Basic Books, Inc., 1975.

Saraskina, L. I., ed. *Besy: Antologiia russkoi kritiki*. Moscow: Soglasie, 1996.

———. *Besy. Roman preduprezhdenie*. Moscow: Sovetskii pisatel', 1990.

———. "Distortion of the Ideal: The Cripple in *Demons*." In *The New Russian Dostoevsky*, edited by Carol Apollonio, 189–216. Bloomington: Slavica, 2010.

Sazonova, L. I. "Emblematicheskie i drugie izobrazitel'nye motivy v *Povestiakh Belkina*." In *Povesti Belkina: K 200-letiiu so dnia rozhdeniia A. S. Pushkina*, edited by N. K. Gei and I. L. Popova, 510–534. Moscow: Nasledie, 1999.

Scanlan, James P. "The Case against Rational Egoism in Dostoevsky's *Notes from the Underground*." *Journal of the History of Ideas* 60 (1999): 549–567.

———. *Dostoevsky the Thinker*. Ithaca: Cornell University Press, 2002.

Scherr, Barry P. "The Topography of Terror: The Real and Imagined City in Dostoevsky's *Besy*." *Dostoevsky Studies* XVIII (2014): 59–85.

Schmid, Wolf. "Narratologiia Pushkina." In *Pushkinskaia konferentsiia v Stenforde: Materialy i issledovaniia*, edited by D. Bethea, A. L. Ospovat, N. G. Okhotin, and L. S. Fleishman, 300–317. Moscow: OGI, 2001.

———. "Three Diegetic Devices in Puškin's *Tales of Belkin*." In *Language and Literary Theory*, edited by Benjamin A. Stolz, I. R. Titunik, and Lubomír Doležel, 505–526. Ann Arbor: Papers in Slavic Philology 5, 1984.

Serman, I. Z. "Dostoevskii i Appollon Grigo'ev." In *Dostoevskii i ego vremia*, edited by V. G. Bazanov and G. M. Fridlender, 33–66 and 130–142. Leningrad: Nauka, 1971.

Setchkarev, Vsevolod. *Gogol: His Life and Works*. Translated by Robert Kramer. New York: New York University Press, 1965.

Shaw, J. T. "The Problem of the Persona in Journalism: Puškin's Feofilakt Kosičkin." In *American Contributions to the Fifth International Congress of Slavists*, 301–326. The Hague: Mouton & Co., 1963.

———. "Puškin's 'The Stationmaster' and the New Testament Parable." *The Slavic and East European Journal* 21, no. 1 (1977): 3–29.

Shklovskii, Viktor. *Za i protiv: Zametki o Dostoevskom*. Moscow: Sovetskii pisatel', 1957.

Sidorov, V. "O *Dnevnike pisatelia.*" In *Dostoevskii: stat'i i materialy (sbornik vtoroi)*, edited by A. S. Dolinin, 110–116. Leningrad and Moscow: Mysl', 1924.

Skvoznikov, V. D. "Zhiznennye uroki povedeniia dvorianina." In *Povesti Belkina: K 200-letiiu so dnia rozhdeniia A. S. Pushkina*, edited by N. K. Gei and I. L. Popova, 535–554. Moscow: Nasledie, 1999.

Slonimsky, Aleksander. "The Technique of the Comic in Gogol." In *Gogol from the Twentieth Century: Eleven Essays*, edited and translated by Robert A. Maguire, 323–274. Princeton: Princeton University Press, 1974.

Sobel, Ruth. *Gogol's Forgotten Book: Selected Passages and its Contemporary Readers*. Washington, DC: University Press of America, 1981

Stanzel, F. K. *A Theory of Narrative*. Translated by Charlotte Goedsche. Cambridge: Cambridge University Press, 1984.

Steiner, Lina. *The Bildungsroman in Russian Culture*. Toronto: University of Toronto Press, 2011.

Sternberg, Meir. *Expositional Modes and Temporal Ordering in Fiction*. Baltimore: The Johns Hopkins University Press, 1978.

Struve, Gleb. "Koe-chto o iazyke Dostoevskogo." *Revue des etudes slaves* 58 (1981): 608–618.

———. "Zametki o iazyke Dostoevskogo." In *Zapiski russkoi akademischeskoi gruppy v SShA (Transactions of the Association of Russian-American Scholars in the USA)*, edited by A. P. Obolensky and N. Natov, 314–323. New York, New York Association of Russian-American Scholars in the USA, 1981.

Sutherland, Steward R. *Atheism and the Rejection of God: Contemporary Philosophy and* The Brothers Karamazov. Oxford: Blackwell, 1977.

———. "Death and Fulfilment, or Would the Real Mr. Dostoyevsky Stand Up?" In *Philosophy and Literature* (Royal Institute of Philosophy Lecture Series) 16, edited by A. Phillips Griffiths, 15–28. Cambridge: Cambridge University Press, 1984.

Terras, Victor. *A Karamazov Companion: Commentary on the Genesis, Language, and Style of Dostoevsky's Novel*. Madison: The University of Wisconsin Press, 1981.

Thaden, Barbara. "Bakhtin, Dostoevsky, and the Status of the 'I'." *Dostoevsky Studies* 8 (1987): 199–207.

Thomas, G. "Aspects of the Study of Dostoevsky's Vocabulary." *Modern Language Review* 77 (1982): 670–678.

Thompson, Diane O. *The Brothers Karamazov and the Poetics of Memory*. Cambridge: Cambridge University Press, 1991.

Todd, William Mills III. "*The Brothers Karamazov* and the Poetics of Serial Publication." *Dostoevsky Studies* 7 (1986): 87–97.

———. *Fiction and Society in the Age of Pushkin: Ideology, Institutions, Narrative*. Cambridge: Harvard University Press, 1986.

———. "To Be Continued: Dostoevsky's Evolving Poetics of Serialized Publication." *Dostoevsky Studies* 18 (2014): 23–33.

Todorov, Tzvetan. *Genres in Discourse*. Cambridge: Cambridge University Press, 1990.

Toichkina, Aleksandra V. "Obraz ada v 'Zapiskakh iz mertvogo doma': K teme Dostoevskii i Dante." *Dostoevskii i mirovaia kul'tura: Almanakh* 29 (2012): 52–66.

Toporov, V. N. "On Dostoevsky's Poetics and Archaic Patterns of Mythological Thought." *New Literary History* 9 (1978): 333–352.

Trahan, Elizabeth Welt, ed. *Gogol's "Overcoat": An Anthology of Critical Essays*. Ann Arbor: Ardis Press, 1983.

———. "*The Possessed* as Dostoevskij's Homage to Gogol': An Essay in Traditional Criticism." *Russian Literature* 24 (1996): 397–418.

Tunimanov, V. A. "Nekotorye osobennosti povestvovaniia v 'Gospodine Prokharchine' F. M. Dostoevskogo." In *Poetika i stilistika russkoi literatury: Pamiati akademika V. V. Vinogradova*, edited by M. P. Alekseev, 203–212. Leningrad: Nauka, 1971.

———. "Podpol'e i zhivaia zhizn'." In *XXI vek glazami Dostoevskogo: perspektivy chelovechestva*, edited by K. Stepanian, 11–22. Moscow: "Graal," 2002.

———. "Priemy povestvovaniia v 'Krotkoi' F. M. Dostoevskogo." *Vestnik Leningradskogo universiteta* 2 (1965): 106–115.

———. "Rasskazchik v 'Besakh' Dostoevskogo." In *Issledovanie po poetike i stilistike: sbornik statei*, edited by V. V. Vinogradov, 86–162. Leningrad: Nauka, 1972.

———. "Satira i utopiia: 'Bobok' i 'Son smeshnogo cheloveka' F. M. Dostoevskogo." *Russkaia literatura* 4 (1966): 70–87.

———. *Tvorchestvo Dostoevskogo: 1854–1862*. Leningrad: Akademiia nauk, 1980.

Tynianov, Iu. N. "Dostoevskii i Gogol': K teorii parodii." In *Literaturnaia evoliutsiia: izbrannye trudy*, edited by V. I. Novikov, 300–339. Moscow: Agraf, 2002.

Tynjanov, Jurij. "Dostoevsky and Gogol." In *Twentieth-Century Russian Literary Criticism*, edited by Victor Erlich, 102–116. New Haven: Yale University Press, 1975.

Tynyanov, Yury. "Dostoevsky and Gogol: Towards a Theory of Parody," Part 1. In *Dostoevsky and Gogol*, edited and translated by Priscilla Meyer and Stephen Rudy, 101–118. Ann Arbor: Ardis, 1979.

Valentino, Russell Scott. *Vicissitudes of Genre in the Russian Novel*. New York: Peter Lang, 2001.

Van Der Eng, J. and J. M. Meijer. "*The Brothers Karamazov* by F. M. Dostoevskij." *Dutch Studies in Russian Literature* 2. The Hague: Mouton & Co, 1971.

Vetlovskaia, V. E. "Alyosha Karamazov and the Hagiographic Hero." In *Dostoevsky: New Perspectives*, edited by Robert Louis, 206–226. Englewood Cliffs, NJ: Prentice Hall, 1984.

———. "Ob odnom iz istochnikov *Brat'ev Karamazovykh*." *Izvestiia Akademii nauk SSSR. Seriia literatury i iazyka* 40 (1981): 436–445.

———. *Poetika romana "Brat'ia Karamazovy."* Leningrad: Nauka, 1977.

———. "Razviazka v 'Brat'iakh Karamazovykh.'" In *Poetika i stilistika russkoi literatury*, edited by V. V. Vinogradov, 195–203. Leningrad: Nauka, 1971.

———. "Ritorika i poetika (utverzhdenie i oproverzhenie mnenii v 'Brat'iakh Karamazovykh' Dostoevskogo." In *Issledovanie po poetike i stilistike: sbornik statei*, edited by V. V. Vinogradov, 163–184. Leningrad: Nauka, 1972.

Vinitsky, Ilya. "Where Bobok is Buried: The Theosophical Roots of Dostoevskii's 'Fantastic Realism.'" *Slavic Review* 65, no. 3 (2006): 523–543.

Vinogradov, V. V. *Gogol and the Natural School*. Translated by Debra K. Erickson and Ray Parrott. Ann Arbor: Ardis Press, 1987.

———. "Iz anonimnogo fel'etonnogo naslediia Dostoevskogo." In *Issledovanie po poetike i stilistike: sbornik statei*, edited by V. V. Vinogradov, 185–211. Leningrad: Nauka, 1972.

———. "Stil' perterburgskoi poemy *Dvoinik*." In *Dostoevskii: Stat'i i materialy*, 1, edited by A. S. Dolinin, 211–254. Petersburg: Mysl', 1922.

Virolainen, M. N. "Mir i stil' ('Starosvetskie pomeshchiki' Gogolia)." *Voprosy Literatury* 4 (1979): 125–141.

Vitalich, Kristin. "*The Village Stepanchikov*: Toward a (Lacanian) Theory of Parody." *Slavic and East European Journal* 53, no. 2 (2009): 203–218.

Vladiv, S. B. *Narrative Principles in Dostoevskij's "Besy": A Structural Analysis.* Berne, Frankfurt, and Las Vegas: Peter Lang, 1979.

Volgin, Igor. "Alyosha's Destiny." In *The New Russian Dostoevsky: Readings for the Twenty-First Century*, edited by Carol Apollonio, 271–286. Bloomington: Slavica, 2010.

Voloshin, G. "Prostranstvo i vremia u Dostoevskogo." *Slavia* 12, no. 1–2 (1933): 162–172.

Voloshinov, N. *Marxism and the Philosophy of Language*. Translated by Ladislav Matejka and Irwin Titunik. Cambridge: Harvard University Press, 1986.

Walicki, Andrzej. *The Slavophile Controversy*. Translated by Hilda Andrews-Rusiecka. Oxford: Oxford University Press, 1975.

Ward, Bruce K. *Dostoevsky's Critique of the West: The Quest for Earthly Paradise*. Waterloo, Ontario: Wilfried Laurier University Press, 1986.

Wasiolek, Edward. "*Aut Ceasar, Aut Nihil*: A Study of Dostoevsky's Moral Dialectic." *PMLA* 78 (1963): 89–97.

———. *Dostoevsky: The Major Fiction*. Cambridge: MIT Press, 1964.

———, ed. *Fyodor Dostoevsky: The Notebooks for "The Brothers Karamazov."* Translated by Edward Wasiolek. Chicago and London: University of Chicago Press, 1971.

———, ed. *Fyodor Dostoevsky: The Notebooks for "The Possessed."* Translated by Victor Terras. Chicago: University of Chicago Press, 1968.

Weiner, Adam. *By Authors Possessed*. Evanston: Northwestern University Press, 1998.

Weinstein, Mark A. *The Prefaces to the Waverley Novels*. Lincoln: University of Nebraska Press, 1978.

Wellek, René, ed. *Dostoevsky: A Collection of Critical Essays*. Englewood Cliffs, NJ: Prentice-Hall, 1962.

Woodward, J. B. *The Symbolic Art of Gogol: Essays on His Short Fiction*. Princeton: Princeton University Press, 1981.

———. "'Transferred Speech' in Dostoevskii's *Vechnyi muzh*." *Canadian-American Slavic Studies* 8 (1974): 398–407.

Yarmolinsky, Avrahm. *Dostoevsky: His Life and Art*. New York: Grove Press, 1957.

Zakharov, V. N. *Sistema zhanrov Dostoevskogo: Tipologiia i poetika*. Leningrad: Izdatel'stvo Leningradskogo universiteta, 1985.

Zaslavskii, D. O. "Zametki o iumore i satire v proizvedeniiakh Dostoevskogo." In *Tvorchestvo F.M. Dostoevskogo*, edited by N. L. Stepanov, D. D. Blagoi, U. A. Gural'nik, and B. S. Riurikov, 445–471. Moscow: Akademiia nauk SSSR, 1959.

Zeldin, Jesse. *Nikolai Gogol's Quest for Beauty: An Exploration into His Work*. Lawrence: Regents Press of Kansas, 1978.

Zhivolupova, Natal'ia V. "'Krotkaia' i evoliutsiia zhanra ispovedi antigeroia v tvorchestve Dostoevskogo." *Dostoevsky Studies* 4 (2000): 129–142.

Zholkovsky, Alexander. "Rereading Gogol's Miswritten Book: Notes on *Selected Passages from Correspondence with Friends*." In *Essays on Gogol: Logos and the Russian Word*, edited by Susanne Fusso and Priscilla Meyer, 172–184. Evanston: Northern Illinois University Press.

Index

Alexander II 157
Alexandrov V. E. 107n37, 111-112
Allen, Elizabeth Cheresh ix, 40n30
Andreeva, A. N. xxiin15
Anxiety 2, 12, 16, 20, 151, 162n36, 163
Apollonio, Carol 92n3, 146n9
Avsey, Ignat 32n8, 32n10, 36n21,
Bakhtin, Mikhail M. xixn12, 37, 43, 43n37, 45n43, 135n42, 141, 147, 150n16
Bakunin, Mikhail, A. 62n3
Balzac, Honoré de 65, 162n36
Barnhard, Joe E. 32n8
Belkin, A. A. 144n2
Belknap, Robert L. 81n53
Berdyaev (Berdiaev), Nikolai 57n62
Bestuzhev-Marlinsky, Alexander A. 63, 63n5, 114n56
Bitsilli, P. M. 45n43
Blackmur, Richard P. xivn8
Bojanowska, Edyta M. 10n22
Booth, Wayne C. xvin11
Brambeus, Baron 35, also see Senkovsky
Braun, Maximilian 145, 152
Bulgarin, Faddei 3-5, 5n12-14, 6, 8-9, 12, 15, 20, 27

Catherine the Great 3
Chekhov, A. P. 126
Chernyshevsky, Nikolai 13-14, 14n31, 15, 77-78, 123
  What is to be Done? 13, 14n30, 32, 15, 77
Chronotope xix-xx, 75-76, 92
Code (encode, decode) xi, xiii, 3-4, 14n31, 26, 93, 131, 134-136, 139-140
Cohn, Dorrit 150, 150n15-16
Comism, comic 32n6, 33, 68, 91-92, 92n3, 102, 106, 114, 154
Coulson, Jessie 38n25
Cravens, Craig 114n55
Dante 47, 47n46
  Divine Comedy, The 47n46
Davydov, Denis 63
Debrezeny, Paul 21n48
Demin, A. S. xivn8
Dickens, Charles 108, 125
Discourse xiii, xix-xxi, 1, 12-13, 20-21, 29, 40, 43, 45-46, 52, 62-63, 66, 68, 72-78, 80, 84-86, 92-93, 97-99, 104, 107-113, 120-123, 126, 131-133, 135n42, 136, 139, 142, 145-147, 150-154, 158-160, 164-169

Index

Disguise 21, 115, 158
Dostoevsky, Fedor Mikhailovich (Fyodor) xi-xviii, xxi-xxii, 1, 6n15, 13, 15, 20, 21n47, 25-170
   Adolescent, The 119, 157n29n, 164, 166
   "Bobok" xiv-xv, xvii, 121-124, 142-143
   "Boy at Christ's Christmas Party, The" xiv-xv, xvii, 120 124-127, 130-131, 142-143
   Brothers Karamazov, The ix, xii-xv, xvii-xvii, 1, 119, 128n20, 143-149, 151-168
   Crime and Punishment 57n62, 81n53, 148, 157n29
   Demons (Possessed, The) xiv-xv, xvii, xix, 30n2, 32n7, 91-111, 113-118, 119n1, 128n20, 140n51, 163-166
   Diary of a Writer, The xiv-xvi, xviii, 1, 6n15, 42n35, 62, 119-143, 156-157, 162, 165, 169
   Double, The 28-29
   "Gambler, The" 164, 166
   "Gentle Creature, A" xiv-xv, xvii-xvii, 123n9, 131-143, 165, 168
   Humiliated and Insulted, The (Humiliated and Injured, Insulted and the Injured) 29n1, 61, 74, 164, 166
   Idiot, The xv, 157n29
   Notes from the House of the Dead ix, xi, xiv-xv, xvii-xviii, 29-30, 38, 40-41, 61, 74-76, 122, 141, 164, 167
   Notes from the Underground xiv-xv, xvii, 15, 21n47, 41n33, 67n16, 69-90, 122, 148, 164, 166-167
   "Peasant Marei, The" xiv-xv, 127-131
   Poor Folk 26, 28-29, 35, 36n19, 41n33
   Village of Stepanchikovo and its Inhabitants, The xiv, xvii-xvii, 29-40, 91, 122, 164-166
   White Nights 26n58, 28
   Winter Notes on Summer Impressions xiv-xv, xvii, 61-69, 80n51, 123
Dostoevsky, Mikhail 29, 31, 41n33, 61, 62n1, 73n29, 85n58
Double-voicing 84, 135, 135n42, 147, 150, 150n16, 151, 156-157, 161, 168
Dowler, Wayne 130n31
Editor, fictional xi, 43, 81, 83-85, 87-88, 91, 122, 147, 154, 167
Eliot, Charles, W. xiiin8
Emerson, Caryl xixn12, 37n22, 43n37, 135n42
Epigraph xxii, 91, 93-94, 105-106, 118, 153, 161
Epokha (Epoch) 61, 70n22, 73, 75, 80n51, 85, 90, 166
Exile xiv, xviii, 27, 38, 40, 61-62, 96, 107, 114, 168
Fanger, Donald 7n17, 31n5, 45n43
Farce 31, 34, 37, 39, 92
Fitzgerald, Gene D. ix, 77n42, 95, 95n8, 98n14, 107n37, 111n46, 112-113, 140n51,
Flaubert, Gustav 153
   Madame Bovary 153
Folklore 48
Foreword xiv-xxi, 1-12, 20-21, 25-27, 32-37, 53, 63, 70, 76n40, 85, 85n59, 86-88, 94, 109, 118, 122, 127, 131-132, 143-164, 164n1, 165-169
Forrester, James 85n60
Fourier, François Marie Charles 98, 109

Framed novel 106
Frank, Joseph 32n8, 35n18, 38, 53n57, 62n1, 72, 73n30, 75n35, 77, 80n51, 81n52, 85n58, 89n62, 89n64, 106n34, 107n35, 111n46, 115n57, 146n9, 147n10
Franklin, Simon 43n38
Frazier, Melissa 35n16
Fridlender, G. M. 50n50
Fusso, Susanne 31n5, 39n30
Garnett, Constance 26n58
Genette, Gérard xiii, xivn9, xvi-xviii, 2, 12, 15, 63, 65n9-10, 145n5, 148, 149n14, 153n22, 161, 162n36, 163, 169
Gertsen, A. I. see Herzen
Ginzburg, E. I. 45n43
Gogol, Nikolai x, xiii, 7n17, 10-12, 13n27, 15, 17, 18n38-41, 19-21, 31, 32n6, 33, 36, 46, 64, 82, 85, 88, 91, 103, 106-108, 147, 154n26, 162, 169
  Dead Souls 10-12, 15, 19-20, 43n38, 103
  Evenings on a Farm Near Dikanka (Dikanka Tales) xiii, 17, 18n41, 19, 147
  Selected Passages from Correspondence with Friends 31, 33, 36
Golosovker, Ia. 149n14
Goncharov, Ivan 27
Gospel 53, 105
  Luke 93-94, 105n32
Greshman, Herbert S. xiiin8
Grigoriev (Grigor'ev), Apollon 75n34, 130n31
Grigorovich, Dmitry 26
Grossman, I. P. 62n1, 146n9
Gutsche, G. J. 95n8
Herzen, Alexander 13, 13n28, 62n3
  Who is To Blame? 13, 13n28

Hingley, Ronald 38n25
Holland, Kate 93, 93n4, 96n10, 98, 105, 119n1
Holquist, Michael xixn12, 43n37, 89, 89n65, 123n9
Hugo, Victor 140, 140n52, 155n27, 162n36
  Last Day of a Man Condemned to Death, The 140, 140n52, 155n27
Iakubova, Rima 92n3
Idealism, idealist 46, 60, 71, 77-78, 80, 90, 107, 116
Immoral (amoral) 7-8, 24, 106
Insecurity 2, 4-5, 12-13, 17, 26, 36, 158, 163
Introductory xiii, xv, xviii, xxi, xxin14, 30, 32-33, 40, 45-47, 57, 60, 70, 72, 76, 76n40, 85, 85n59, 86-87, 101-104, 109, 118, 145, 165
Irony, ironic 7, 12, 15, 17, 24, 43, 45-46, 54, 57, 63-66, 79, 82, 84, 86-88, 90, 124, 162
Isenberg, Charles 30n2, 75, 79, 85n59, 90n67, 103-105, 116, 133n36,
Irving, Washington 15
Jackson, Robert Louis 44, 47n45, 70-72, 86n61, 119, 120n3, 130n31, 141n53
James, Henry xivn8
Janda, Laura, A. 48n49
Jonas, Florence 63n5
Jones, John 72, 72n28, 74, 142, 142n54
Jones, Malcolm V. 43n39, 74n53, 91n1, 93n5, 99n18
Kantemir, Antiokh 3
Karamzin N. N. 63, 63n5, 64n7, 103
  Poor Liza 103
Karaulov, Iu. N. 45n43

Index

Karlova, T. S. 50n50
Katz, Michael R. 13n28-29
Kent, Leonard J. 17n37
Khagi, Sofya 66n13
Kirpotin, V. Ia. 43n36, 47n45, 78n46, 84n57
Kleepsies, Ingred 64n7
Lacanian 32n8
Lantz, Kenneth 119n2, 122n8,
Leatherbarrow, W. J. 89n63
Leighton, L.G. 95n8
Lermontov, Mikhail 5-9, 12, 15, 20, 22-27, 40-41, 46, 52n55, 67, 124, 146, 169
  Hero of Our Time, A 5, 6n15, 7-9, 20, 22, 23n54, 24-25, 40-41, 52n55, 67, 114, 146
Lesage, Alan René 1-3
  Gil Blas 2-3
Lewin, Jane E. xiiin7
Lounsbery, Anne S. 13n27, 117n62
Mackler, Mary 62n1
Maguire, Robert A. 32n6
Manipulation, manipulate 14n31, 15, 64, 92, 112-113, 116, 116n60
Marivaux, Pierre Carlet de Chamblain 64-65
Martinsen, Deborah A. 66n13, 107n38, 116n60
Marvels of the East xix, xxi, 109-110
Matejka, Ladislav 150n16
Matlaw, Ralph, E. 6n15, 25n57, 71, 89
McCracken-Flesher, Caroline 16n34
Meijer, Jan M. 152n21
Meyer, Priscilla 31n5
Milne, Lesley 81n53
Mirsky, D. S. 44
Moore, Gene M. 97n12, 113
Moral (morals, moralist) 4, 6-10, 49-52, 54-55, 57-58, 63, 88, 108, 121n5, 126, 151, 153

Morson, Gary Saul 32, 32n9, 42, 71-72, 79, 81n53, 89, 89n63, 119-121, 121n5
Monas, Sidney 5n14
Mystification (mystify) 19, 21, 28, 168
Nabokov, Dmitrii 6n15
Nabokov, Vladimir 6n15
Narezhnyi, Vasily 1, 1n1, 2-5, 6n15, 9, 10n22, 12, 15, 20
Narrator xii-xii, xvn10, xvi, xxin14, 17, 19, 21-26, 30, 32-42, 45, 52n55, 68-69, 71, 83-89, 91-93, 94n6, 95-101, 103-107, 109-117, 122-125, 129, 132-142, 145, 147, 149-163, 164n1, 165
Natov, Nadine 115n59
Nechaeva, V. S. 73n29
Nekrasov, A. N. 123
Nicholas I 5, 5n14
Nihilism (nihilistic, nihilists) 107, 107n35
Odoevsky, Vladimir F. 6n15, 25-26
  Russian Nights 6n15, 25
Olienikov, Olga 6n15, 25n57
Paperno, Irina ix, 14n31, 15
Parodist, parody 22-23, 32n8, 33n12, 72, 77, 82-83, 86, 89-90, 154n26
Pascal, Roy 69n20, 150n16, 151, 152n19, 153-154
Pedrotti, Louis 35n16
Peschio, Joe x, 5n14, 7n18, 22n51
Pervushin, N. V. 36n21
Peter the Great 3, 80n51
Petrashevtsy 115
Pevear, Richard xiin6, 67n16, 70n22, 92n2, 144n2
Pike, Chrisopher R. 43n39
Poetics xxiin15, 5n14, 6n15, 7n18, 22n51, 37n22, 45, 66n13,

81n53, 135n42, 146n8-9, 147, 147n10, 161n35
Pobedonostsev K. P. 152n20
Pope, Richard 91n1
Post-exile xiv, 63, 74, 76, 90-91, 150, 169
Preface ix, xiii-xxii, 1-27, 29-32, 35, 40, 62-65, 68-71, 91-92, 94, 100, 106, 109, 118-124, 131-132, 140, 140n52, 141-143, 145n5, 146-149, 153-154, 157, 161, 162n36, 163-169
Prologue xii, xiiin8, xvii-xxi, 26, 69-72, 75-76, 83, 86-91, 94, 109, 120, 163, 167
Protagonist xi, 8, 29-30, 33, 40, 47, 57n62, 94, 164n1, 167
Pushkin, Alexander xiii, 5n12, 15, 20, 20n46, 21, 21n47, 22, 27, 40, 46, 94, 147, 154n26, 167, 169
  Tales of the Late Ivan Petrovich Belkin, The xiii, 20-23, 40-41, 147, 167
Patterson, David 63n4
Rational Egoism 77-78, 90
Raymond, William 74
Reader xiv, xvin11, xviii-xxi, 2-28, 31n5, 33-36, 39-44, 47, 53, 61, 63-66, 71-74, 76, 80, 83, 85-94, 97, 103-104, 107, 109, 112-113, 122-124, 127-143, 148-168
Rousseau, Jean-Jacques 23, 114
  Confessions 23
Ryleev, Kondraty 114n56
Said, Edward xi, xiin1, xiii
Saltykov-Shchedrin, N. E. 27
Sarcasm, sarcastic 54, 65, 82
Satire, satiric 3, 3n7, 4, 22, 31, 33, 37, 72, 82-83, 84n56, 86-94, 96n10, 97, 104, 106, 114, 116, 116n60

Scanlan, James P. 71, 77-78, 78n46-48, 81
Scott, Walter xiiin8, 15-17, 20-21, 40, 65
  Ivanhoe 16
  Prefaces to the Waverley Novels by Sir Walter Scott xiiin8, 16-17, 65
Senkovsky, Osip Ivanovich 35n16
Shevyrev S. P. 12
Shklovsky, Viktor 44
Siberia, Siberian xi, xiv, 28, 38, 41, 46-58, 61, 114n56
Sidorov, V. A. 133n35, 143
Slonimskii, Alexander 32n6
Sobel, Ruth 31n5
Steinbeck, John xiii
  Tortilla Flat xiii
Stepanov, N. I. 43n36, 47n45, 144n2
Strakhov, Nikolai 72-73, 73n30
Stromberg, David 101n23, 115n59
Templeton, Laurence 15-17, 21
Terror, terrorist 65, 108, 110
Terry, Garth M. 43n39, 93n5
Thompson, Diane 146n8-9
Time (Vremia) 61-62, 73, 73n29, 75, 80n51, 166
Titunik, Irwin 150n16
Todd, William Mills III ix, 5n12, 5n14, 6n15, 145n10, 161n35
Toichkina, A. V. 47n46
Tolstoy, Lev xii, xiin5, xviii, 13, 27, 40n30, 62
Toporov, V. N. 81n53
Trahan, Elizabeth Welt 107n36
Tragi-comic 100, 107
Tunimanov, V. A. 58n62, 97, 98n15, 115
Turgenev, Ivan S. 13, 27, 103-104, 107n35, 116n60, 126
  Fathers and Sons 103, 107
  First love 103-104, 126

Tynianov, Iu. N. 33, 36n21,
Valentino, Russell Scott 96n10
Vaudeville 33, 38, 39n30, 92n3
Ventriloquist act 36, 85, 90
Vetlovskaia, V. E. 146n8, 154n24, 162n37
Viazemsky, Petr 20n46
Vinogradov, V.V. 97n13
Vitalich, Kristin 32n8
Vladiv, Slobodanka B. 95n8, 98, 101, 115
Volgin, Igor 146n9
Volokhonsky, Larissa xiin6, 67n16, 70n22, 92n2, 144n2

Voloshinov, N. 150n16
Vremia, see *Time*
Warnock, John 43n40
Weiner, Adam 94n6, 111n44-45, 112-113, 113n52, 114, 115n59, 117n61
Weinstein, Mark A. 16n34
Whitworth, Kernan B. xiiin8, 16n34
Yarmolinsky, Avraham, 144
Young, Sarah 81n53
Zholkovsky, Alexander 31n5, 37n22
Zola, Emil 162n36

www.ingramcontent.com/pod-product-compliance
Lightning Source LLC
Chambersburg PA
CBHW071740150426
43191CB00010B/1649